AMERICAN DREAM GLOBAL NIGHTMARE

The Dilemma of
U.S. Human Rights Policy

COUNCIL ON
FOREIGN RELATIONS BOOKS

The Council on Foreign Relations, Inc., is a non-profit and nonpartisan organization devoted to promoting improved understanding of international affairs through the free exchange of ideas. The Council does not take any position on questions of foreign policy and has no affiliation with, and receives no funding from, the United States government.

From time to time, books and monographs written by members of the Council's research staff or visiting fellows (like this book), or commissioned by the Council, or written by an independent author with critical review contributed by a Council study or working group are published with the designation "Council on Foreign Relations Book." Any book or monograph bearing that designation is, in the judgment of the Committee on Studies of the Council's board of directors, a responsible treatment of a significant international topic worthy of presentation to the public. All statements of fact and expressions of opinion contained in Council books are, however, the sole responsibility of the author.

AMERICAN DREAM GLOBAL NIGHTMARE

The Dilemma of U.S. Human Rights Policy

Sandy Vogelgesang

A Council on Foreign Relations Book

W · W · NORTON & COMPANY

NEW YORK LONDON

Published simultaneously in Canada by George M. McLeod Limited, Toronto. Printed in the United States of America.

All Rights Reserved

First Edition

Library of Congress Cataloging in Publication Data

Vogelsang, Sandy.
  American dream, global nightmare.
  The Dilemma of U.S. Human Rights Policy.
  Bibliography: p.
  Includes index.
  1. United States—Foreign relations—1977–
2. Human rights. I. Title.
JX1417.V63 1980   327.73   80–10351
ISBN 0-393-01363-4

1 2 3 4 5 6 7 8 9 0

Contents

Foreword

Few declarations of policy in the history of twentieth-century diplomacy produced more mixed reactions and confusion than Jimmy Carter's 1977 pronouncements on human rights. It was more than a year, in fact, before the president's position was explicated in a way that was fully understood by both our friends and antagonists abroad.

The Carter administration's original statements in 1977 were widely construed as an effort by the administration to score points in the international game of advantage-seeking rather than as an attempt to accomplish a genuinely felt objective. The president went beyond governing principles and broad objectives to a denunciation of sinners—in particular, the Soviet Union. He called attention to the plight of the Soviet dissidents and the need to increase emigration of Soviet Jewry.

One reaction of the Soviet Union to America's declaration was to criticize the United States publicly for its own violations of human rights. Thus the issue of human rights became something of an international propaganda football. Whatever the reaction of the world to the Soviet charges, it is doubtful if Moscow's criticism had any greater practical effect on U.S. policies than our public criticism had on theirs.

How, then, can the United States advance the cause of human rights in the world? A valuable clue is furnished by our own history. No document in world history has had wider influence than the American Declaration of Independence. Next in order of influence would be the United States Constitution. Not even *The Communist Manifesto* has had a more direct or profound effect on the shaping of nations than these two American documents. The reason is clear and highlights the difference between persuasion by exhortation and persuasion by example. The American documents were tied to specific events. They served as a model. When the American colonies tore themselves free from colonial rule, they provided a powerful inspiration for all human beings. By bearing witness to the principles defined in the Declaration of Independence and the Constitution, the Americans helped set millions of other people in motion too. The inspiration persisted. As late as 1955, when the Asian and African nations met at Bandung, Indonesia, to celebrate their newly won independence from outside rule, the ideas that lit up their minds and that informed their actions were linked to the American Declaration of Independence—a fact they had no reluctance to acknowledge.

The evidence is clear, therefore, that America's ability to protect and enlarge human rights inside the United States still represents the most potent means available to us for improving the condition of other human beings on this planet. Sandy Vogelgesang recognizes the relevance of the internal situation of the United States to its public aims in the world. She sees the difficulty of applying a single governing principle with respect to human rights in our foreign policy. Different countries represent different problems in relationships and in the engineering of international consent.

The entire subject of moving the world toward a higher plateau for human rights is one of enormous complexity and subtlety. Ms. Vogelgesang defines and deals with this complexity with wide knowledge and sensitivity. She recognizes that separate parts of the world give rise to special problems. The interaction and interrelationship of the nations may reveal unusual trends and tropisms; the expression of these forces may differ sharply. Her book deals with an essentially new situation in the world, a world that has become a single geographic unit the effects of which are widely and often wildly interactive—and in which the demand for human rights may well represent the most dynamic and volatile challenge of the age. By delineating this challenge so expertly, Ms. Vogelgesang puts us all in her debt.

NORMAN COUSINS

Acknowledgments

This book began as a private odyssey, but ended—somewhat to my surprise—with a public destination. I started in the early 1970s to worry about what role human rights should play in American foreign policy. I did so partly because of questions I had raised but not answered for myself while writing a book on the response of the American intellectual left to the Vietnam war. I also did so because, like many of my fellow foreign service officers, I could not reconcile much of what the United States was doing abroad with the ideals that had first drawn me to public service.

Thus troubled by the gap between expectation and reality, I backed gradually into the idea of reading and writing about human rights. The opportunity to do so—and learn as I went—I owe to more people and organizations than I can mention. Even so, I would like to name some of them.

To Winston Lord, now president of the Council on Foreign Relations and the former director of the State Department's Policy Planning Staff, I remain more indebted personally and professionally than I can ever convey. The Council itself—by awarding me an International Affairs Fellowship and opening the programs of the Harold Pratt House to me—provided a superb setting for reflection and discussion. I am thus most honored that the Council has endorsed this book as one of its own. Although the entire Council staff went out of its way to help me, I am particularly grateful to Grace Darling Griffin, who gave me the confidence to seek publication; to William Bundy, James Chace, and Jennifer Whitaker of *Foreign Affairs*, who prodded my early thought processes on the subject of human rights; to Alton Frye, director of the Fellowship Program, and John Temple Swing, vice president of the Council; and to Catherine Gwin, executive director of the 1980s Project, Andrew Pierre, acting director of the Studies Program, and Helena Stalson, senior fellow, who were kind enough to review the entire manuscript. Early discussion series on human rights and basic human needs, held by the Council, contributed to much of my early education on human rights. For the opportunity to participate, I am most grateful to Richard H. Ullman, Theodore M. Hesburgh, and Tom Farer.

Colleagues in the federal government have gone gallantly out of their way in my behalf. I am especially beholden to those with whom I worked on the Policy Planning Staff of the Department of State during the tenure of both Henry Kissinger and Cyrus Vance; to members of the staff of the National Security Council; to former Ambassador Andrew Young and his staff at the U.S. mission to the United Nations; to those such as Patt Derian, Mark Schneider, Stephen Cohen, Michele Bova, Roberta Cohen, and John Salzberg in the Bureau of Human Rights and Humanitarian Affairs; to members and staff of the Senate Foreign Relations Committee and the House International Relations Committee; to those in the bureaus of Congressional Relations, Economic and Business Affairs, and Public Affairs, and the office of the Legal Adviser; and to officials in the Agency for International Development and the staff of the State Department Library and the Library of Congress.

Several foundations and other organizations have been most generous, either in terms of providing financial support for my work or by including me in their programs. Among those, I must note the Ford Foundation and such helpful friends as Bruce Bushee and Felice Gaer; the Rockefeller Foundation and those such as Joel Colton; the Council on Religion and International Affairs and those such as James Finn and Kenneth Thompson; the Johnson Foundation, which enabled me to participate in a Wingspread Conference chaired by Harvard law professor Louis Sohn; and the Center for Philosophy and Public Policy at the University of Maryland, where I learned from Henry Shue, Peter Brown, and others. The list could and does go on.

Other individuals gave generously of their time and expertise. Among them were Stephanie Grant and David Hawk of Amnesty International; Laurie Wiseberg and Harry Scoble, the parents of the "Internet"; Judith Bruce at the Population Council; Donald Ranard, Bill Goodfellow, and Jim Morrell at the Center for International Policy; and Tom Buergenthal and Judy Torney, wearing their *International Studies Quarterly* hats. Donald Lamm, president of W. W. Norton, and Mary Cunnane have been remarkable in their commitment to publishing a book on human rights.

Finally, of course, I am indebted to friends, who know best who they are because they endured with me the roller-coaster ride of the writing process, and my family, who has always asked the least and given the most to me.

What I have written I had not expected to become a book. Now that it has, I alone assume full responsibility for its contents. I hope only that some of what others have imparted to me helps clarify part of U.S. foreign policy and makes human rights matter for more Americans.

AMERICAN DREAM GLOBAL NIGHTMARE

The Dilemma of U.S. Human Rights Policy

Introduction

There are those who will say that the liberation of humanity, the freedom of man and mind, is nothing but a dream.
They are right. It is the American Dream.

Archibald MacLeish

Human rights—like God, Mother, and Country—claim proverbial rev-
erence among Americans. The average citizen sees the U.S. Bill of
Rights as an article of faith at home and an item for emulation abroad.

The main question is thus *not* whether most Americans applaud
stress on human rights in U.S. foreign policy. It is what they are ready
to *do* about it. The perennial questions that have plagued the attempted
marriage of morality and American diplomacy persist. Whose morality,
and at what cost to whom?

Most Americans are solid in their general support for human rights,
but soft on specifics. And with some good reason.

Many do not understand what their own government means by
"human rights." The term often assumes a chameleon cast, changing
color with the advent of each new administration. You were pink if you
touted the cause in the 1950s and yellow, without the guts for higher office, if you criticized violation of human rights in Biafra, Bangladesh,
or Vietnam in the 1960s. In the 1970s, advocacy of human rights was in
the Bicentennial spirit of red, white, and blue, and true to the proclaimed tradition of the Republic. In the 1980s, the hue may be less
bold, colored by growing appreciation for the cost and complexity of
commitment to human rights.

It is not clear what American "tradition" implies or how it applies. Is
Henry Kissinger correct that promotion of human rights is a crusade
that exposes the "impotence" of American policy? Or is Jimmy Carter
closer to the mark in calling human rights the "soul of our policy"? Do
Americans have any business pushing liberal democracy in poor na-

tions, where people may not share so-called Western values, or where more may worry about food on the table than parliamentary fare? Should Americans work as hard to promote human rights at home as abroad? If so, with what consequence for those who have arrived at the upper reaches of income distribution and authority in the United States, those in the Great American Middle seized by the animus of Proposition 13, and those on the bottom for whom the American Dream seems a cruel hoax?

Many Americans do not understand how promotion of human rights serves the U.S. national interest. Put bluntly, why bother, and what's in it for us? Most Americans say that they feel better about taking the high road for human rights. That said, some see no direct benefit for themselves from U.S. efforts to espouse fundamental freedoms abroad. It is hard to gauge or appreciate the longer-term, more indirect impact of stress on human rights—the dimension that may be most crucial in assessing the ultimate worth of the policy. Still others see significant risks in stressing human rights. For example, one eventual goal of an activist human-rights policy could be the overthrow of repressive regimes. So seen, Jimmy Carter could have more revolutionary effect on Latin America than did Che Guevara. While potentially advantageous for the United States in the long run, toppling conservative governments could carry stiff short-term political and economic costs.

There are thus caveats on U.S. public commitment to human rights. Public-opinion polls since Carter took office in 1977 reveal that the majority of Americans, while pleased by the President's stress on human rights, draw the line when that policy seems to undercut other national objectives. For instance, according to most surveys made in the late 1970s, fewer than 10 percent of Americans thought that the U.S. government should put more emphasis on condemning the Soviet Union's treatment of its Jewish dissidents, than on seeking the successful conclusion of SALT II. Moreover, special U.S. interest groups challenge what they see as moralistic excess. For example, American farmers balk at U.S. legislation that denies food aid to countries guilty of serious human rights violations. Such actions put promulgation of human rights above promotion of U.S. grain shipments. The domestic boomerang from diplomatic *démarches* on human rights can mean higher costs for other American producers and steeper prices for American consumers.

Many Americans, while convinced that the U.S. government should stress human rights, stop short on the issue of implementation. What can or should be done? Americans may want to come to the rescue of human rights elsewhere, but to what avail? It is possible that one country's campaign for reform in another may provoke a backlash and thus do more harm than good. The arrest of Soviet dissident Andrei Sakharov in 1980 could suggest just that. There is, further, the problem of consistency. Most Americans do not like what smacks of a double standard. Often, U.S. officials seem to wink at lapses by leaders in countries such as South Korea and the Philippines because of alleged U.S. security ties there, while looking askance at nations less essential to the United States. There is understandable confusion when the U.S. Government asks less of a leftist totalitarian government than of others. Critics of the Carter administration faulted the president in 1979 when he found elections held in Zimbabwe Rhodesia insufficiently fair to merit recognizing the government there and lifting sanctions, while, at the same time, normalizing relations and moving to expand trade with the People's Republic of China. On the other hand, can any one human-rights standard and any one approach fit all cases and countries at all times? If the ultimate U.S. goal is to gain increased respect for human rights, consistency may not be only the "hobgoblin of small minds," but also a false issue for foreign policy.

Beyond official action, what can or should the average American citizen do? There is some evidence that those outside government can accomplish more for human rights than can any battalion of bureaucrats. But will it do any good if labor leaders, business executives, or academics shun contacts with their counterparts in countries condemned as international pariahs? Can the individual help achieve majority rule in the Republic of South Africa by refusing to own stock in any U.S. company that operates there? Or is that the option of the ostrich, burying its head in self-righteousness and leaving South African blacks alone with *apartheid*?

To address such questions requires some sense of what human rights—or, more to the point, human wrongs—are. And there is the need to know how violations of internationally recognized rights affect and are affected by Americans. For many in the United States, proclamations on human rights remain bland abstractions, a line from the national litany to which politicians give lip service. Torture is something distasteful in a distant land, a practice detached from U.S. influence or interest.

Several points thus deserve emphasis.

First, repression of human rights is a brutally concrete expression of man's continuing inhumanity to man. Human rights are about human beings, not some eighteenth-century reflection of the Enlightenment or some twentieth-century incarnation of strategic calculus. Amnesty International, winner of the 1977 Nobel Peace Prize for its work in behalf of what it calls "prisoners of conscience," warns that serious violations of human rights occur in over one hundred nations. Genocide recurs in Southeast Asia and elsewhere on a scale to rival that practiced by Stalin or Hitler. Torture, thanks partly to new technology that lets secret police break a prisoner's will and leave no mark, creates a pervasive subculture of terror. The victims are often the prototypic next-door neighbor: a student, a lawyer, a labor leader, a journalist. Government-sanctioned abuses include rape of women by trained dogs and use of devices such as the "Parrot's Perch," a horizontal stick from which the prisoner is hung by the knees, with hands and ankles bound together, and prodded with electric shocks.

Second, repression of human rights can and does affect Americans. As philosopher Martin Buber would have it, there may be no ultimate distinction between I and Thou. There are links, direct and indirect, between violations of human rights abroad and the well-being of Americans.

Iranian mobs underscored the connection between the fight for human rights and the fate of Americans when they stormed the U.S. embassy in Teheran on November 4, 1979, and seized sixty hostages. Enraged because the Carter administration had let the deposed Shah of Iran come to New York for emergency medical treatment, they chanted, "Death to Carter," and "Kill the American dogs." They reflected the bitter anti-Americanism of the stern Islamic leader, the Ayatollah Ruhollah Khomeini, who blamed the United States for supporting the Shah. The Shah was, according to their charges, a ruler guilty of torturing political opponents, killing thousands of Iranians, and plundering the nation's wealth.

Khomeini's inflammatory rhetoric helped fan Muslim fervor and anti-Americanism across and outside Iran. There were demonstrations from Turkey to India and beyond. Angry crowds stormed the U.S. embassy in Pakistan and left two marines dead and the U.S. compound a gutted ruin. There were to be, in addition, emergency sessions of the United Nations Security Council and rising political temperatures inside the United States to match the escalation in international tension. The crisis was to color the presidential campaign of 1980 and raise hard questions for the American public. There was to be a stunning effect on U.S. interests, ranging from oil prices to national security—with consequences continuing to unfold through the 1980s.

Dramatic as the Iranian reaction to alleged U.S. complicity in the Shah's human-rights record was, there are other telling reflections of the global nightmare that transcends national borders.

Example: Agents for Chile's secret police struck in downtown Washington, D.C., in broad daylight during 1976. In a gangland-style political execution, they blew up a car carrying Chile's former ambassador to the United States and his American aides. Subsequent inquiry by the Federal Bureau of Investigation traced the blame to the highest levels of the Chilean junta and the legacy of U.S. training of anti-Castro Cubans.

Example: Operatives for the Korean Central Intelligence Agency (K.C.I.A.) kept tabs on actual and alleged opponents of President Park Chung-hee—whether they were inside or outside South Korea. They did so on the orders of Park, who came to power in a military coup in 1961 and brooked few challenges to his authority. He was, somewhat ironically, to meet a bloody end at a dinner party arranged by the head of the K.C.I.A. in October 1979. By then, however, the U.S. Department of State had collected a thick file of complaints from Koreans living in the United States—many of them American citizens—who had reported frequent harassment by the K.C.I.A. The "Koreagate" scandal of the 1970s, in which Park and his K.C.I.A. advisers decided to buy American favor through contributions to members of the U.S. Congress and compaigns in support of former President Richard Nixon, sprang partly from Park's concern that his poor record on human rights could lead to cuts in U.S. military and economic appropriations for South Korea.

Example: An estimated 1.5 million so-called "illegal aliens" arrive in the United States each year. They come, sometimes via a leaky fishing boat from Haiti or by crawling through drainage pipes from Mexico, because their own governments have failed to fulfill rights set forth in the U.N. Universal Declaration. In southern Florida alone, there are over 15,000 Haitians who have fled both stark poverty and arbitrary arrest and torture by the *tontons macoutes* of President Jean-Claude ("Baby Doc") Duvalier.

Example: Over 250,000 refugees from Southeast Asia have come to the United States since 1975. Many have come because the threat to life and livelihood was so great that they risked probable death, rather than remain in their own countries. When the flow of refugees reached flood proportions by mid-1979—and spokesmen for Malaysia and Thailand announced that new arrivals in their countries would be shot on sight—the United States was among those nations forced to decide their fate.

Crimes against what the United Nations terms "security of person"—that is, murder, torture, or detention without trial—hit home in other ways. Although the United States ranks high in the international community for the respect it accords human rights within its own borders and efforts made abroad, it *is* open to some criticism.

Alleged U.S. complicity with repression is cause for concern. Promoting respect for human rights often clashes with the *raison d'être* of the Central Intelligence Agency. Former C.I.A. agents claim publicly that the agency has worked or continues to work closely with security police of authoritarian governments, from South America to southern Africa. Officials at the highest levels of the agency confirm the same point. As one put it, "We don't let policy questions that bother the rest of the U.S. government clog our business; our job is to recruit agents and get information."

Another index to apparent complicity is the number of governments put into power by the United States or closely allied with Washington that are notable for their poor performance on human rights. An illustrative list, from the past and present, includes the governments of Rafael Trujillo Molina and Joaquin Balaguer (Dominican Republic), Fulgencio Batista (Cuba), Park Chung-hee (Republic of Korea), Ferdinand Marcos (Philippines), Shah Mohammed Reza Pahlavi (Iran), Mobuto Sese Seko (Republic of Zaire), Haile Selassie (Ethiopia), Antonio de Oliveira Salazar and Marcello Caetano (Portugal), Francisco Franco (Spain), and George Papadopoulos (Greece). Revolt against the former government of Anastasio Somoza Debayle in Nicaragua put Washington on the spot because of deep U.S. involvement in that country. American marines had occupied Nicaragua several times in the early twentieth century. Somoza's father came to power with their help. The United States established, trained, and armed Nicaragua's national guard. Until the late 1970s, the United States discouraged political opponents to what seemed a solid bulwark against communism in the Caribbean. It was, after all, from Nicaragua in 1961 that the United States launched the invasion of Cuba's Bay of Pigs.

Past U.S. policy haunts the present. Authoritarian allies wonder why the United States no longer puts top priority on fighting communism. Why do U.S. officials now criticize them for imprisoning "Marxist agitators"? Memories die hard of many years when the U.S. ambassador served as *de facto* proconsul in much of Central America and the Caribbean and when American troops could and did land to restore "stability." It is no wonder that U.S. policymakers and members of the Sandinist National Liberation Front that overthrew Somoza in 1979 were and remain wary of each other. The front was named in honor of Augusto César Sandino, the Nicaraguan national hero who fought against American occupation in the 1930s and who was assassinated by the U.S.-backed founder of the Somoza dynasty.

Skeptics from elsewhere in the so-called Third World of less developed countries doubt that U.S. leaders are suddenly serious about human rights. Revived attention to that subject strikes them as a replay of the Cold War. It is a gimmick for the West to gain an ideological edge over the East and, in the process, practice what they call "moral imperialism" in the recently decolonized nations. Further, noting U.S. opposition to one-time dictator Idi Amin and the belated American response to black cries for racial justice in southern Africa, one Nigerian delegate at the United Nations asked, "How can Americans expect us to believe that you mean what you say about human rights when U.S. representatives advocate economic sanctions against black Uganda, but not against a regime most Africans consider far worse, that of the white-dominated government in South Africa?"

The alleged double standard of American diplomacy—preaching one thing, while practicing another—has a domestic counterpart. To help establish more credibility for U.S. policy on human rights, Americans themselves may have to reassess what they are prepared to *do* for victims of violations at home and abroad. There have been some egregious gaps between what Americans say they believe and how they act. Although on record against mass killings, Americans have not pressed the Senate to ratify the U.N. convention outlawing genocide—even though that document was approved by the United Nations in 1948 and signed by President Harry Truman in 1949. Nor did they do much for the Cambodian victims of genocide in the mid-1970s. Further, there have been—and are—lapses in American concern for violations of human rights within the United States. Exposés of the "counter-intelligence program" of the Federal Bureau of Investigation during the 1960s and early 1970s undercut confidence in the rule of law and the government's respect for the individual. Recollections of U.S. incarceration of American residents of Japanese descent during World War II, sanctioned by all three branches of the U.S. government, still give pause. So do pictures of blacks and whites pushed with cattle prods into prisons during the 1960s for seeking voter registration in the American South and current reports of near-slave conditions common for migratory laborers throughout the United States.

* * *

Portrayal of human rights and wrongs is thus not a pretty picture. The view of violations reveals not only acute suffering for the victims but, sometimes, a troubling reflection of Americans themselves.

This book is an effort to sharpen focus on the complex subject of human rights and their role in the formation of U.S. foreign policy. It draws on extensive review of primary documents and secondary literature, several years of direct involvement with the issue within the Department of State, and hundreds of interviews—including discussion with senior officials in the U.S. government and other national governments, members of the U.S. Congress and their staffs, executives of major U.S. multinational corporations and banks, representatives of human-rights organizations, and individuals living in exile within the United States because of opposition to repression elsewhere. Names are often withheld, for the sake of candor—or for the protection of those non-Americans reportedly on their governments' "death lists."

This book is a look behind the scenes: whether from the perspective of a "patient" in a Soviet psychiatric hospital or that of a U.S. congressman trying to help that Jewish dissident. It is a look at the often controversial dilemmas of policy faced by men as different as Henry Kissinger and Jimmy Carter. Finally, it is a look to the longer term: what are the larger issues, and what is to be done?

This discussion amounts to a trilogy on human rights. It consists of three parts, each of which presents one perspective on policy in this area, but which, together, contribute to some overarching themes and conclusions. Since trends and policies on human rights constitute a moving target, this discussion does not pretend to be comprehensive in coverage or up to the latest count on political prisoners. It draws primarily from problems faced and decisions made by the U.S. government in the 1970s to illustrate questions raised by stress on human rights for the 1980s and beyond.

A case-study of one individual, against the backdrop of the country in question and U.S. efforts there, provides an introduction to each of the three parts. Since it is often hard to relate the rhetoric of human rights to the reality of what violations mean for a specific human being, reports on a Cambodian refugee, a Soviet dissident, and a peasant from El Salvador furnish a "face" for each facet of U.S. policy on human rights: diplomacy, politics, and economics.

* * *

The first face belongs to Ly Linn. A woman without a country, she has survived escape from Cambodia and reached a refugee camp in Thailand. Her plight illustrates the "diplomacy of human rights"—that is, what governments and international organizations can say and do through foreign policy about human rights. Her situation also shows why governments violate the rights of their own citizens and how national sovereignty conflicts with international concerns.

The imperative for power cuts two ways: the attempt by a leader such as the Cambodian prime minister to keep control, and the effort by others, such as the U.S. president or the U.N. secretary general, to use their power to effect change. But, change itself is fraught with dangers. Revolution, as Mao Tse-tung said, is no dinner party. Neither is counterrevolution. Further, it is not clear how or if the United States, though itself of revolutionary origin, can deal with fundamental political change. Ly Linn's flight from fear thus leads her to Thailand; it leads the U.S. policymaker to larger choices between two poles of alleged contention: pragmatism and principle.

* * *

The second face is that of Viktor Isaakovich Fainberg. He, too, is an exile. Because of his political protest against Soviet authorities, he was sent to an insane asylum. He won release and an exit visa to Israel when world outrage made his threatened suicide embarrassing for the U.S.S.R.

Fainberg's story sets the stage for the "politics of human rights"—or how U.S. domestic political considerations shape American reaction to human rights abroad. Special emphasis by U.S. leaders on Jewish dissidents suggests how good politics may or may not be good overall policy. The clarion call of human rights brings all principal U.S. political actors into play: the president, the Congress, the public, and special-interest groups. It serves as many purposes as there are protagonists.

Promoting human rights often plays well in Peoria. Jimmy Carter found that making Americans feel proud again, through stress on morality in U.S. foreign policy, drew consistent applause during the 1976 campaign. Henry Kissinger learned that lesson too late to help shore up domestic support for *détente* or Gerald Ford. Touting human rights also has a long and mixed political history in the United States. And it has some less obvious costs and potential consequences. Recent U.S. reaffirmation of human rights, begun because of distress with executive branch excess and the Vietnam war, may boomerang against its advocates—including Jimmy Carter. On the other hand, it may lead to a fundamental reevaluation of national priorities that amounts to a second American Revolution.

*   *   *

The third face belongs to Rosa Maria Caceres Zeyalandia. Her situation is both the least known to most Americans and the most typical of most people in the world. A peasant in El Salvador, she has no decent shelter, diet, or medical care—and no easy way out. She enjoys neither political and civil liberties nor, of most immediate concern to her, the economic and social rights spelled out in the U.N. Universal Declaration.

Her case helps illuminate the "economics of human rights." There are two distinct dimensions to this economic aspect of the human rights issue. First are the arguments behind promotion of economic and social rights and their implications. There is fierce debate over whether fulfillment of such basic human needs as food and clean water is, for governments, an objective or an obligation. Is deprivation of political freedom a necessary price for economic development in the Third World? Second are the types of economic measures available to advance all human rights and their consequences. U.S. policymakers are not sure which economic measures work and who gains by their use. Language alone, while important, may be an expedient catharsis for humanitarian sentiment, but without significant impact. Yet economic sanctions, as applied so far, have rarely achieved their intended effect. The record for foreign aid is, at best, spotty. What else is at hand to help governments put words into action?

However the economics of human rights is pursued, there is a question of capacity. For example, it is not clear how those who have long controlled El Salvador can cease to view peasant protest as a communist plot and see it for what it is in fact: an outcry of an aggrieved citizenry for a roof over the head and food in the belly. And, even if the conservative oligarchy were to decide to deal with these rudimentary needs of El Salvador's impoverished majority, it is not clear that that nation, with or without outside help, could marshall enough resources for sustained reform.

Nor is it clear how the United States could or should react to the economic dimensions of the human-rights question. What kind and amount of foreign aid should the U.S. provide to help make economic and social rights a reality in nations like El Salvador? And, more broadly, should the United States use *all* available means, including the "stick" of economic sanctions and the "carrot" of official development assistance, to help support the full spectrum of human rights? For the United States, the cost of that latter course could necessitate a sweeping reexamination and readjustment of national priorities. It could also lead to blurring more of the traditional lines between the public and private sectors. The size of the U.S. government's program for foreign aid is minute, compared to the scope of operations by major U.S. multinational corporations and banks. Further, the fact that U.S. private investment fast filled the void created by U.S. legislation blocking more official aid to the repressive government in Chile is just one of many instances where government and business work at apparent cross purposes. To be effective, should the reach of U.S. policy on human rights extend into the private sphere? If so, with what implications, short- and long-term, for human rights and U.S. economic interests? The economics of human rights may boil down to the bottom line of political will and the bottom billion of the world's poor—and what connection U.S. policymakers make between the two.

* * *

Taking stock on human rights thus misses the point if it turns into taking any one administration to task. Concern about human rights did not begin when "Jimmy Who?" became President Carter. Nor do the problems disappear with his departure from office. Repressive regimes do not wither away willingly. As one seasoned spokesman for Amnesty International observed, "We will not live to see the day when there are no more violations of human rights."

Beyond the regnant cliché and current moral chic, there are issues that are both urgent and enduring. Must improved respect for human rights develop from within a society, or can the catalyst for lasting change come from without? Are national boundaries more sacred than human rights, or has protection of human rights become a global problem with attendant global responsibilities and approaches? Is liberty a luxury for the poor, or is the lesson from the Indian election of 1977 (in which the overwhelming majority of citizens reacted against Indira Gandhi's invocation of emergency powers by voting her out of office) that economic rights begin with politics? Is there an inevitable clash between U.S. promotion of human rights and pursuit of national security, or does advocacy of human rights suggest some essential link between the two concepts? Should pursuit of human rights provide new perspective on national priorities at home and abroad? Much that is implicit in full furtherance of human rights suggests that the amorphous term, *the national interest*, may itself be ripe for reinterpretation.

In the broad view, there can be a human-rights dimension to most choices made by the U.S. government. For example, sales of police equipment to a Third World dictator may bolster short-term U.S. relations with that government, fend off revolt that might disrupt U.S. public and private interests, and boost the U.S. balance of trade. But, in the longer term, if local security forces of repressive regimes use U.S. weapons against political opponents and if that opposition comes to power, there can be a bitter backlash against the United States and its interests. The virulent anti-Americanism and seizure of U.S. hostages in post-Shah Iran reflect just that. Further, increased U.S. dependence on such emerging world powers as Brazil and Saudi Arabia—where many human rights are not respected—poses what U.S. policymakers call a "tough trade-off." Should the United States forego close relations with nations important because of their strategic location or resources, for the sake of making a point in behalf of human rights? If so, so what? As one member of President Carter's Cabinet observed, "If we stop arms sales to a dictator and France steps into the void, it is not clear that we advance anything except our moral purity."

Dilemmas of the most fundamental character have confronted the two men most often cited as the main contemporary protagonists on U.S. human-rights policy—Henry Kissinger and Jimmy Carter. The former secretary of state expressed concern about the choices posed by stress on human rights. "Peace," he asserted, "is the overriding moral objective." The plight of Israel, important to Kissinger partly because of his own Jewish background, joined the issues of peace and freedom. In the early 1970s, some of Kissinger's advisers urged him to dissociate the United States from the authoritarian regimes of Franco and Caetano in Spain and Portugal, respectively. Kissinger hesitated because he thought that antagonizing those leaders might mean losing access to bases the U.S. would need if war were to erupt in the Mideast. The choice before Kissinger: Should he trade the likely short-term risk to Israel's survival, for the possible long-term advantage of more friendly relations with those who might oppose Franco and Caetano and accede to power in Iberia?

Jimmy Carter has faced comparable quandaries, decisions that seem to pit pursuit of peace against protection of human rights. The U.S. stance toward the authoritarian government of South Korea's former president, Park Chung-hee, is a key case in point. When Carter announced plans to visit South Korea after the Tokyo Economic Summit in mid-1979, impassioned debate took place inside and outside the U.S. government. Advocates of human rights saw Carter's trip as a presidential stamp of approval on the despised Park government, a sign that human rights took a sickly second place to concern about national security. The State Department's Bureau of East Asian and Pacific Affairs, on the other hand, applauded the visit as a means to repair tattered ties with South Korea. To that end, the issue of human rights was to be raised only quietly, if at all. Proponents of human rights, incensed by what they considered "knee-jerk clientism," moved to outflank that bureau. They persuaded influential members of the Congress and others to press the issue at the White House. The result: Carter's assertion in Seoul that South Korea's position on human rights had direct bearing on short- and long-term U.S. security interests.

Is the issue of human rights the hapless handmaiden of geopolitical calculations and a hindrance to Big Power politics? Or, is stress on human rights the real stuff of *Realpolitik?*

The points posed by Kissinger and Carter—underscored by the deterioration of détente after the Soviet invasion of Afghanistan—suggest that promotion of human rights may be most significant, not for the answers it gives, but for the questions it raises. President Carter —together with other national leaders, members of the U.S. Congress, and human-rights activists outside government—has helped bring a neglected issue to the fore. He has raised world consciousness and opened the door to new directions. He has made an important beginning. But just that. The next steps depend on the American people. Are they ready—faced by the global nightmare of human-rights violations—to give full credence to the American Dream?

PART I

I

---◄••••►---

Cambodia
Escape from Genocide

Ly Linn looks older than her twenty-five years. She is also stronger than she appears, since she has survived escape from both Cambodia and Vietnam. Today she waits, with thousands of other Cambodians crowded into a monsoon-soaked refugee camp in Thailand, for word on her future.

There was little in Ly Linn's past to prepare her for this turn of events. She was a member of the upper middle class—born into privilege and educated in French by Roman Catholic nuns during her childhood in Phnom Penh, the capital of Cambodia. She had led a life of unsuspecting tranquillity.

All that changed on April 17, 1975. On that date, the Communist Khmer Rouge came to power in Cambodia, just five days after the U.S. mission evacuated Phnom Penh at the end of the Vietnam war. Soldiers from the new regime broke into Ly Linn's home. They forced her, her husband and two small children, and her sister-in-law and her father—along with thousands of their compatriots—to join the immediate exodus from Phnom Penh. As Ly Linn looked at the unwieldy mass of humanity around her, she saw the very young, the old, and the sick—some had apparently been interrupted in the middle of surgery—carried by their relatives. Still, the soldiers shouted, "Fast, fast, fast, the Americans are coming to bomb Phnom Penh."

Ly Linn's elderly father-in-law died on the road, as did thousands of others. Huan Sour Lai, her sister-in-law, said, "We got so used to corpses we were no longer afraid of them; we slept among them."

It took Ly Linn and Huan Sour Lai a month to reach their designated destination, a small rural village in southeast Cambodia near the Vietnamese border. There they were separated from other family members, assigned to groups by sex and age, and put to work tilling existing fields and carving new ones out of the jungle. Both women were often harnessed to buffalo carts and made to draw them. Although weakened by fatigue, lack of food, and disease, they resisted going to the primitive local hospital. Once the village pagoda, it seemed to be a place from which no one returned alive. Ly Linn's eight-month-old son did die, because he was too young to eat the banana tree roots and leaves which were the family's only food. Seven months after arriving in their new place of exile, Ly Linn's husband was seized by Communist soldiers. They had discovered that he had been a lieutenant in the army of the government headed by Lon Nol, prime minister of Cambodia from 1970 to 1975. "I never saw him again," said Ly Linn. Nor does she expect to.

The seizure of her husband convinced Ly Linn that she might be next. The wives of former officers most often came to share their husbands' fate. Escape, while dangerous in a situation where no one was allowed away from the guards or outside the commune without specific authorization, seemed the only alternative.

Ly Linn arranged to have her sister-in-law and her remaining two-year-old son use the cover of darkness to slip out of the compound. They then started the long trek to Vietnam. The women used jewels hidden on their bodies to bribe village officials into letting them stay overnight along the way. Traveling by separate routes, they took work in some of those villages, until they reached Saigon and found each other in the Cambodian pagoda where many refugees were sheltered.

Though life seemed better in Vietnam than it had been in Cambodia, both women became convinced that they could not stay. Ly Linn said, "I have to think of the future of my child. I am very afraid of communist regimes." She therefore made contact with another Cambodian refugee, a fisherman who was arranging escape for twenty-nine Cambodians and twenty-five ethnic Chinese. The two sisters-in-law hid in a sugar-cane field for three days and nights while a boat was made ready. Ly Linn kept her small son drugged with barbiturates so that his crying would not betray their mosquito-infested hiding place.

The boat crossing from Vietnam to Thailand took three days. After three more days in a Thai police jail, they were brought to an open field ringed with coiled barbed wire and kept under constant guard. Food was short. The small tents kept out neither the rain nor the intestinal parasites that plagued many of the refugees.

There was and is no indication of where Ly Linn can go next. Her name, low on the long lists of those who have applied for emigration to the United States, may be high, she fears, on lists held by Thai officials who could send her, at gunpoint, back to Cambodia and probable death. She waits, a woman without a country and with little hope.[1]

*   *   *

The story told by Ly Linn coincides with the reports given by thousands of Cambodian refugees. It also reflects the main questions raised by the situation in Cambodia:

« What did, in fact, happen in Cambodia?
« What explained the behavior of Cambodia's leaders?
« What did those outside Cambodia do about the situation there—and with what effect?
« What does the case of Ly Linn, writ large, suggest about the "diplomacy of human rights"?

What really happened in Cambodia—called Democratic Kampuchea by the Khmer Rouge who ruled there from 1975 to 1979—has been difficult to discern. At first, outsiders could see Cambodia only through the prism of propaganda. Within the United States, writers for the conservative *Reader's Digest* and the leftist Indochina Resource Center drew diametrically opposed conclusions from early accounts.[2] The U.S. government had little direct access to information about events inside Cambodia. Most information was gleaned from interviews held in the Thai refugee camps by members of the staff from the U.S. embassy in Bangkok. Inquiries to the Cambodian government from nongovernmental organizations such as Amnesty International went unanswered.[3]

Despite the difficulty in getting reliable information, the body of data, like the Cambodian death count, grew after 1975. Too many refugees told the same stories with too much detail to discount the overall thrust of their accounts. This comment, one of hundreds submitted to the United Nations, was representative:

There are no rights in Cambodia, not even the right to smile. I would have preferred to have remained in Cambodia, but I could not endure such a life. I wanted just a little bit of freedom, to be happy again, and to have enough to eat. [4]

The cumulative picture from such statements—together with the reports from the few foreign correspondents who remained in Phnom Penh for several weeks after the Communist takeover, the few diplomats and journalists allowed entry during the rule of the Khmer Rouge, official Cambodian news releases, and Radio Hanoi—confirmed the initial impression conveyed by individuals like Ly Linn. Cambodia, for the period from 1975 to 1979, turned into a vast rural work camp where murder was a frequent means of imposing control. [5] (Life thereafter was to be comparably cruel because of strife between the Vietnamese invaders and the remnants of the Pol Pot regime and the massive starvation of the Khmer people who were caught in the middle of what many considered a proxy war between the Soviet Union and the People's Republic of China.)

Cambodia's leaders attempted a fundamental restructuring of that nation's society and life. To that end, they forced as many as three to four million people to evacuate the cities in the spring of 1975, and to travel by foot to distant areas in the countryside. A second migration occurred in late 1975 when thousands were shifted from one rural location to another. Phnom Penh, swollen to a wartime population of two to three million by 1975, shrank to an estimated twenty to fifty thousand by 1979. The rulers compelled the evacuees to work twelve or more hours a day cultivating rice under the watchful eye of Communist guards (often indoctrinated teenagers) and then to attend evening political sessions where they were exhorted to work harder. Individuals who consistently failed to fulfill their work quotas were called before the local Angka or Communist "organization." Laziness was provocation for summary execution.

There were other means to mobilize radical reform. Officials enforced total collectivization of life in the countryside. The result was no ownership of private property; no money; no food besides the daily ration of one cup of rice from Angka; no religious observance (monks were defrocked); and no marriage without political permission (extramarital sex was considered grounds for execution). The nation's new constitution, ratified on January 3, 1976, called for the "constructive education" of those who engage in "activities regarded as dangerous and in opposition to . . . the people's state."[6] And, finally, the Khmer Rouge exterminated opponents of the regime. There was, according to one diplomat based in the area, a "centrally-directed policy with implementation at the whim of regional leaders who eliminate certain 'categories' of people."[7] The main targets for early elimination were former government employees, soldiers, and those called "intellectuals"—that is, persons with higher education.

A new element in this extermination was the increasing campaign in 1977 and 1978 to seek out the wives and children of men already killed. According to one report, 108 wives and children of former soldiers were led to a dike. Their arms were tied to their sides and they were pounded to death with large sticks. (Soldiers were under orders to conserve scarce bullets.) Some of the small children were thrown into the air and impaled on bayonets; others were held by their feet and swung to the ground until dead.

The toll from this revolutionary restructuring of Cambodian society was high. Estimates for the total loss of life—from both the liquidation campaigns against those associated or thought to be associated with the former Khmer Republic and the malnutrition and disease connected with forced evacuation and harsh working conditions in the countryside—range from "hundreds of thousands" (the U.S. government figure) to over one million in a population of about seven million.[8] Jean Lacouture thus concludes:

> Ordinary genocide (if one can ever call it ordinary) usually has been carried out against a foreign population or an internal minority. The new masters of Phnom Penh have invented something original, auto-genocide. After Auschwitz and the Gulag, we might have thought this century had produced the ultimate in horror, but we are now seeing the suicide of a people in the name of revolution; worse: in the name of socialism.[9]

*   *   *

Why? What caused the Khmer Rouge to take this revolutionary course? None of the available accounts, impressive as some of them are, provide a wholly satisfactory explanation.[10]

What little that *is* known about men such as former Cambodian Prime Minister Pol Pot and President Khieu Samphan suggests that they themselves have furnished the most concise rationale for their program. In their words: "We must burn the old grass and the new will grow."

Implicit in that statement was a drive for self-sufficiency, security, and, as noted, restructuring of Cambodian society. According to some accounts, the new leaders undertook the mass evacuation of the cities and collectivization of rural rice paddies in part because they believed that citizens in most urban areas, crowded by the influx of war refugees and dependent on U.S.-supplied rice, faced starvation. They thought that there was sufficient food for all in the countryside and that there could be even more in the future if more people could be mobilized to expand irrigation and planting. Since the leaders saw no easy way to move enough food fast enough to the people, they moved the people to the food.[11]

Whether or not the Khmer Rouge were genuinely concerned about a food crisis, they did have two related objectives. They wanted to revert to Cambodia's traditional peasant society, and they wanted to do so without outside help. Important members of the government, while students in Paris in the 1950s, had written doctoral theses on such topics as "Cambodia's Economy and the Problems of Industrialization" and "The Cambodian Peasantry and Projects of Modernization." Their strategy, developed in the fifties and refined during long years of political exile, was to build a strong agricultural base, supported by local cottage industries and handicrafts, on which industries could develop over time. Because of their own experiences, they did not trust anyone outside their organization. Nor did they believe that any other country could or would help Cambodia. Further, they equated the acceptance of such aid with subservience. Hence their decision to limit most contacts with the Chinese and to refuse most assistance, even in the face of the massive cholera epidemic of 1976.

Building a self-sufficient agricultural society required total control of the Cambodian people. The government thus stressed its second major task, assuring security. It was not clear how a new, inexperienced, and outnumbered coterie of Communists could organize, discipline, and direct the potentially hostile population that had been administered by Lon Nol. That citizenry included half a million men who had worn the government uniform, as many more who had worked as civil servants, thousands of Buddhist monks (with their network of temples, which were the centers for social life in rural areas), large numbers of peasant families who owned their own land and prospered from their farming, merchant groups (mostly of Chinese or Vietnamese blood), and hundreds of intellectuals (students, teachers, and writers) who might resist Communist domination. Potential opponents had the rallying point of Norodom Sihanouk—deposed as chief of state by the Cambodian National Assembly in 1970 and exiled to Peking—who was still technically head of state. And there were active resistance groups who continued to use the weapons and ordnance scattered about the countryside.

To deal with these millions—at a time when the new rulers had a small army, few civilian cadres, and the need to work people to the bone—called for a drastic solution. Mass evacuation of the cities served the dual purposes of getting people to food and breaking up the population into a mass of disoriented individuals—without roots, resources, or significant will to resist.

*   *   *

This recourse to self-reliance by the Khmer Rouge left outsiders with few means to learn what was going on inside Cambodia or to do much about it. Even so, one of the most remarkable aspects of the Cambodian case is how few *tried* to learn what was happening and to speak or act accordingly. Until 1977, no government or international body attempted to penetrate what Chaim Herzog, Israeli ambassador to the United Nations, called "a deep, black, echoless hole."[12] When Freedom House, the human-rights–monitoring organization, filed an appeal with the United Nations Human Rights Commission, that body took three months to respond, and then only to decline action. It was not until the 1978 session of that commission that a decision was made to look more intensively at the Cambodian situation. Great Britain proposed and got acceptance for a procedure whereby the U.N. secretary general would inform Cambodia of allegations made about human-rights violations there and have all relevant information available for the next session of the Human Rights Commission. The Cambodian government subsequently informed the U.N. secretary general that "the imperialists were trying to interfere in the internal affairs of Democratic Kampuchea to defeat the independence struggle of the people." In a letter dated November 7, 1978, to the president of the U.N. Security Council, the

Cambodian government stated further that—because of the "aggressive war" waged by the United States against Kampuchea, resulting in the death of one million Khmer and the destruction of 80 percent of the country—such alleged imperialist U.N. member nations as the United States were "not entitled" to raise the issue of human rights.

U.S. response to the human-rights situation in Cambodia had matched the slow pace of world reaction. There was only sporadic press or media commentary in 1975 and 1976. The executive branch released a few general statements noting the loss of life in Cambodia. President Carter made no public statement until April 21, 1978. No congressional hearings were held until May 1977. Some congressional resolutions, expressing "deep concern over the disregard of basic human rights in Cambodia," followed in August 1977 and April 1978. Statements on the Cambodian situation were entered into the Congressional Record in 1978. That concern over genocide in Cambodia did not, however, lead the Congress to take what Senator William Proxmire considered a logical and possible step: ratification of the United Nations Convention on Genocide. Former Congressman Donald M. Fraser stated in 1977, "We continue to be confronted with the fact that the United States' own performance in many respects has fallen far short of what we might have wished."[13]

What explained the slow and limited U.S. response to genocide in Cambodia? There were several factors.

First and most important was the lack of leverage with the government of Cambodia. Richard Holbrooke, assistant secretary of state for East Asian Affairs, explained to a congressional subcommittee in mid-1977 that the United States had little influence because "we don't have relations with Cambodia." He observed further that "our legislation does not permit aid to Cambodia," that "we have no intention of offering it," and that "our export and finance controls prohibit any licensed transactions."[14] Charles Twining, the state department's "Cambodia watcher" at the U.S. embassy in Thailand from 1975 to 1977, believed that the United States had a "moral imperative" to speak out, but that he was "not sure that the Cambodian leadership would care a hoot about what we or anyone else would have to say."[15] Further, many officials inside the executive branch and the Congress believed that speaking out too strongly would jeopardize prospects for future contacts with the Cambodian government. U.S. officials were still concerned about acquiring information from that government on the status of American servicemen and civilians listed as missing in Cambodia. That nation, unlike Vietnam, expressed no interest in normalizing relations with the United States. In fact, as one member of the National Security Council staff at the time explained, the United States remained "Phnom Penh's favorite whipping boy in its propaganda which portrays America as a threat to Cambodia and as the arch foe of the Third World."[16]

A second, less readily understood factor in U.S. reaction to the Cambodian situation was the backdrop of American involvement in Southeast Asia from 1965 to 1975. There was much in the American mood of this last decade that leaned toward putting Indochina behind us.

That may have been particularly true with regard to Cambodia. Former President Richard Nixon's decision to send U.S. troops into Cambodia in April 1970, and to attack North Vietnamese troops after Cambodia's Prince Sihanouk was overthrown in a coup, provoked an uproar in the United States. Hundreds of thousands of demonstrators descended on Washington for a protest march circling the White House. Government officials—including some staff members of the National Security Council, such as Anthony Lake, who was to return to the government as Director of Policy Planning for Secretary of State Cyrus Vance—quit in protest. Violent campus demonstrations culminated in the slaying of students by national guardsmen at Kent State University in Ohio. U.S. planes dropped an estimated 500,000 tons of bombs on Cambodia and caused, according to U.S. Senate investigators, a reported half-million Cambodian deaths. Some U.S. journalists faulted Secretary of State Kissinger for a policy calculated to save American face and "fight to the last Cambodian." They criticized other senior officials who justified U.S. action as necessary for the "re-election of the President."[17]

The net result was the contention by some critics of U.S. policy in Southeast Asia that the United States was directly or indirectly responsible for the sequence of events in Cambodia and thus all the more obliged to try to halt further killing there. One State Department expert on Cambodia argued that the United States did have a significant role in the ultimate Khmer Rouge victory, though "not with malice aforethought." The United States supported Lon Nol, though a "loser," and encouraged him to believe that he would receive full U.S. support if he opposed the North Vietnamese. Although U.S. bombing of Cambodia may have kept the Khmer Rouge from winning control of Cambodia in 1973, it did give them a tool to "foment revolutionary rage" against the United States. Subsequently, many of the first victims of execution by the new Cambodian government were those who had been associated with the U.S.–supported the Lon Nol government.

Regardless of what effect U.S. actions before April 17, 1975 may have had on subsequent developments in Cambodia—a debate that was to erupt anew with the publication in 1979 of Henry Kissinger's memoirs and the critique of his Cambodian policy by British journalist William Shawcross—U.S. policymakers came full circle to the question of real and hypothetical options for action. Because of congressional constraints and the absence of a U.S. embassy in Phnom Penh, they did lack many traditional means of influence. The few choices left included such possibilities as clandestine efforts to infiltrate the Khmer Rouge (perhaps leading to assassination of the government officials responsible for the killing), to efforts to get nations such as the People's Republic of China, which did have diplomatic relations with Cambodia, to intercede. U.S. domestic opposition to C.I.A. assassination of foreign leaders was just one of several factors that foreclosed serious consideration of the former. On the latter, some attempts were made. Zbigniew Brzezinski reportedly expressed U.S. concern about the human-rights situation in Cambodia to Chinese leaders during his visit to Peking in May 1978. Several congressional delegations had already voiced comparable concerns and asked the Chinese to help. Although it is possible that the Chinese, worried about Cambodian treatment of ethnic Chinese within Cambodia, had tried and failed in such efforts with the Khmer Rouge, they told U.S. congressmen that internal affairs in Cambodia were not a Chinese problem.

Even if the Chinese had agreed to intervene in behalf of human rights in Cambodia, it was not clear what effect they could have. Although China and North Korea were the main sources of outside aid for the Cambodian government, the amount of that assistance was not significant. To threaten its withdrawal as a *quid* for a human-rights *quo* seemed more likely to make the Cambodians sever ties with the Chinese—and thus deprive outside nations of a valuable source of information and some possible future influence—than to help the human-rights situation. Thus, U.S. congressmen who played the "China card," including some who suggested tying U.S. normalization of diplomatic relations with the People's Republic to Chinese intercession in behalf of human rights in Cambodia, met frustration. Efforts with other nations that had missions in Phnom Penh, such as those from Eastern Europe, were similarly fruitless.

The United States found little support for its concern among many other Asian nations. Those, including Japan, were loath to make much of the human-rights issue in Cambodia. They considered U.S. concern "interference" in Cambodia's internal affairs and took care themselves not to jeopardize potential normalization of relations with Cambodia and expansion of trade. Thus, as the Cambodians sought expanding markets for such items as their surplus rubber, they encountered no obstacles, on human rights grounds, from the rest of Asia.

Cambodia's conflict with Vietnam provided the critical crack in the dike of prior disregard for international opprobrium. As tension mounted between those two traditional enemies after 1977 and the threat to the Khmer Rouge grew, Cambodia's leaders apparently decided that they needed to rally world opinion to counter Vietnam's vitriolic attacks against their alleged mass killings. For example, they invited Western journalists to visit Cambodia in late 1978 for the express purpose of reviewing the human-rights situation there. Closed as that society was, its leaders—like many elsewhere—revealed concern about their image when hostile world opinion seemed to undercut their perceived national interest.

The fact that Phnom Penh did fall to the Vietnamese invaders in early 1979 left several major questions unanswered. How or whether international opinion and pressure might have significantly modified the human-rights performance of the Cambodian leaders remains an open question. More to the point of U.S. policy, the quandary that beset the Carter administration hangs in tantalizing abeyance. During the period 1977–78, some government officials wondered, Why expend time and effort on a situation that the U.S. seemed unable to affect? Why try to do so, moreover, when Cambodia had little strategic or economic importance to the United States? Others countered that there was a moral compulsion to act, but admitted that they had no idea how to improve on the policy set by 1978. That range of activity included maintaining a watching brief on Cambodia's expanding ties with other nations, continuing efforts to mobilize public awareness about the human-rights situation in Cambodia, and helping spur multilateral action.

Although the gist of U.S. policy toward Cambodia was to suggest that

Americans could do little in the short term to stop the killing there, the question of U.S. response to refugees from Cambodian repression remained. The United States had most latitude in treating the result, not the cause, of human-rights violations in Cambodia.

The record of reaction to the major area where the United States *could* have effect fell far short of the ideals expressed by the Carter administration. Although the U.S. did accept over 175,000 Indochinese refugees in the period 1975–78, it was slow to help Cambodian refugees. Special U.S. parole authority and interim measures from the Carter administration did break the log jam of many stranded in Thai refugee camps, but the special criteria for admission to the United States excluded most Cambodians. Many, unlike the Vietnamese, could not fulfill the requirement of having close relatives in the United States or having worked directly for the U.S. government.

The reason for the relatively meager U.S. response to the plight of Cambodian refugees during the devastating rule of the Khmer Rouge lay, in large measure, with the American people. Rabbi Marc Tannenbaum, an eminent leader in the American Jewish community and member of a special citizens' committee that visited Southeast Asia in 1978 because of concern about the refugees there, said that U.S. public interest was "virtually non-existent."[18] In touring the United States after his visit to the refugee camps, he found an "epidemic of callousness" that reminded him of disregard in the 1930s for Hitler's holocaust of Jews. Economic worries suppressed humanitarian instincts. Many Americans feared that the Indochinese would take their jobs or compound the welfare burden for hard-pressed taxpayers. Blacks and Hispanics especially resented increased competition at the lower end of the job scale and for social services. For such reasons, neither the Congress nor the executive branch had the political will to seek prompt assistance for the Cambodians when they needed it most.

*   *   *

The composite picture from Cambodia—the specific plight of Ly Linn, the larger scope of human-rights violations in that country, the rationale for violent revolution, and the record for external redress of the situation—suggests the complex considerations that come to bear on the diplomacy of human rights. Cambodia under Pol Pot may have been, as President Carter said, both "the worst violator of human rights in the world today" and the one least open to reform. There was international agreement that the Cambodian government was guilty of officially sanctioned murder, torture, and detention without trial, as well as denial of fundamental economic and social rights and political and civil liberties. Its actions had chilling parallels to those in Nazi Germany. One used modern technology to achieve racial purity and the other used agricultural primitivism to attain political purity.

The case of Cambodia leaves questions that haunt both advocates and skeptics of human-rights diplomacy. What of the belated diplomatic jockeying that condemns a people to extinction? Is there nothing that can be done by outside nations or organizations when a determined government decides to kill its own citizens? Does national sovereignty include the right of any nation to dispose of its people as it wants? Does international law provide grounds for international investigation, condemnation, or intercession? If the United Nations can do nothing about what observers of Cambodia have called "murder of a gentle land," of what worth is the charter born out of outrage against genocide?

There are, moreover, some especially agonizing questions for the United States. Have U.S. actions contributed to the tragedy? Given both the devastation of Cambodia during American intervention in Indochina and the disruption of the area after the U.S. departure in 1975, both opponents and proponents of the Vietnam war can answer, "Yes." With that division of opinion over cause and consequence, how can any U.S. president define the nation's responsibility for further action? What, finally, can any alleged American moral imperative amount to when there is no clear means to end the holocaust?

Notes

1. The story of Ly Linn is true. It is her own report, as told to *New York Times* correspondent Henry Kamm, who won a Pulitzer Prize in 1978 for his reporting on Indochinese refugees. This account draws from one of Kamm's releases (*The New York Times*, December 23, 1977), as well as publicly available corroborative data on comparable cases gathered by U.S. embassy officials at Cambodian refugee camps in Thailand.

2. That clash of perspectives dominated the first set of congressional hearings. See "Human Rights in Cambodia," Hearing before the Subcommittee on International Organizations of the Committee on International Relations, House of Representatives, May 3, 1977 (Washington, D.C.: U.S. Government Printing Office, 1977).

3. *Amnesty International Report* (London: Amnesty International Publications, 1977),

pp. 190–92; *Amnesty International Report* 1978 (London: Amnesty International Publications, 1979), pp. 167–70.

4. Quoted from an interview with a Cambodian refugee in Surin, Thailand, conducted by an officer at the U.S. embassy, June 1978. The transcript of this interview, as well as scores of others, was included in material assembled in response to Decision 9, "Human Rights Situation in Democratic Kampuchea," at the Thirty-fourth Session of the U.N. Human Rights Commission in the Spring of 1978. This material was provided for consideration by the U.N. Sub-Commission on Prevention of Discrimination and Protection of Minorities.

5. William Shawcross, writer on foreign affairs for the London Sunday *Times*, has done some of the most thoughtful analysis of developments in Cambodia and evaluation of recent writing on that country. See: "Cambodia Under Its New Rulers," *New York Review of Books*, vol. 23, no. 3 (March 4, 1976), 24–27; "The Third Indochina War," *New York Review of Books*, Vol. 25, No. 5 (April 6, 1978); 15–22; and his controversial book, *Side Show: Kissinger, Nixon and the Destruction of Cambodia* (New York: Simon and Schuster, 1979).

6. Congressional Research Service, Library of Congress, "The Status of Human Rights in Selected Countries and the U.S. Response," Prepared for the Subcommittee on International Organizations of the Committee on International Relations, U.S. House of Representatives, July 25, 1977 (Washington, D.C.: U.S. Government Printing Office, 1977), p. 6.

7. Timothy Carney is a foreign service officer who was with the U.S. embassy staff in Phnom Penh at the time of the closing of the American mission in April 1975. He served subsequently as the state department's Cambodia desk officer and has written extensively on political events and leaders in Cambodia.

8. Data on both population and the death toll are, at best, estimates since there is uncertainty about how many died during the war period, 1970–1975, and about the loss of life during the period since then.

9. Jean Lacouture, "The Bloodiest Revolution," *New York Review of Books*, Vol. 24, No. 5 (March 31, 1977), 9.

10. See François Ponchaud, *Cambodge année zéro* (New York: Holt, Rinehart and Winston, 1978); Timothy Michael Carney, ed., *Communist Party Power in Kampuchea: Documents and Discussion* (Ithaca, New York: Southeast Asia Program, Department of Asian Studies, Cornell University, 1977); John Barron and Anthony Paul, *Murder of a Gentle Land: the Untold Story of a Communist Genocide in Cambodia* (New York: Reader's Digest Press, 1977); and George C. Hildebrand and Gareth Porter, *Cambodia: Starvation and Revolution* (New York: Monthly Review Press, 1976).

11. William Goodfellow, of the Center for International Policy in Washington, challenged the characterization by the Western press of such evacuations as a "death march." He argued that "it was a journey *away* from certain death by starvation, for at the time the former Phnom Penh government surrendered, starvation was already a reality in the urban centers, and widespread famine only a matter of weeks away. . . ." Reported in *The New York Times*, July 14, 1975. However, Shawcross noted that Cambodian Prime Minister Pol Pot made no mention of food shortages as the motive for evacuating Phnom Penh. He said that the decision to clear the city was made "before the victory was won, that is, in February 1975, because we knew that before the smashing of all sorts of enemy spy organizations, our strength was not enough to defend the revolutionary regime." *New York Review of Books*, Vol. 25, no. 5 (April 6, 1978), p. 21.

12. Quoted by Leo Cherne, "The Terror in Cambodia," *The Wall Street Journal*, May 10, 1978.

13. "Human Rights in Cambodia," Hearing before the Subcommittee on International Organizations of the House Committee on International Relations, July 26, 1977 (Washington, D.C.: U.S. Government Printing Office, 1977), p. 24.

14. *Ibid.*, pp. 3 and 16. The one exception, on humanitarian grounds, to the congressionally imposed embargo was the shipment of $50,000 worth of anti-malarial materials in 1976–77. The fact that the Environmental Protection Agency demanded, but later withdrew, a request for an "environmental impact statement" for that DDT illustrates just one of the many complications in U.S. government efforts to respond to the situation in Cambodia.

15. *Ibid.*, p. 15.

16. Kenneth M. Quinn, "Cambodia 1976: Internal Consolidation and External Expansion," *Asian Survey*, vol. 17, no. 1 (January 1977), p. 51.

17. Anthony Lewis of *The New York Times* and Richard Strout of the *Christian Science Monitor* were representative of those expressing this view. Many officials within the U.S. government, however, believed that it was not the U.S. bombing campaign, but rather the failure of the U.S. public and Congress to make emergency supplies available in 1975, that made victory by the Khmer Rouge inevitable and thus opened the door to predictable atrocities. John Gunther Dean, U.S. Ambassador to Cambodia when Phnom Penh fell in 1975, made that point in congressional testimony reported by the *Washington Post*, May 6, 1976.

18. Quoted in *The New York Times*, February 19, 1978.

2

Diplomacy
of Human Rights

The case of the Cambodian refugee captures what is most compelling about the international diplomacy of human rights. Foreign policy is first and last about people—whether expediting a visa for their escape or warding off the war that makes their escape essential. Foreign policy is also, like politics, the pursuit of the possible through the application of power and persuasion. Efforts to promote human rights through diplomacy join the issues of individual welfare and international negotiation. In so doing, they bear upon the most fundamental questions of U.S. foreign policy: What are the means and ends of American diplomacy, what difference can or should the United States make, and at what cost or benefit to whom?[1]

United States stress on human rights provides a microcosm of concerns of another magnitude. The diplomacy of human rights touches on such perennial tensions of U.S. foreign policy as the alleged conflict between power and morality. At the same time, it encompasses such newly eminent global issues as economic development and terrorism. The diplomacy of human rights is as timeless as the appeal of the Declaration of Independence and as timely as the latest arrest of a political dissident. And it is likely to continue to raise questions that require response, not just by the U.S. government, but by the American public. These issues have clear implications for the victims of violations of human rights. They have less obvious, but no less important, significance for the related course of East-West and North-South relations. Finally, the handling of human rights is part of the continuing redefinition of national priorities.

The thrust of argument here is that stress on human rights is important for U.S. foreign policy on two counts. First, violations of human rights constitute an increasing global problem. Second, response to that problem affects U.S. national interests.

This discussion starts with the assumption—contrary to the popular myth, but based on commentary in the media and data on public opinion—that there are more skeptics than true believers when it comes to making human rights a focal point of U.S. foreign policy. The scope, nature, and significance of the human-rights problem are not apparent to many Americans. Torture of students by the Chilean secret police, although abhorrent in the abstract, is often just that—a remote abstraction. Nor are the pressures that can be brought to bear on that problem known to the average U.S. citizen. There has been much talk about the commitment of the Carter administration to human rights, but less indication of what effect that policy has had, in fact, for victims of human-rights violations. If the record so far looks mixed, why? What questions complicate promotion of human rights in general, and in the specific case of American diplomacy? Finally, what does the human-rights issue suggest for present and future U.S. policy?

With an eye to such questions, this discussion addresses the following issues:

《 What is the international human-rights problem?
《. What can be done about it?
《 What problems complicate treatment of human rights?
《 What conclusions emerge?

What is the international human-rights problem?

Genocide in Cambodia is just one reflection of the human-rights problem. "There is," according to former Congressman Donald M. Fraser, "a worldwide growing abuse of human rights, with violations of international standards so widespread that we are, indeed, facing a global human rights crisis."[2]

The standards are clearly stated in the "international bill of human rights" of the United Nations. That collection includes the U.N. Charter; the Universal Declaration of Human Rights; the International Covenant on Economic, Social, and Cultural Rights; and the International Covenant on Civil and Political Rights.[3] The main rights proclaimed in this international lexicon range from concern about crimes committed against the person, such as torture, to concern about civil liberties and economic needs. The documents prohibit slavery and provide for access to due legal process. They endorse freedom of movement within and among nations; freedom of thought, religion, and assembly; the right to take part in government directly or through freely chosen representatives; the right to work and to a standard of living adequate for health and well-being; and the right to education.

The Carter administration drew its human-rights policy directly from that international framework. It was not, as some critics charged, something made up out of whole cloth—or manufactured to reflect only American ideals. The scope of U.S. concern, stated by President Carter and Secretary of State Vance, encompassed, by explicit design, those rights already part of accepted international parlance on the subject. Those rights were set forth as three sets of what Vance called "complementary and mutually reinforcing" rights:

> The "right to be free from governmental violation of the integrity of the person. Such violations include torture; cruel, inhuman or degrading treatment or punishment; and arbitrary arrest or imprisonment," as well as "denial of fair public trial and invasion of the home";
>
> The "right to the fulfillment of such vital needs as food, shelter, health care, and education";
>
> The "right to enjoy civil and political liberties," such as freedom of thought, religion, assembly, speech and the press, as well as freedom of movement within and outside one's own country and freedom to take part in government. [4]

The magnitude of both the U.S. roster of concerns and the international bill of human rights is more than matched by the enormity of the problem at hand. The extent of repression and deprivation is staggering. Freedom House, an organization located in New York that monitors human-rights performance around the world, reports that twice as many governments today are authoritarian as are democratic. Death squads, tacitly or openly approved by governments, kidnap and kill students, labor leaders, lawyers, journalists, and others who threaten their claim to power. Thousands of political prisoners, from Argentina to Zambia, remain behind bars. They are often denied access to legal defense; visits by their families; and adequate food, water, or medical treatment.

The violations recur, regardless of region, race, ideology, or level of development. There are documented accounts of reigns of terror on every continent. Blacks kill blacks, for example, in the Central African Republic where the deposed Emperor Bokassa I bashed children to death in a widely-publicized massacre in 1979. Whites kill blacks in countries such as the Republic of South Africa. Whites kill whites in Northern Ireland and elsewhere. And Orientals kill their own, as the Cambodian case illustrates. The abuses persist from the left, as in Cuba, and the right, as in Chile. The situation in Argentina, where terrorism and counter-terrorism have become mutually reinforcing phenomena, illustrates the fragility of democracy at even advanced stages of development. Concern with security, not human rights, preoccupies most of Argentina's twenty-five million citizens—people who enjoy the highest living standard in Latin America and cultural development similar to that in Mediterranean Europe.

State-sanctioned torture has become what Amnesty International calls a worldwide "social cancer" in the body politic. Despite U.N. declarations against torture, reports suggest that its use has spread dramatically since the time of Hitler's concentration camps and Stalin's Gulag Archipelago.[5] This growing phenomenon of the times has a ritual and language of its own. Use of the Wet Submarine means near-suffocation of the victim by immersing him or her in water or urine. The Dry Submarine is the same procedure, but with a plastic bag tied over the victim's head to cut off oxygen. In the Grill, a massage of shocks racks the body of the victim stretched out on a metal frame. Throughout, sexual abuses are prevalent. They include inserting rats into women's vaginas and hanging bricks on men's testicles.

Other violations—less dramatic, but no less devastating—occur. Over one billion people live below what officials in the United Nations call the "absolute poverty line." They have no likely way out of a life blighted by poor food, housing, and medical care. The denial of economic and social rights is all the more galling for those who see a growing gap between rich and poor and who, moreover, suffer their poverty in urban slums at the foot of luxury high-rises. At the most serious and extreme level of deprivation are those who face threats to their very existence. Hunger and malnutrition, for example, are a major cause of death for approximately ten million people, mostly infants and small children.

Other violations of economic rights, albeit of less immediate threat to survival, merit mention. Among the victims of such violations are laborers and trade-union leaders who are often beaten and imprisoned because they seek higher pay and better working conditions. Democracy ceases to be an abstract principle when workers get too little pay to buy enough food for their families. For example, those South Koreans whose hard work and low wages have helped fuel that nation's export boom often flock to protest meetings. Those sessions can become stormy affairs, with fists thrust into the air and a familiar tune with unfamiliar words filling the room: "Uri Sugni Harira" ("We Shall Overcome"). One government response to such labor discontent is to dispatch stick-swinging agents who dump buckets of human excrement on the protesters, to fire those workers, and to label them Communist agitators.

Violations of human rights—whether in death arbitrarily decreed, a minimum standard of living denied, or freedom of expression denounced—often lead to a rash of reaction and counterreaction that spreads across borders. There are several increasingly obvious examples of this phenomenon.

Resort to terrorism is one. Many made desperate by their government's refusal to permit access to the political process or to open the door to economic opportunity turn, more and more, to violence. Governments respond in kind. A frequent result is a perverse *pas de deux* between the government and the governed, with sequences of escalating terrorism and counterterrorism. U.S. businessmen, caught in the middle in such countries, must wear bulletproof vests and travel in armored cars. Further, as events in South America demonstrate, repressive rulers in different nations collaborate with one another, as do the guerrillas. Secret police can and do follow, from one country to another, those advocates of human rights marked for death. A national problem thus turns international.

A second manifestation of how the human-rights problem transcends national boundaries is the movement of the world's homeless millions. Refugees, as President Carter noted during White House ceremonies commemorating the thirtieth anniversary of the U.N. Universal Declaration, are the living reflection of the world's failure to live by the principles of peace and human rights.[6] Unemployment rates of over 50 percent in Mexico or beatings by Haitian police translate into over 1.5

million so-called illegal aliens pouring into the United States each year. There is a continuing trickle of Berliners from East to West over the Wall and there is the far larger number of persons leaving Eastern Europe in general for new homes in the West. The flow of refugees seeking relief from violence in Africa and Asia has become a flood. There are over three million displaced because of extended fighting in southern Africa and the Horn of Africa, and there is no end in sight to the hundreds of thousands fleeing from Cambodia, Laos, and Vietnam.

There is nothing new about man's inhumanity to man. Historical texts abound with chilling accounts, whether from Suetonius's biographies of the twelve Caesars or medieval records of heretics burned at the stake during the Inquisition. Nor is expression of governmental concern new. For example, Gelon, Prince of Syracuse, defeated Carthage in 480 B.C. and made it a condition of peace that the Carthaginians abandon their custom of sacrificing their children to Saturn.

What *is* new is the known scale of violations. Modern communications—whether through nightly television coverage of dissidents' trials in the Soviet Union or dispatches from an Associated Press stringer in a Central American village—make possible global coverage for once-unknown victims of repression. Organs of international institutions, together with the worldwide network operated by nongovernmental organizations, have been galvanized since World War II to expose previously ignored cases of brutality. For example, Amnesty International provides information through the efforts of the expanding research staff at its London secretariat and its approximately two thousand groups in over 35 countries. Each group works to obtain information on and the release of three adopted prisoners of conscience and often takes part in urgent appeals to heads of state to save prisoners in imminent danger of torture or execution. Missionaries for churches around the world, quietly but effectively, provide data on lapses from the Universal Declaration to their central offices and home congregations, as well as sometimes to representatives of nongovernmental organizations and U.S. embassy officials.

Reports from such sources, as well as other indicators, suggest that abuses are likely to increase. That projected increase in violations of human rights is another new consideration, which underscores the need for the U.S. government and the international community to devote more attention to the problem.

There is a revolution of rising expectations among victims of violations, coinciding with a revelation of decreasing capacity of governments to deal effectively and fairly with them. Riots against former Nicaraguan President Somoza and the murder of Italian leader Aldo Moro in 1978 illustrate variants on the crisis of governance that pervades both developing and developed societies. The problem is now most acute in the Third World. In most less developed countries, the gap between rich and poor, powerful and powerless, is growing. A relationship exists there between economic and political oppression that poses fundamental questions, such as this one: Can we, given the underlying nature of the human-rights problem and the increasing interdependence among nations, expect to achieve sustained global economic growth? (Part III will explore this and related questions.)

Without a major and still unforeseen shift of direction by Third World leaders, current failures to fulfill human rights could feed upon themselves—with devastating consequence for those inside and outside the immediate realm of repression. The most likely outcome is a growing difficulty within the developing nations to satisfy demands for a minimum standard of living and, within the developed nations, to maintain an accustomed quality of life. One worse case scenario for several developing nations suggests the range of danger implicit in poor performance on human rights. As peasants find it impossible to satisfy their basic human needs in the countryside, more and more of the rural poor may move into urban shantytowns. Government leaders and elites, without easy access to resources to meet the needs of the poor or, more likely, with little inclination to reform, are apt to tighten the screws. They may, in the not-too-distant future, turn to new technology to maintain control. The repertoire of repression may expand to include such new techniques as the use of chemicals to modify behavior and so facilitate even greater control of the citizenry. For their part, the citizens could also invoke technological advance, with a twist to terrorism that includes nuclear blackmail.

What can be done?

"Diplomacy can be a rich mix"—as one senior official in the Carter administration put it—when it comes to doing something about human rights. [7] The diplomacy of human rights can be private or public, multi-lateral or bilateral, punitive or positive. And, it can be one, several, or all of the above at the same time. The challenge is to find the means that can help victims of violations most, at the least cost to all concerned. A brief survey suggests the range of specific tools and tactics.

So-called "quiet diplomacy" is the course most governments prefer. It entails working behind the scenes, whether in an unpublicized discussion between a junior U.S. embassy official and his or her counterpart at the host-country foreign ministry or a discreet exchange between the U.S. president and another head of state. The medium of the message can be low key or blunt, depending on the point to be made.

Quiet diplomacy has much to recommend it. It lets the government in question respond with, for example, the release of political prisoners, without seeming to capitulate to outside pressure. Governments, like individuals, do not relish losing face. Moreover, private approaches can get results. West German Chancellor Helmut Schmidt has attributed his success in repatriating thousands of ethnic Germans and facilitating family visits in Berlin to discreet *Ostpolitik*. [8]

Private talks carry additional deterrent value: if quiet diplomacy is not possible or if it lacks sufficient force, the next step may be to go public. Such was the case in Cambodia under the Khmer Rouge, when the United States had no diplomatic representation in Phnom Penh. Such was also the case, to a large extent, in Iran after the departure of the Shah. The Ayatollah Khomeini's paranoia about U.S. intervention precluded direct contacts with him or his immediate entourage. With no other way to register its concern about the toll taken by what some U.S. officials privately called "holy fascism," the Carter administration made public statements objecting to the wave of summary executions in the Islamic republic. The move to public diplomacy may also be part of an effort to mobilize world opinion, as occurred in October 1979 when U.S. officials denounced Czechoslovakia for convicting of "subversion" six members of the Charter 77 human-rights movement. It may be an expression, not of disapproval, but of approval—exemplified by plaudits from the Carter administration to several military governments in Latin America that held long-delayed elections, released political prisoners, or opened their borders to outside inquiry about human-rights conditions in their jails. Shifting priority for human rights in programming by the International Communication Agency (formerly the U.S. Information Agency) and the Voice of America represents another facet of public diplomacy.

This public side of human-rights diplomacy also involves a good deal of symbolism. Some examples of this sort include President Carter's decision to meet with opposition leaders during his visit to Brazil, attendance by U.S. embassy officials at trials of Soviet dissidents, and the friendly wording of the White House toast to former Indian Prime Minister Desai in 1978. Symbolic gestures can also be used to opposite effect. President Gerald Ford seemed to signal a disinclination to stress human rights when he refused to meet with exiled Soviet writer Aleksandr Solzhenitsyn in 1976.

Upping the diplomatic ante through public statements and gestures has advantages and disadvantages. On the one hand, it helps dissociate the United States from a repressive regime. Distancing Washington from a dictatorship can help establish U.S. *bona fides* on human rights at home and abroad. Jimmy Carter used this theme in the 1976 presidential campaign with telling political success against the Ford administration and the "quiet diplomacy" of Henry Kissinger. On the other hand, public diplomacy can decrease maneuvering room on human rights. Public condemnation raises hackles in the target country, risks backlash against either victims of violations or other U.S. goals, and unleashes powerful and often unpredictable forces. The siege mentality of the government in South Africa during the 1970s reflected international censure of *apartheid* there. President Carter's stress on human rights in the Soviet Union made the fate of dissidents like Anatoly Shcharansky a test of national wills and matter of mushrooming public protest in the West.

Both public and private diplomacy tend to be most effective when pursued by more than one country and when sanctified by the status of an international forum. Thus, U.S. policymakers have long contended that respect for human rights depends on "multilateralizing" the issue: developing regional or global consensus, getting groups of countries to work together, and following up with enforcement machinery. Three arenas are most important to the United States in this regard: the United Nations, the Organization of American States, and the Conference on Security and Cooperation in Europe. Since discussion on all three abounds elsewhere, a quick survey suffices to suggest the range of legal and institutional instruments.[9]

The United Nations is the most significant focus for multilateral diplomacy. The fact that it has over 150 member states helps give its statements and actions the most nearly universal stamp of authority. It has what is recognized as a body of international law and documentation on the subject. In addition to the international bill of human rights already noted, this collection includes the Genocide Convention, the International Convention on the Elimination of All Forms of Racial Discrimination, and a host of other declarations and conventions.[10] And the United Nations has mechanisms in place to facilitate compliance and implementation of those documents. The most significant in which the United States now participates are the U.N. Commission on Human Rights and the Subcommission on Prevention of Discrimination and Protection of Minorities.[11]

The sum total of these U.N. efforts represents a critical turning point in the history of human rights. The horrors of World War II, especially the slaughter of six million Jews by the Nazis, suggested to many in the world community that protection of human rights must become a collective responsibility. The U.N.'s documents and organizations dealing with human rights thus represent a relatively new international recognition of the human-rights problem and the first stated international acceptance of obligations on that question.

Some recent efforts suggest that the United Nations may be moving to fulfill the promise implicit in that unprecedented mandate. The Human Rights Commission receives over fifty thousand communications every year, many from individuals who risk their lives to convey concern about violations. For the first time, the commission announced in 1978 that it had taken decisions—according to Resolution 1503 of the Economic and Social Council, which establishes a procedure for dealing with complaints by individuals and nongovernmental organizations—on Bolivia, Equatorial Guinea, Malawi, the Republic of Korea, Uganda, Ethiopia, Indonesia, Paraguay, and Uruguay. At its 1979 session, the commission held the first extended hearing on cases raised by the Resolution 1503 procedures. A precedent was set when the commission decided to examine the case of Equatorial Guinea in open session. Further, in 1979, the commission approved measures to strengthen human-rights machinery in the United Nations. For example, it endorsed longer sessions for itself and approved planning to give itself an intersessional role. There is significant support for a proposal, initiated by Costa Rica, for a U.N. High Commissioner or Coordinator on Human Rights and for another proposal, set forth by India, for the creation of national institutions to serve as forums for revealing human-rights violations. Although little known publicly, the United Nations Educational, Scientific and Cultural Organization (UNESCO) has adopted a new procedure which enables individuals to file complaints about violations of their rights to the areas under UNESCO's jurisdiction. Governments are then called upon to respond.

The Organization of American States (O.A.S.), like the United Nations, has impressive declarations and committees dealing with human rights. The O.A.S. is the most important regional organization concerned with human rights in which the United States participates directly.[12] The O.A.S. Charter, drawn up in 1948 and revised in 1967, declares that "the American states proclaim the fundamental rights of the individual without distinction as to race, nationality, creed, or sex." It designates the Inter-American Commission on Human Rights an O.A.S. consultative organ responsible for promoting the observance and protection of human rights. Since its establishment, the commission has developed from an organ charged only with preparing studies to an institution that can act. The commission receives petitions from individuals who believe that their governments have violated their rights and makes on-the-spot inspections, which may take place in prisons and alleged torture chambers. Its reports name names and specify actions taken. For example, one commission report on accusations filed against the government of Brazil identified the army captain who was accused of beating a woman until her lips bled, in an effort to have her perform a striptease, and of grinding out a cigarette and a match on her bare abdomen.

There is evidence that efforts by the commission and others are making an impact. There is increased support for giving more authority to the commission. Its budget has been tripled. Human rights has become a central focus for discussion at the O.A.S. General Assembly. Because of human-rights violations in Uruguay, O.A.S. member states voted to shift the 1978 meeting from Montevideo to Washington. (In contrast, Henry Kissinger did go to Santiago for the 1976 meeting of the O.A.S. General Assembly, even though atrocities by Chile's military junta were widely criticized at the time.) President Carter stated before the opening session of the O.A.S. General Assembly, June 21, 1978: "My government will not be deterred from our open and enthusiastic policy of promoting human rights; . . . where nations persist in serious violations of human rights, we will continue to demonstrate that there are costs to the flagrant disregard of international standards." After the 1978 meeting, one member of the U.S. delegation marveled at the strong spotlight beamed on human rights, stating: "There is now a far greater acceptance of the legitimacy of such regional attention to concern for human rights—far more willingness to allow the Commission to maintain its watch."[13]

In a somewhat paradoxical twist to progress, the United States helped speed hemispheric approval of the American Convention on Human Rights—while itself refusing to ratify it. President Carter signed the convention, but the Senate has not acted on it. Nor is it likely to do so in the foreseeable future, for reasons that are explained in Part II. Yet, Carter's signature did revive momentum for ratification elsewhere. With Grenada's ratification of the convention in 1978, the way opened for the Inter-American Court of Human Rights to hold its inaugural session in July 1979. That court, similar to its Western European counterpart, offers victims of violations yet another forum for protest and redress. There is a further twist to this development. Since the United States is not a party to the convention, it was Costa Rica that nominated a U.S. citizen to serve on the seven-judge tribunal. Appropriately enough, given the often close connections among human-rights issues and activists, he is Thomas Buergenthal, the immigrant son of Jewish-German parents and one of the youngest survivors of Auschwitz.

The Conference on Security and Cooperation in Europe (C.S.C.E.) is one of the most recent and most significant arenas for promotion of human rights through multilateral diplomacy. The Final Act for the conference, begun in 1973 largely at the instigation of the Soviet Union, was signed on August 1, 1975, at a summit meeting held in Helsinki, Finland. It was attended by the chiefs of state of thirty-three European nations, the United States, and Canada. President Gerald Ford led the U.S. delegation to the summit. The Final Act called for improving East-West relations on a range of issues—including cooperation in European security; in economics, science and technology, and the environment; and in humanitarian and other related fields. Implementation of that third section of the Final Act, together with General Principle VII of the document, provided the handle for often blunt exchanges on human rights at follow-up meetings held in Belgrade, Yugoslavia (1977–78), and a raft of human-rights–related activity in all signatory states.

In fact, the Helsinki Final Act has surprised almost everyone with its impact. At the time of the Helsinki summit, much of the U.S. press and many American politicians were disturbed by the apparent blessing to postwar borders in Europe. They saw that meeting as a symbol of the Ford Administration's sell-out to the Soviet Union. But since then, dissidents throughout the U.S.S.R. and Eastern Europe have seized the Final Act as a means to press their human rights case or seek escape to the West. The Act has acquired a life and momentum of its own. Monitoring groups have sprung up in most communist countries. Delegates at Belgrade agreed to follow up on their work at a meeting in Madrid in 1980. Despite interim setbacks, the central fact remains: thirty-five nations are accountable to each other for how they treat their own citizens.

Multilateral diplomacy, while impressive and essential in an area that thrives best on international consensus and cooperative action, has not been an unqualified success, as later discussion will suggest. There is thus the need for bilateral measures, above and beyond the private and public approaches already sketched.

What additional tools are available to the United States? When words do not work and multilateral organizations fail to act effectively, Washington must, as several policymakers argue, "put its money where its mouth is." The U.S. Congress, with its power of the purse, turned to such tactics in the 1970s as a way to distance the United States from some repressive governments and make clear that the United States was serious about human rights. It mandated or threatened cuts in economic aid, trade, and security assistance, including arms sales, to countries which practiced, in legislative parlance, "a consistent pattern of gross violation of internationally recognized human rights."

There is also a *positive* counterpart to this punitive diplomacy. The option is open to the United States to reward respect for human rights. That, according to many senior spokesmen, is the preferred course of the Carter administration. Converting the stick into a carrot means granting more security or development assistance to those who do promote human rights. There are other possibilities, such as: a reorientation of U.S. aid programs to nations that stress economic and social programs; more money for cultural-exchange programs that bolster "progressive" elements in other societies; greater allocations for refugee relief; tax incentives for U.S. companies that help foster human rights abroad; and more support for nongovernmental organizations concerned with human rights. For example, encouraging the Ford Foundation to continue funding for the International Commission of Jurists, the Geneva-based organization dedicated to the rule of law, may do more to elicit accurate information on prison conditions and promote due process than would the most ambitious U.S. government exchange program.

The Carter administration has not been the first to use the mixture of diplomatic methods just described to deal with human rights. All of them have been invoked intermittently since the founding of the Republic. Indeed, Henry Kissinger, often posed by his critics as the arch-enemy of human rights, began much work that came to fruition after he left the State Department. Because of losing over a dozen of his own family during the Nazi holocaust of the 1930s, Kissinger was sensitive to the issue of human rights. He thus worked behind the scenes to facilitate the emigration of Soviet Jews.

What the Carter administration *did* do is begin to demonstrate, more actively and often than previous administrations, what can be accomplished for human rights through diplomacy. Officials in the administration first established the fact that human rights was to figure prominently in their foreign policy. They then worked to refine their approach. That meant taking due note of such factors as the pattern and trend of violations, the degree of responsibility by the government concerned, its openness to outside inquiry, the utility of U.S. action, and the effect on other U.S. concerns.

Members of the Carter administration have used the full array of diplomatic approaches to help promote human rights. By meeting with Chilean opposition leaders or sending official U.S. observers to trials of dissidents in Thailand, South Africa, and the Soviet Union, they have made a symbolic gesture, with both real and symbolic impact. They have, as in the case of ending grant military matériel for Ethiopia, moved from symbolism to sanctions. They have made U.S. views known quietly behind the scenes—for example, with the former Shah of Iran. They have blended private and public diplomacy—for instance, during President Carter's official visit to South Korea in mid-1979. By turning over privately compiled lists of the names of more than a hundred alleged political prisoners to the South Korean foreign minister and calling for an investigation and their release—and then making that action public—Secretary of State Vance sent an unprecedented signal to South Korean leaders. And, in addition to bilateral exchanges, the administration has stressed multilateral initiatives. Secretary Vance's call before a meeting of foreign ministers of the Organization of American States in June 1979 for the departure of Somoza from Nicaragua helped break new ground for U.S. policy and developments in Central America.

The Carter administration has also tried, according to senior officials, to "institutionalize" the process of decision making on human rights within the U.S. government. Such efforts are intended to help assure more consistent application of human-rights criteria to foreign-policy decisions and to help the stress on human rights to endure after Jimmy Carter's departure from the White House. Efforts to bolster that process of institutionalization include expansion of an independent State Department Bureau of Human Rights and Humanitarian Affairs, directed by Patricia Derian, a determined political appointee with direct access to the president; inclusion of human-rights concerns in most major strategy papers and statements of objectives; a directive to all ambassadors, assigning them personal responsibility for policy follow-up; and creation of an Interagency Group on Human Rights and Foreign Assistance, chaired by Warren Christopher, the discreetly effective Deputy Secretary of State.

Some further specifics underscore what happens when a U.S. president makes a conscious choice to try to advance international human rights. As Carter's visits abroad have illustrated, he and members of his family and the Cabinet have made human rights an important point of discussion with foreign leaders. The administration has also backed its expressed policy with some leverage. It has made human rights a factor in the allocation of funds or materials through bilateral aid, PL 480 Title I food-aid agreements, the Overseas Private Investment Corporation, and the Export-Import Bank. It has also complied with U.S. law and a perceived spirit of Congress to use its "voice and vote" to try to channel funds from major multilateral banks away from countries that are serious violators of human rights. To that end, the United States had, by 1980, delivered *démarches* to scores of countries, abstained on loans to others (including South Korea and the Philippines), and voted against over fifty loans to more than 15 nations.

What U.S. bureaucrats call the "bottom line" for foreign policy is impact. What difference does American diplomacy make for the individual victim of human-rights violations? Sometimes the answer is "not much." Changes in performance may be more superficial than real. For example, Argentine authorities ignored appeals from over four thousand families who wanted information on those who had "disappeared" in the last five years—but painted the prisons, where many of those people were reportedly held, in preparation for a visit by the Inter-American Human Rights Commission.

Sometimes, on the other hand, the changes are substantial. Although it is hard to know how much credit the United States can or should take, the latest annual reports from Freedom House and the International League for Human Rights do confirm that respect for human rights has improved in many countries and that some of those improvements reflect emphasis placed on human rights by the Carter administration. According to David Hawk, formerly of Amnesty International, "Anyone who worked in the field of human rights before Carter became president can appreciate the difference he makes."[14] Thanks in part to U.S. efforts, thousands of political prisoners have been released since early 1977 in such nations as Cuba, Indonesia, South Korea, the Philippines, Poland, Morocco, Bangladesh, Pakistan, and Tanzania. As part of an effort to regain prestige at home and abroad and to make better use of skilled manpower for modernization, the government of the People's Republic of China reportedly released in 1978 about 110,000 persons who had been detained since an "anti-rightist" campaign in 1957. In 1979, it began work on a broad range of legal reforms that could provide more protection of individual rights.

Why do these changes occur? Part of the answer lies in an explanation offered by Zbigniew Brzezinski, Assistant to the President for National Security Affairs. He has stated that "there is today not a government in the world that does not know that how it behaves in regard to human rights will affect its relationship with us."[15] In fact, even though there are clearly examples of other nations' thumbing their noses at U.S. efforts in behalf of human rights, there are numerous instances of just the opposite. Many governments, often for the first time, have begun to weigh the costs of oppression and to assess those costs—in their relations with the United States, their ties with other governments, and their image in the international community. For example, the military rulers of Bolivia agreed, after seven years in power, to hold elections—

largely because they believed that doing so would impress the Carter administration and help assure continuing foreign aid to Bolivia. To gain most-favored-nation trade status and the return of the Crown of St. Stephen, the government of Hungary promised to maintain emigration practices satisfactory to the United States.

The case of the Dominican Republic may be a particularly noteworthy example of the impact of changing U.S. policy. In 1965, then Deputy Secretary of Defense Cyrus Vance went to Santo Domingo while that capital city was reeling from civil war. He was part of a mediating team whose goal, at least temporarily, was to install Antonio Guzmán as interim president. That effort failed and was followed, in part because of armed U.S. intervention, by twelve years of rule by the dictatorial Joaquin Balaguer. The underlying assumption of that U.S. action, according to critics, was that what U.S. officials called "stopping communism" made the Dominican Republic more stable for American investment.

In 1978, Vance returned to the Dominican Republic, this time as head of the U.S. delegation attending Guzmán's presidential inauguration. The U.S. government had helped thwart an apparent attempted *coup* after the electoral defeat of Balaguer. President Carter had expressed prompt support for President-elect Guzmán and threatened U.S. sanctions if Balaguer were to thwart the shift of government in the Dominican Republic. To reinforce that message, then U.N. Ambassador Andrew Young and Major General Dennis McAuliffe, chief of the U.S. Southern Command in Panama, accompanied Vance to the inauguration. The presence of McAuliffe was particularly significant: it underscored for those Dominican generals known to be unhappy with Guzmán that U.S. armed forces now stood behind the democratic aims of the popularly elected president.

There are other examples of the use of U.S. influence in behalf of human rights. The Carter administration built on prior initiatives and achieved some movement toward the newly emphasized U.S. goal of attaining racial justice in southern Africa. It did so first through the U.S.–U.K. plan for majority rule in Zimbabwe Rhodesia and later through support for the Thatcher government's lead in seeking compromise among rival African factions. It also demonstrated its good faith in this regard through repeal of the so-called Byrd Amendment allowing chrome imports from Zimbabwe Rhodesia, initiatives to speed Namibian independence, support for the 1977 mandatory U.N. arms embargo against the Republic of South Africa, and President Carter's politically difficult decision throughout most of 1979 to buck congressional pressure and continue the economic embargo against the government in Salisbury.

More has been done elsewhere—such as making U.S. arms sales contingent on recipient-nation release of political prisoners or more general improvement in the human-rights situation—that cannot be made public without jeopardizing progress under way or hurting already delicate bilateral relations. Indeed, the fact that many effective efforts in behalf of human rights fall into the category of quiet diplomacy accounts for the dilemma of public relations faced by any administration that tries to make human rights a key factor in its foreign policy. How can the president both achieve progress on human rights abroad—and make voters at home believe that he is actively promoting the cause, when his most telling work is often done without headlines?

Finally, the Carter administration has found that it need not be, as originally claimed by critics, perched at the end of a unilateral limb. International initiatives—some from the Carter White House, some begun by the Nixon-Ford administration, and some by other nations—have begun to bear fruit. Of note, in addition to the previously noted efforts in the United Nations, Organization of American States, and Conference on Security and Cooperation in Europe, are actions in still other quarters.

Many West European nations are increasing their attention to human rights. Indeed, it is important to recall that they discovered the issue long before Jimmy Carter came to the White House. They consistently ostracized Spain during its authoritarian rule by General Francisco Franco. In the late 1960s, the Council of Europe suspended Greece from participation in its activities because the European Commission of Human Rights found the ruling military junta in Athens to have violated the human rights of Greek citizens. More recently, the government of the United Kingdom admitted before the European Court of Human Rights that its handling of certain prisoners in Ulster amounted to inhuman treatment and torture—in short, a violation of the European Convention on Human Rights. Spokesmen for Western European nations took the lead—against the strong resistance of Henry Kissinger—in advocating the human-rights provisions for the Helsinki

Final Act. And Western European nations have often outdone the United States in the percent of Gross National Product devoted to foreign aid. They have thus frequently paid a relatively larger share of the bill for fulfilling the economic and social rights of the Third World poor. All this said, Carter's stress on human rights and increased consultations with European leaders on the subject have helped move several European nations to take further actions. For example, nations such as Sweden have voted "no" on international loans to major violators on explicit human-rights grounds, something they did not do before—even in the case of Chile, which they condemned in the strongest terms.

Governments and international organizations are not the only advocates of human rights. There has been an explosion of unofficial activity within the United States and elsewhere to complement the moves of official actors. The major nongovernmental organizations have consultative status with such intergovernmental bodies as the U.N. Economic and Social Council; the International Labor Organization; UNESCO; the Council of Europe, and the Organization of American States.[16] For example, the International League for Human Rights, organized by the venerable Roger Baldwin in 1942, has a secretariat in New York, near the United Nations, and includes groups ranging from the American Civil Liberties Union to the Moscow Human Rights Committee. The International Commission of Jurists—with Niall MacDermot as Secretary-General in its main office in Geneva—has national sections of lawyers and judges in over fifty countries. The World Council of Churches, which also has its headquarters in Geneva, is well financed and sponsors activities around the world. It often acts in Catholic countries, where the Vatican, because of an often conservative hierarchy, cannot. Some of its actions, such as budgeting support for guerrilla groups in southern Africa, have aroused protests from U.S. congregations that thought their weekly donations were destined for Albert Schweitzer-like missionaries.

What hurdles hinder promotion of human rights?

Although there are many means to further human rights and although the United States has helped achieve some movement toward that end, much remains to be done. There are both general questions and specific issues that challenge U.S. policymakers.

GENERAL QUESTIONS. Promotion of human rights falters, first, because of an alleged dilemma of definition. Skeptics argue that there is no international agreement over what human rights are, which ones deserve priority, and what standards to apply.

Those challenging or exploring the universality of human rights come from different eras, regions, and ideological persuasions. John Stuart Mill, the philosopher most often invoked as the authority on so-called "natural rights," wrote: "To suppose that the same international customs, and the same rule of international morality can obtain between one civilized nation and another, and between civilized nations and barbarians, is a grave error and one which no statesman can fall into. . . ."[17] More recently, former Secretary of State Dean Acheson warned, with regard to the question of morality in foreign policy, that "when we look for standards, we find that none exist."[18] And still more recently, some Third World leaders have argued that the U.N. international bill of rights neither constitutes nor creates a consensus. They point out that it came into being in the 1940s when Western states and ideas dominated the United Nations and when many present members were still colonies. Others argue that the U.N. documents do not go far enough. Thus, the demand, in the name of human rights, for everything from more career opportunities for women, to promotion of gay rights, to protection against what Princeton Professor Richard Falk calls "ecocide."

Are some rights more basic than others? If so, which ones, and why? Some of those inside the U.S. government, in other governments, in human-rights organizations, in the academic world, and elsewhere espouse a selective approach. For example, Rita Hauser, outspoken former U.S. representative to the U.N. Human Rights Commission, argues that genocide in Cambodia represents the kind of situation that merits first call on limited reserves of national and international political capital. It is a clear instance of a crime against the security of person, and none can dispute the right to live. Further, condemnation of the Cambodian situation draws on both Western values and the Buddhist tradition of Cambodia itself, which holds as its highest moral tenet the "respect for all sentient beings." Others, however, argue that there can be no descending scale of wrongs and that all human rights deserve comparable concern. Hence, the effort to place equal priority on providing breakfast for a poor peasant in El Salvador, assuring freedom of speech for a Soviet dissident, and stopping officially sanctioned murder in Cambodia—not to mention meeting Falk's concern about the depletion of global ozone by aerosol sprays.

Whatever the legitimate range of human rights, nations can and do disagree over whether to accord primacy to the individual or the group, to promote the prerogative of the state or protect the citizen from the state. There is thus a philosophical and operational gap between most Americans who are most concerned about the individual freedoms specified in the U.S. Constitution, Bill of Rights, and Declaration of Independence and many spokesmen for communist or developing nations who stress the role of the state, the working class, or society as a whole. Within the international bill of rights, there are documents, such as the Covenant on Civil and Political Rights, that define basic rights protecting individuals *against* their governments, and those, such as the Covenant on Economic, Social and Cultural Rights, that define rights as actions by governments *for* their citizens.

Most Americans differ with their counterparts from communist and developing nations over a related point: whether to put more emphasis on economic and social rights or political and civil liberties. Even though Franklin Roosevelt's "Four Freedoms" (which provided an intellectual backdrop to the Universal Declaration) included "freedom from want," the average American considers such items as freedom of speech, assembly, and press the crux of human rights. For many citizens in the Third World, such freedoms do not make sense until they have food in their stomachs and a roof over their heads. Ernst Haas, prolific writer on international issues, summarizes the cumulative conundrum:

> How will American policy adjust to the patent fact that the traditional American emphasis is no longer shared by many other countries? The logic of collective rights violates the notion of individual rights, but the logic stressing individual political rights may jeopardize the enjoyment of some economic rights, while the commitment to certain collective economic and social rights makes impossible the full enjoyment of all individual political rights.[19]

Whatever the answer, there is an apparent ideological clash. Western liberalism strikes its Third World critics as an ideology of abundance. It appears preoccupied with violations committed by the state and impervious to violations committed against society as a whole. According to Princeton's Professor Fouad Ajami, "If political rights constitute the 'comparative advantage' of the First World's liberalism, economic rights are its Achilles' heel: it is here that liberalism is most vulnerable as an ideology of the affluent in a world seeking greater material equality."[20]

Finally, those seized by the definitional dilemma argue that there can be no one standard for all nations. Any judgment must take into account the level of economic and political development in the country concerned, its history and culture, the control its government has over the human-rights situation, and the extent of a genuine threat to the nation's security.

Advocacy of human rights flounders, in the second instance, because of the underlying reason for official oppression. To put it bluntly, governments violate human rights because their leaders believe it is in their interest to do so. Dictators need not be diabolical devotees of torture to conclude that it is often cheaper or easier to jail opponents or terrorize the citizenry, rather than meet popular demands. Because of real or imagined threats to security, love of wealth or power, ideological stance, or personal idiosyncrasy, such states and leaders do not disappear without a struggle.

Thus, for yet another reason, the U.N. Universal Declaration of Human Rights is often anything but universal in practice. Most nations consider foreign criticism of their performance on human rights an unacceptable assault on their sovereignty. Philippine President Ferdinand Marcos has asked rhetorically, "How would you feel if a foreigner walked into the White House and told the President how to run his Government?"[21] Few nations outside Western Europe are willing to submit to the U.N.'s complaint procedure. There is tension within the U.N. Charter itself, repeated in the Helsinki accords, because of attention to human rights (Articles 1, 55, and 56) and reference to the principle of noninterference by one state in the internal affairs of another (Article 2).

Implicit in the notion of noninterference is emphasis on national sovereignty. Stress on sovereignty recurs in statements made by repressive leaders because of their preoccupation with survival on one of two levels (or both): the individual leader of the state and the state itself. On the one hand, a survey of the season of Caesars in South Korea and the Philippines indicates that Park Chung-hee and Ferdinand Marcos invoked so-called emergency powers primarily to perpetuate their own personal power and not, as asserted, to serve national ends.[22] On the other hand, some Third World leaders, such as Indian Prime

Minister Indira Gandhi, appear to be concerned with both the question of national development and personal power. Many Indians, although critical of Indira Gandhi's suspension of political liberties, have argued that some of her efforts to slow the nation's population explosion and deal with India's enormous economic problems were necessary.

Revolution, according to many national leaders, has its presumed prerogatives. The case of Cambodia under the Khmer Rouge illustrates how a movement for national liberation or experiment in democratic centralism can turn into a mechanism for new repression.

Even without revolution, stress on national security, combined with the quest for rapid industrialization, can mean that other considerations fall by the wayside. For instance, government officials in Brazil have argued that the need for greater Gross National Product overrides traditional Western notions of freedom. According to their reading of *raisons d'état*, the West has no license to use such issues as human rights to change the rules of the game. That, they say, is unfair to latecomers to development and new aspirants to global power. [23]

The imperative of power cuts two ways in the diplomacy of human rights. It is, as noted above, part of the explanation of the human-rights problem. It is also part of the solution to that problem. To wit: it takes power to influence or remove those in power. The third obstacle to promoting human rights is thus one of effective implementation of expressed policy.

Leverage by one nation against another is often elusive. It is hard to find a way to force reform. The history of sanctions provides few examples of success. Indeed, sanctions can be as costly for the nation imposing them as for the target of concern. If Great Britain were to impose a trade embargo as a means to help end *apartheid* in South Africa, the U.K. might lose a market critical to its own troubled economy and encounter political backlash, both because of increased economic problems and the blood ties between many British citizens and South Africans.

External pressure to achieve reform may produce just the opposite effect. A referendum in Chile, held in early 1978 because of U.N. condemnation of human-rights violations there, suggests how both government leaders and citizens rally round the call to national pride and prerogative. There was overwhelming support for President Augusto Pinochet's stand against "international aggression," despite apparent

Chilean popular disdain for the double-speak of Pinochet's "authoritarian democracy."[24] Resentment against alleged outside interference can also lead to a backlash against the intended beneficiaries of human-rights diplomacy. Leaders of the South African government responded to increased outside criticism in the late 1970s by clamping down on blacks and retreating into the laager—much as their ancestors, the migrating Boers of the eighteenth and nineteenth centuries, took shelter at night inside a circle of ox-drawn wagons.

* * *

PROBLEMS IN MULTILATERAL DIPLOMACY. Actions such as those in the Republic of South Africa and the Republic of Chile belie easy optimism about the promotion of human rights. Indeed, despite some clear achievements, the United Nations, the Organization of American States, and the Conference on Security and Cooperation in Europe are sometimes more remarkable for what they have *not* done. There is, in these major multilateral arenas, what may be two sides of the same coin: too much politicization of the human-rights issue and too little political will to do enough about it.[25]

Human rights may be most conspicuously politicized in the United Nations. There national spokesmen, of whatever ideological persuasion, condemn those countries where they have other political axes to grind. According to Senator Daniel P. Moynihan, former U.S. Ambassador to the United Nations, the new majority of communist and developing nations has adopted "selective morality." Until 1978, such nations concentrated their condemnation of human-rights violations almost entirely on Chile, South Africa, and Israel. They had the preponderant voting strength in the United Nations—a change from the early days of the U.N. when Western influence prevailed—and could thus make their bias binding. Consequently, the United Nations has often turned a blind eye to blatant abuses in such nations as the People's Republic of China and most of black Africa. When the United Nations did begin to break away from selective morality—as in the case of Uganda in 1977 and Cambodia in 1978—the Human Rights Commission did no more than recommend "study" of the situation.

If that politicization of human rights rankles in the West, representatives from developing and communist nations are no less concerned—albeit for different reasons. Many delegates from the Third World see recent U.S. revival of human rights as a political gimmick. It is, they say, a reincarnation of despised paternalism. They interpret U.S. promotion of human rights as an ideological extension of past colonialism and present foreign interference by U.S.-based multinational corporations. They view U.S. stress on human rights as part of the West's effort to win propaganda points at the expense of the East. Many representatives of developing nations, moreover, are inclined to side with the East because they appreciate the support they have received from the Soviet Union and Eastern European nations on issues most important to the Third World (such as the New International Economic Order, decolonization, and opposition to South African *apartheid*) and because many applaud the apparent fulfillment of economic and social rights in communist nations.

Further, given the past U.S. record of alleged support for right-wing dictatorships, many Third World representatives are loath to put much credence in what they see as a sudden reversal of U.S. policy on the subject of human rights. For example, because of U.S. actions in Ethiopia, where the United States gave $400 million in military aid and training to 25,000 Ethiopians during the repressive reign of Emperor Haile Selassie, or in Chile, where U.S. public and private efforts "destabilized" the leftist government of Salvador Allende (1970–73), the U.S. record remains suspect. The result of such suspicions on all sides is, all too often, little serious attention to the promotion of human rights.

Henry Kissinger warned in his statement before the General Assembly of the Organization of American States in 1976 that "procedures alone cannot solve the problem." There must be the political will to use those procedures. That will has often been as weak in the O.A.S., despite the belief that a regional approach holds the greatest promise for effective multilateral action on human rights, as in the United Nations. Bryce Wood, academic observer, has called that organization's Inter-American Commission on Human Rights "a self-induced, benign boil upon the body politic of the O.A.S., no less resented because of the legitimacy and impartiality of its prickling."[26]

What has gone wrong in an institution with such apparent promise? One answer lies in the change in political climate throughout Latin America. The overthrow of several notorious Latin American dictators in the late 1950s helped create a political and social environment conducive to human rights. Hence, the creation of the Inter-American Commission on Human Rights in 1959. Subsequent deterioration of that *ambiente*—with the quantum jump in military-controlled governments, mounting challenges from the left, and the spread of terrorism—has eroded some of the political base for the commission's operation. There has been a pronounced shift throughout Latin America toward institutionalization of rule by the military. All the military regimes have the same related goals: stress on fast economic development, maintenance of internal security and order, and the defense of the military as an institution. The argument put forth by Brazil's leaders is typical: opposition to the government constitutes disloyalty and a threat to the stability and progress of the Brazilian state. According to Ernesto Geisel, the fifth general to rule Brazil since the 1964 *coup* that toppled the civilian administration of President Joao Goulart, Brazil should guard against "hypocritical, irresponsible and demagogic populism and the utopias of full democracy and outdated liberalism."[27] Leaders such as Geisel defend their actions against political opponents on moral grounds: they are upholding the rights of their citizens to enjoy peace and order.

In such an environment, the commission becomes a political threat and institutional anomaly in a contest for power, where the winner takes all and the loser is left poor, exiled, or dead. The result of the conflict between claims made by many Latin American governments and those presented by human-rights advocates has been little real implementation of O.A.S. declarations and little impact on the reported increase in human-rights violations in the Western Hemisphere. Countries such as Brazil have blocked the commission from investigating conditions in their prisons. The O.A.S. has taken little action to follow up on those inquiries that have been conducted, such as that in El Salvador in 1978.

There are comparable frustrations in follow-up for the Conference on Security and Cooperation in Europe. President Gerald Ford concluded his address to the Helsinki summit in 1975 by saying, "History will judge this conference, not by what we say here today, but by what we do here tomorrow; not by the promises we make, but by the promises we keep." Although the returns on the Helsinki Final Act are far from complete and action in the C.S.C.E., as in the U.N. and O.A.S., may be most important for the *process* underway, some interim results have been disappointing. There was no reference to human rights in the summary document at Belgrade in 1978. Reports compiled by the U.S. Commission on Security and Cooperation in Europe, headed by Congressman Dante Fascell, indicate that the Soviet Union and nations of Eastern Europe have fallen far short of commitments made to promote human rights.[28] Work on the sequel to the review meeting in Belgrade, a high-level conference in Madrid in late 1980, has indicated that there is cause for both optimism and pessimism. The good news is that national representatives and individual citizens within the participating countries persist in raising concern about human rights. The less cheering news is that progress is agonizingly slow.

*   *   *

SOME BACKGROUND ON AMERICAN DIPLOMACY OF HUMAN RIGHTS. Human rights has traditionally been one of the neglected stepchildren of U.S. foreign policy. Ernest Lefever, outspoken director of the Ethics and Public Policy Program at Georgetown University, has summed up one alleged reason for this situation: "A consistent and single-minded invocation of the 'human rights' standard in making United States foreign policy decisions would serve neither our interests nor the cause of freedom."[29]

The charge, since serious, deserves elaboration. Hence, a brief step back to summarize past U.S. policy on human rights and to survey why human rights has posed such a challenge to American diplomacy, in principle, in practice, and in relation to the rest of U.S. foreign policy.

First, a look at the record.

Jimmy Carter did *not* discover human rights. Concern with a moral tone, if not policy, has dominated American diplomacy since the Declaration of Independence invoked a universal appeal for "unalienable rights." Woodrow Wilson's call to make the world "safe for democracy" and John F. Kennedy's pledge to "bear any burden, pay any price," anticipated the line from Carter's inaugural: "Because we are free, we can never be indifferent to the fate of freedom elsewhere."

The sense of a special American mission to humanity has recurred throughout U.S. history. Benjamin Franklin wrote, "Establishing the liberties of America will not only make the people happy, but will have some effect in diminishing the misery of those, who in other parts of the world groan under despotism, by rendering it more circumspect, and inducing it to govern with a light hand."[30] In his inaugural, Andrew Jackson told the American people, "Providence has showered on this favored land blessings without number, and has chosen you as the guardians of freedom, to preserve it for the benefit of the human race." Referring in 1898 to U.S. annexation of the Philippines, William McKinley marked the imperial turn of U.S. fortunes with the observation: ". . . We must take up and perform, and as free, strong, brave people, accept the trust which civilization puts upon us." As war came to Europe in 1914, Woodrow Wilson anticipated the time when "America will come into the full light of day when all shall know that she puts human rights above all other rights, and that her flag is the flag not only of America, but of humanity."

American idealism was to serve as the foundation of a new world order. Interests, after the turn of the century, were to coincide with ideals. The point was picked up subsequently by Franklin Roosevelt. After the Japanese attack on Pearl Harbor in 1941, Roosevelt explained to the American people, "We are fighting in defense of principles of law and order and justice, against an effort of unprecedented ferocity to overthrow those principles and to impose upon humanity a regime of ruthless domination by unrestricted and arbitrary force." Harry Truman accepted the connection between, on the one hand, the expansion of freedom and human rights, and, on the other hand, international peace and stability. At the closing session of the United Nations conference at San Francisco in 1945, he stressed that "the Charter is dedicated to the achievement and observation of human rights and fundamental freedoms" and thus argued that "unless we can attain those objectives for all men and women everywhere—without regard to race, language, or religion—we cannot have permanent peace and security." In his address at American University in 1963, John Kennedy captured the sentiment subsequently seized upon by Jimmy Carter: "And is not peace, in the last analysis, basically a matter of human rights?"

Significant as such proclamations were, they clashed with another central theme in American diplomacy—preoccupation with what was variously interpreted as U.S. national interest. For that reason, declarations notwithstanding, morality has enjoyed ephemeral fashion in U.S. foreign policy.

One of the first tests of the nation's moral priorities was whether the United States would help the French revolutionaries in the late eighteenth century. The United States chose *Realpolitik* over human rights. George Washington refused to commit U.S. resources to the French revolutionary cause because of the alleged need to look to more permanent national interests. In his Farewell Address of 1796, Washington advised his fellow Americans that "the nation which indulges toward another an habitual hatred or an habitual fondness is in some degree a slave."

For the following century, the United States refused to undertake any foreign crusade for freedom—despite much public focus on human-rights causes abroad and many politicians' efforts to capitalize on that popular fervor. The sentiment expressed by John Quincy Adams in 1821 prevailed:

> Wherever the standard of freedom and independence has been or shall be un-furled, there will be America's heart. . . . But she does not go abroad in search of monsters to destroy. She is the well-wisher to the freedom and in-dependence of all. She is the champion and vindicator only of her own.

When President James K. Polk tried in 1845 to universalize American interest in the Western Hemisphere under the guise of the Monroe Doctrine, conservatives, such as John C. Calhoun, argued successfully that "true dignity consists in making no declaration which we are not prepared to maintain." American leaders, from Thomas Jefferson and James Madison to Henry Clay and Abraham Lincoln, limited the United States to trying to set an example for the world during the nineteenth century and resisted U.S. involvement in revolutions abroad.

During the twentieth century, efforts by the United States to make democracy universal and peace part of an international structure have been most significant, not for their humanitarian thrust—considerable as that has been—but for their coincidence with U.S. interest. The United States was therefore in the vanguard of efforts to establish the United Nations and set its early course because of the perceived contribution that organization could make to global and American security. The U.S. played a strong role in drafting the charter, which included promotion of human rights as one of the U.N.'s primary purposes. Eleanor Roosevelt served as chairman of the U.N. Human Rights Commission during its early years.

Yet, even in that commitment, the United States fell short of its professed goals. The late 1940s proved to be a fast-receding high-water mark for U.S. leadership on human rights in multilateral arenas. Since then, the United States has failed to provide a good example for participation in many international programs. The United States has, for example, adhered to few human-rights agreements of any importance. It has not ratified the legally enforceable Covenant on Civil and Political Rights, which has created a Human Rights Committee to review human rights reports from each signatory state. Nor has it signed the optional protocol to that covenant, which permits private citizens of ratifying states to submit complaints against their own governments directly to the committee once they have exhausted all available domestic remedies.

* * *

CHALLENGES TO PRINCIPLES AND PRACTICES. This dichotomy in American diplomacy, between profession of general principles and preference for particular practices, has haunted past U.S. advocacy of human rights. It continues to do so. Further, some influential critics of human-rights diplomacy challenge the concept at its core. They consider any general moral principles suspect in foreign policy. George Kennan believes that the United States has exaggerated the role of moral and legal principles in its considerations and neglected the constructive pursuit of its own national interest. He, like other so-called realists in American foreign policy, scorns the zealotry often unleashed by moral crusades.[31] Hans Morgenthau claims that "in politics, the nation and not humanity is the ultimate fact."[32] There is a difference between the principles which govern individual lives and those that affect the behavior of states. The late Reinhold Niebuhr argued that foreign policy be based on man as he is—the mix of "children of light and darkness"—and *not* as we want him to be. The central conclusion of the realist critique is that the deliberate effort to act on principle may lead to the ultimate wickedness. For many in the realist school, ousting the Shah of Iran—only to have the Ayatollah Khomeini come to power—suggests that promoting human rights abroad may undercut its expressed purpose. Women, among others, have lost human rights in a state dominated by Islamic fervor. Those such as Henry Kissinger also assert that the Carter administration hurt more fundamental U.S. national interests by its criticism of the Shah's human-rights record.

Those who criticize the principle behind an active human-rights policy also condemn its practice. They fault the Carter administration for its misreading of American power, excesses of style, and lack of strategic design. Skeptics, noting what Denis Brogan once called "the illusion of American omnipotence," argue that the United States alone cannot change the rules of the international game.

Critics also blame the Carter administration for the alleged inconsistency of its human-rights policy—and, hence, its lack of credibility. Principle crumbles in practice when U.S. officials appear to mute criticism of human-rights violations in countries ranging from Saudi Arabia to the People's Republic of China and many one-party states in black Africa. In the case of the Philippines under Ferdinand Marcos and elsewhere, the moving finger points but, having pointed, moves on.

Problems of principle and practice in human-rights diplomacy, together, incur some serious costs for the rest of American foreign policy. Haas argues that "the measure of morality is, not the loud espousal of strongly held beliefs, but the principle of proportionality between ends and means, the principle of weighing competing but legitimate ends and choosing the most moral among them for priority attention, while doing the least harm to nations, groups, and individuals who may get in the way."[33] He concludes that letting human rights take first place would make attainment of most other objectives of U.S. foreign policy, such as *détente*, "quite impossible."

Some experience from the Carter years confirms the worst fears of the critics. At the least, the record so far raises some questions. Stressing respect for human rights has led to complications in U.S. relations with traditional allies, with some newer allies among the so-called emerging middle powers, with adversaries, and with a large number of developing nations. In all those cases, there have been new threats to interests that transcend strictly bilateral relations. To illustrate:

Pressing hard on human rights has upset important NATO allies. Particularly in early 1977, many considered Carter's "moral crusade" ill-conceived, naive, and harmful to East-West rapport, which, in turn, affected *détente* in their own backyard. West German Chancellor Helmut Schmidt minced no words at that time. He feared that a U.S. frontal attack on Soviet repression might undermine his quietly effective efforts to ease movement between East and West Germany. The Western Europeans also found many U.S. efforts to reform Third World leaders unrealistic and contrary to their own overriding economic interests. The European Community thus responded to sharp criticism from developing countries, where its member states valued access to markets and resources, by paring back reference to human rights in the Lomé II renewal agreement for trade and aid with African, Caribbean, and Pacific nations.

Some critics believe that the alienation of allies gives aid and comfort to Moscow which more than offsets any good that human-rights diplomacy may achieve. That problem, they say, is especially serious when U.S. criticism of human-rights violations in nations such as South Korea, the Philippines, and several South American nations undercuts their ability to counter communist expansion. It is wrong to criticize these *authoritarian* regimes, the argument goes, since doing so may mean that they fall under even worse *totalitarian* rule.

Treating Argentina like a moral outcast has hardened anti-U.S. attitudes in right-wing circles throughout Latin America and has threatened other U.S. objectives. Officials in the Carter administration have feared that Argentina could accelerate efforts to develop its own capability to reprocess nuclear fuels, without proper safeguards. Further, the legislative requirement to end all new arms transfers to Argentina by October 1978 helped push that nation toward European markets, thus losing export sales for the United States, and to increase efforts at self-sufficiency, thus exacerbating the spiral of global arms expenditures and feeding international tension.

Countries such as Saudi Arabia, Brazil, Iran, Nigeria, and other nations rising to global prominence pose particular problems for U.S. policymakers. Thomas Hughes, president of the Carnegie Endowment for International Peace, claims that American foreign policy must provide for the "management of contradictions."[34] If so, Washington may be on a collision course. It is not obvious how the United States can cultivate nations newly important to its interests and, at the same time, advocate more respect for human rights in those countries.

Embracing Soviet dissidents has struck some as a dagger thrust to *détente*. The fact that President Carter answered a letter from Soviet dissident Sakharov and received another dissident in the White House in early 1977 angered the Kremlin leadership and seemed to sour the atmosphere for Secretary Vance's presentation of a new arms-control package in Moscow in March 1977. (Others have argued that the Soviets simply used the Carter administration's stress on human rights, as an excuse to accelerate a crackdown on dissidents already under way and to veto an arms proposal that they did not find in their national interest.) American insistence on the right of Ludmilla Vlasova, the ballerina wife of a defecting Bolshoi Ballet star, to decide in a non-coercive atmosphere whether to remain in the United States or to return to the Soviet Union, raised the fundamental question of freedom to choose where one lives. It also worsened already delicate U.S.–Soviet relations in 1979. At the same time, exempting the People's Republic of China from stress on human rights, because of the fragility and value of new U.S.–Chinese ties, has baffled other nations and many Americans. Why, for example, grant Most Favored Nation trading status to the People's Republic of China and continue to withhold it, on human-rights grounds, from the U.S.S.R.? Soviet leaders, although hardly noteworthy proponents of fundamental freedoms, have been understandably piqued by perceived U.S. favoritism for Peking.

Invoking human rights as reason to vote against loans from major international financial institutions plays havoc with many avowed U.S. objectives. The case of Romania illustrates one dimension of the dilemma. The U.S. government wants to encourage Romania in its independent foreign policy (Romania is one of the few Eastern European nations to challenge Soviet directives), but discourage its internal oppression (Romania is one of the most restricted societies in Eastern Europe). Will opposing a World Bank loan to the Romanian government, because of Amnesty International's reports of forced labor in Romania, drive that country out of Western institutions such as the Bank and back into greater dependence on the Soviet Union? The situation in the Third World reflects another part of the problem. Voting against bilateral or multilateral loans to developing nations that violate human rights may, according to Henry Kissinger and others, lead the United States to indulge in inadvertent isolationism. Few governments in the Third World respect human rights. If the United States were to press dissociation from repressive regimes to its logical conclusion, it might cut off all foreign aid to such governments. The United States would thus abdicate much responsibility for developments there and leave the poor and oppressed to fend for themselves.

What conclusions emerge?

Promoting human rights seems to create so many problems and raise so many questions that some wonder, "Why bother"? There are several answers. At the most obvious level, most of the points posed by the skeptics are, as the rest of this chapter will argue, false issues. On a more fundamental plane, a case can be made for the contention that active advocacy of human rights both serves U.S. national interest and spurs needed reevaluation of that concept. This discussion thus concludes with a review of what Americans gain from stress on human rights, how promotion of human rights suggests some new priorities for American policy, and what remains to be done.

RATIONALE FOR HUMAN-RIGHTS DIPLOMACY. There are a number of reasons why promotion of human rights should be a fundamental factor in the formulation of U.S. foreign policy. Those include five major considerations.

First, the simplest answer may be that the United States cannot ignore a problem that is so big, so well-known, and so apt to grow. The governments of over two-thirds of the U.N. member states are authoritarian or totalitarian. Violations have reached, if not record levels, at least unprecedented notice. Nightly telecasts bring reports of torture abroad into U.S. living rooms. Church and student activisits make *apartheid* in South Africa a pocketbook issue for millions of American stockholders and business executives. According to sociologist Peter Berger, once-distant "others" become neighbors in a morally uncomfortable way and the protective walls of traditional worlds break down so that "modernization makes reluctant moral philosophers of us all."[35]

Oppression is expected to increase. That is partly because it is not a phenomenon unto itself. Case histories ranging from Chile to Czechoslovakia suggest that it is significant as both a cause and effect of more fundamental problems within and among societies. Further, trends afoot in the 1980s may tempt governments to increase their violations of human rights. Population growth and all the problems attendant to it—such as food shortages and uncontrolled movement of people from the countryside to urban slums—will put more pressure on governments. So will the higher costs of energy imports that will add yet another hurdle to economic development in the Third World. Those costs will show up in price hikes for fertilizer used by the individual peasant farmer and the need of national governments to tighten domestic belts in order to deal with massive external debt. The safety valve provided by migration may disappear as governments bar entry to those seeking better political and economic conditions. Technological progress may enable governments to hone their capability for far-reaching surveillance and to use hitherto unknown techniques to control the behavior of their citizens.

Second, the United States has legal obligations to help promote human rights. Those obligations are spelled out in the United Nations Charter, the Helsinki Final Act, and other international instruments, as well as in U.S. domestic legislation. The United States is accountable to other nations for its performance on human rights and has an internationally endorsed responsibility to help further fundamental freedoms abroad.

Third, the human-rights problem affects the United States. The average American may think he is immune to the process described by Berger. In fact, he is not. For example, one nation's freedom fighter can become another's terrorist, with predictable tragedy for the innocent U.S. traveler caught in an airport bombing. Even more significant is the relation between violations of human rights and international tension that affects the United States as a whole. Former Secretary of State George Marshall argued in an address before the U.N. General Assembly in 1948 that deliberate denials of basic human rights underlay most of the troubles of the times and threatened the work of the United Nations. He stated that "governments which systematically disregard the rights of their own people are not likely to respect the rights of other nations and other people and are likely to seek their objectives by coercion and force. . . ."[36] That general argument applies to specific challenges before the United States. For example, U.S.–Soviet agreements on strategic and conventional arms depend, in part, on effective provision for inspection. Many means to that end are lacking now because of restricted movement into and out of the U.S.S.R. and strict control of Soviet society. More sustained progress on arms control may not occur until the Soviet system opens up and allows unfettered travel. Next steps in the Strategic Arms Limitations Talks may thus be integrally related to greater protection of human rights.

Fourth, promoting human rights can serve the U.S. national interest—particularly over the long run. The relationship between protection of human rights and promotion of American interest emerges in several ways.

Since states are often judged by the company they keep, the United States can refurbish its tarnished international image by distancing itself from repressive governments. Preliminary returns from the Carter administration's human-rights policy do indicate increased respect for the United States. According to reports received from around the world, the comment from one Brazilian journalist is representative. He asserted that "from the moment Latin Americans, Africans, and Asians started looking at President Carter as a politician interested in human rights, the United States Embassy ceased being seen by thousands of Third World liberals as a headquarters for conservative maneuvers; it became identified with the nation it represents."[37]

Since economic grievances are central to concerns in the Third World, the United States can improve its standing there if it puts high priority on furthering economic and social rights. Leaders from developing nations have warned that U.S. reluctance to take steps to facilitate their nations' economic development—and thereby help fulfill the economic and social rights of their poor—through increased foreign aid, rescheduling of debts, and preferential trade agreements could result in decreased U.S. access to increasingly important Third World markets and resources. According to spokesmen for developing nations, a viable world order must encompass concern for their priorities. Otherwise, they may try to rebel against or withdraw from a Westernized order and slip into the global margin where anomie prevails. As one scholar put it, "The subculture of ghetto violence has a global equivalent."[38] Nations that are ignored have no stake in the prevailing order and attack accessible strategic points.

Since violations of human rights are usually an index to deeper problems within a society, attention to them can alert the United States to underlying instability and help align the United States with progressive forces for change. Doing so can, in turn, help prevent dangerous outbreaks of anti-Americanism and extensions of influence hostile to U.S. interests. Southern Africa is an example of this phenomenon. Past U.S. alignment with white supremacist forces against the black majority—while the Soviets were providing arms and military training for outlawed black nationalists—helped give an unnecessary toehold in southern Africa to the U.S.S.R. and Cuba; lead to an unnecessary bloodletting within Zimbabwe Rhodesia and the Republic of South Africa; and heighten regional tension, as government troops and guerrillas trade retaliatory strikes across borders. U.S. miscalculations in Nicaragua and Iran have had comparably serious consequences.

In most such cases, the fundamental error, for which sensitivity to violations of human rights provides some insight, is to equate apparent stability with order and thus to lose sight of long-term U.S. national interest for the sake of short-term advantage. In his criticism of the Carter administration's human rights policy, Ernest Lefever argued that "in the Third World, we seek inter-state stability, which is conducive to peaceful development and normal diplomatic and economic intercourse among states."[39] However, inter-state stability derives, in large measure, from *intra*-state stability. Although oppression can impose a stability of sorts—that is why dictatorial regimes have been viewed traditionally as "good for business"—it often cannot.

Several questions thus assume increasing urgency for U.S. policymakers. Does short-run preoccupation with stability ignore present realities and prevent longer-term access to strategic real estate, vital resources, or the next generation of leaders? At what price does the United States accommodate dictators, such as Ferdinand Marcos in the Philippines? To what extent do all parts of the U.S. government pursue the same national interest? John Stockwell, former chief of the C.I.A.'s covert operations in Angola, has observed that the Central Intelligence Agency often establishes bonds of influence that contradict official policy. Since its operations are based on special relationships with local security personnel, Stockwell has charged that the agency's sympathies "lie with the police forces, not with the world's peoples." He considers South Africa the classic example of this phenomenon: "With every indication that South Africa's white minority rule is smoldering tinder, the C.I.A. continues to support the white redoubt in the name of our national interest."[40]

Reevaluating national interest in light of the questions posed by concern about human rights suggests that U.S. support for authoritarian governments may lead to the very totalitarianism that policy is supposed to prevent. For the United States, the wisdom of one era, the 1950s, may have become the anachronism of another, the 1980s. The U.S. government may be embarrassed increasingly by its close association, past and present, with right-wing regimes. Once most significant as foes of communism, many are now most notable for an authoritarian nature that fosters communist agitation. The United States is perceived by the opposition within such countries and elsewhere as the accomplice to oppression.

U.S. policy toward the Republic of Korea (South Korea) has been and may remain a case in point. Both Henry Kissinger and Cyrus Vance have stressed the importance of that nation, both to U.S. security interests in Asia and as an alternative to the communist government to the north. Compelling as those arguments may be, at least for the short term, Leonard Meeker, former legal adviser at the State Department, has raised a question which, though it applied specifically to an assassinated leader, still casts some doubt on the conventional wisdom. He wonders "if there is not a greater long-term risk of instability, turmoil, and perhaps substitution of a totalitarian regime of the left from the continued repression by the present Park Government, generously and strongly supported by the United States, than from a sustained U.S. effort to bring about in Korea a more open and humane political system."[41]

Such questions and other factors make the alleged *Realpolitik* of Henry Kissinger suspect. The former secretary of state has talked about the need to address dangers, like the polarization of the world into rich and poor, before they become realities, and of the need to shape an international role that the American people can support over the longer term. At no point has he recognized the possibility that his own relative disregard for human rights worked at cross purposes to that perspective. His emphasis on good relations with some repressive regimes, while explicable in immediate terms of defense, offended American public sensibility and risked damage to longer-term interests. For example, his stress on close ties with the previous conservative government in Portugal put the United States on the losing side both in that country and in its African colonies—with effects that are still unfolding.

The emphasis on order, implicit in many of Kissinger's speeches and actions, missed the point of some change in a changing world. Although human rights is probably not "the genuine historical inevitability of our times"—as Brzezinski has argued—perennial human aspirations for certain basic rights and the impact of communications, literacy, and education on the political consciousness of men and women do underscore the increasing relevance of human rights to U.S. and international calculations about change.[42] To ignore violations of human rights may be to disregard one of the major causes and symptoms of domestic and global tension and thus, as noted previously, undercut the pursuit of peace. It is a short-run reading of national interest that lacks long-term perspective. *Realpolitik*, posited by the realist school as the prudent alternative to idealism, is anything but that. In fact, true *Realpolitik* does not reject moral considerations; it reflects them. In that spirit, Marshall Shulman has identified the underlying point suggested by the conjuncture of human rights and U.S. national interest:

> If security means that what we seek to protect is not only territory but a system of values, then we need a broader and more enlightened understanding of our real security interests than now prevails. . . . It is not a question whether or not to act upon the national interest, but whether we perceive and define that national interest in terms broad enough to respond to the actual determinants of political behavior.[43]

Finally, whether or not promoting human rights puts America on the side of the angels, the winners, or the future, it often does help Americans support their own foreign policy.

By the early 1970s, a majority in the U.S. Congress concluded that most Americans opposed giving aid and arms to governments that oppressed their citizens and that they would not support a foreign policy that mocked traditionally expressed American values. Even though Americans have not always acted on those values, they do consider their country to have been uniquely conceived to promote respect for human rights. President Carter could thus assert with some justification that "human rights is the soul of our foreign policy . . . because human rights is the soul of our sense of nationhood."[44] In that regard, promoting respect for human rights abroad helps dissociate the United States from oppressive governments. Americans feel better and hold their heads higher in the international community when the United States avoids direct or indirect responsibility for the odious practices of other governments. As one senior official in the State Department argued, "We should not sell military equipment to those who torture innocent people—if for no other reason, than it is wrong and we should not shoulder that shame."

Alexis de Tocqueville called Americans the most pragmatic of people, and George Santayana said that "being American is, of itself, almost a moral condition." The foregoing arguments suggest that U.S. policy on human rights falls somewhere between their two perspectives, and between those perennial poles of alleged contention, power and morality. Promotion of human rights may mean that the two coincide and that the national interest becomes a matter of both pragmatism and principle. Therein lies what may be the most important reason for making human rights a factor of major concern in American diplomacy. It is important because it is *right*—in the fullest selfish and selfless sense of that word.

PUTTING HUMAN RIGHTS INTO PERSPECTIVE. Progress toward fulfillment of fundamental freedoms need not be as improbable as some skeptics suggest. The dilemma over defining human rights and building an international consensus is, in many respects, more apparent than real. Before World War II, international law was all but silent on the subject of human rights. Since then, there has been a dramatic internationalization of human rights. No nation can now claim *not* to know what human rights are or assert freedom from international inquiry. The fact that many *do* reflects more of a political choice, admittedly significant in its own terms than a sustainable legal position. Both the consensus of international lawyers and much U.N. practice undercut those who contend that there is no agreed catalogue of rights and no binding obligation. For example, Louis B. Sohn, professor of international law at the Harvard Law School, has stated that "the Declaration not only constitutes an authoritative interpretation of the Charter obligations but also a binding instrument in its own right, representing the consensus of the international community on the human rights which each of its members must respect, promote and observe."[45]

Cultural relativism is more an excuse than a justification for inaction on human rights or resistance to outside scrutiny. It is possible to discern in the major traditional cultures and religions repudiation of such egregious violations as torture. The physical extermination of entire categories of people or separation of children from their parents, as practiced in the People's Republic of China, is not just a violation of what some Chinese leaders consider Western "bourgeois morality." It runs counter to Chinese tradition, which holds that government should be "human-hearted" and that "filial piety" is one of the highest values. One of the posters put up in Peking in early 1979 called on President Carter to "pay attention" to the problem of individual rights in China and justified Carter's involvement by emphasizing the cross-cultural nature of those rights. In like manner, acts of cruelty by a Muslim ruler offend not just the Judeo-Christian tradition but the ethical core of Islam.

Every call to prayer, from every minaret, begins with an invocation of God, who has compassion and commands men, too, to be compassionate.

Others confirm this consensual moral scope of all the major human civilizations. Raúl S. Manglapus, former foreign minister and presidential candidate in the Philippines and now an exile in the United States and the president of the Movement for a Free Philippines, argues, "Human rights are not a Western discovery." The development of customary law, whether in the *adat* among the Malays or the Common Law among the British, reflects long-standing efforts by various societies to hedge against centralized repression. The All-African Conference of Churches has stressed "the roots of civil and political rights in African traditions: checks and balances on the strongest ruler, power dispersion that allowed for a modicum of social justice, and values concerned with individual and collective rights."

Although there may be more of a moral consensus among world cultures and religions on the violations of core human rights noted above, and not on such specific civil liberties as freedom of speech, the record-breaking turnout for the 1977 elections in India casts some doubt on even that distinction. When asked why he was voting, an Indian farmer replied: "Just because I am poor and cannot read does not mean I do not care for human rights."[46]

International discourse already suggests growing convergence on the issues of shared values and responsibilities. There is, for instance, a relationship among the following statements. Julius Nyerere, president of Tanzania, wrote in July 1977: "Organized denial of human rights to all but seventeen percent of its people on the grounds of their race, make South Africa's 'internal affairs' a matter of world concern."[47] Jimmy Carter said at the United Nations in March 1977:

> All signatories of the U.N. Charter have pledged themselves to observe and respect basic human rights. Thus, no member of the United Nations can claim that mistreatment of its citizens is solely its own business. Equally, no member can avoid its responsibilities to review and to speak when torture or unwarranted deprivation occurs in any part of the world. . . .

Kurt Waldheim, secretary general of the United Nations, stated before the opening of the World Conference to Combat Racism and Racial Discrimination (Geneva, August 14, 1978) that "there is an inescapable link between respect for human rights and the maintenance of international peace and security, and no nation can justifiably claim immunity, under Article 2(7) of the Charter, from international scrutiny and expression of concern about flagrant and systematic abuses of the human rights of its citizens."

Implicit in those statements and others is a critical new fact of foreign policy: human rights—like the environment and nuclear proliferation—is a *global* issue. It requires nations to act accordingly. As with other such issues, there is a waning logic to the maximalist claim of the nation-state: this wealth is ours; these dissidents are our concern. The roll call of repression suggests that the rights of nationals cannot be left solely to the control of governments, since those governments are themselves the perpetrators of the injustice and since their actions impinge on other nations.

That fact suggests to some that there is cause to tread cautiously in behalf of human rights. Stanley Hoffmann has argued that the issue of human rights breeds confrontation.[48] Others, such as Ernst Haas, claim that an activist human-rights policy, like that pursued by the Carter administration, leads logically and unwisely to mounting intervention abroad.

Although those the critics call "crusaders" may take large chances, there may be even greater risks if they do not and fewer choices than is thought. The effort of ultraconservative, anticommunist governments in Central America to keep a cap on growing and legitimate demands by their poor citizens has already led to more, rather than less, disorder. Such disorder, as events in Nicaragua have demonstrated, exacts a higher price from all concerned than would have been paid if human rights had received earlier and fuller respect. That price for procrastination may, in fact, be one of the most compelling reasons for stressing attention to human rights. Further, beginning to deal with violations of human rights can help limit the damage already done by years of disregard for fundamental freedoms and may build the basis for reform that serves long-term U.S. interest.

Whether the United States chooses an active or passive approach to the human-rights problem, isolationism is not an option. As one U.S. official admitted, "We're like an elephant in a sitting room; even if we don't move, you can't ignore us." In addition, giving human rights a low priority, for whatever reason, will not stop the problem or its impact on the United States. Without sustained efforts to get at the roots of repression, there will continue to be a flow of political and economic refugees and the regional and international tension and terrorism often attendant to violations of human rights.

Whatever the need for a U.S. policy that tries to deal with rather than deny the human-rights problem, it is important to put the process into perspective. The accomplishments of the last thirty years should be measured, not against utopian goals, but against the gains of the last three thousand years. For most of that period, all but a tiny elite lived in serfdom and misery. It is not realistic to expect all new nations to guarantee human rights that many older nations, including the United States, have achieved only recently, if at all. Indeed, some veterans of the human-rights effort in the United Nations believe that pushing too far too fast can be counter-productive for both human rights and the U.N. "You can't rush in like a lot of messiahs," warned one delegate from India. Rallying world opinion against South African *apartheid*, which many Third World representatives consider the most significant U.N. achievement in the area of human rights, has been due to more than two decades of slowly mounting pressure.

Advancing toward fulfillment of fundamental freedoms must be seen as part of a long-term and sometimes painful process. The "hell of good intentions" described by Hoffmann is often the time it takes to achieve them. Americans themselves are notoriously impatient. Just as most turned against the Vietnam war because they were tired and saw no "light at the end of the tunnel," so might they turn on the policy envisaged as the moral antidote to that war. If stress on human rights provides few quick fixes, as seems likely, or costs too much, as seems possible, it could boomerang in the United States and elsewhere.

To avoid that reversal constitutes the overriding challenge for U.S. diplomacy on human rights. It was with good reason that Cyrus Vance invoked Archibald MacLeish when he gave the Carter administration's first comprehensive statement on human-rights policy: "The cause of human liberty is now the one great revolutionary cause. . . ." The question now is how the United States, born in revolution, can deal with those revolutionary implications. The answer depends, in part, on the degree to which Americans accept the argument that promotion of human rights both serves their national interest and contributes to its overdue redefinition.

Notes

1. An adaptation of parts of this chapter appeared in the *International Studies Quarterly*, vol. 23, no. 2 (June 1979), 216–45. Material used in that article is used with the permission of Sage Publications.

2. Donald M. Fraser, "Freedom and Foreign Policy," *Foreign Policy*, No. 26 (Spring 1977), 140. Fraser, the eight-term Democratic Representative from Minnesota defeated in a bid for the Senate in 1978, was responsible for much congressional attention to human rights through his landmark hearings on the subject before the Subcommittee on International Organizations of the House International Relations Committee.

3. Articles 1, 55, and 56 are the most important human-rights provisions of the charter, a multilateral treaty to which all U.N. member states are party. The Declaration is the first comprehensive codification of internationally recognized human rights. Adopted and proclaimed by the U.N. General Assembly with no negative votes in 1948, it is, technically, a nonbinding resolution. The two covenants, formally adopted by the U.N. General Assembly in 1966 and brought into force in 1976, were designed (a) to transform the principles proclaimed in the Universal Declaration into binding treaty obligations and, together with the Optional Protocol to the Covenant on Civil and Political Rights, (b) to establish international machinery for supervision and enforcement. See the Appendix for the text of the Universal Declaration and the relevant portions of the charter.

4. Quoted from an address by Secretary of State Cyrus Vance in Athens, Georgia, April 30, 1977. That speech was the first comprehensive discussion of human-rights policy by a senior member of the Carter administration.

5. For elaboration on the question of contemporary torture, see: "Torture as Policy: the Network of Evil," *Time*, Vol. 108, No. 7 (August 16, 1976), 31–34; and Fay Willey, "The Push for Human Rights," *Newsweek*, Vol. 89, No. 25 (June 20, 1977), 46–61. For representative surveys of the larger scope and nature of human rights violations, see the annual and special reports of Amnesty International, Freedom House, and the International Commission of Jurists, as well as the annual reports on human-rights conditions abroad submitted by the Department of State to the Congress and the hearings held by Congressman Donald Fraser.

6. Address at the White House, December 6, 1978, to commemorate the thirtieth anniversary of the adoption of the U.N. Universal Declaration of Human Rights.

7. Warren Christopher, "The Diplomacy of Human Rights: the First Year," address before the American Bar Association, New Orleans, February 13, 1978. For a more recent assessment of U.S. policy, see the testimony by Deputy Secretary of State Christopher before the International Organizations Subcommittee of the House Foreign Affairs Committee, "Implementing the Human Rights Policy," May 2, 1979.

8. Chancellor Schmidt stated:

> *Détente* has brought success for the Germans in particular, in a manner and to an extent which could not have been expected at the beginning of the road. I am thinking of the extraordinary expansion in contacts between people in the two German states that has been brought about in recent years and which has given the people in East Germany so much hope and moral support. I am thinking also, of the remarkable increase in the number of people of German descent returning from the Soviet Union and from Romania over the past three years.

Quoted in *The New York Times*, July 17, 1977. Over seventy thousand Germans have been permitted to emigrate from Eastern Europe to the Federal Republic since the Helsinki summit in 1975.

9. See the Bibliography for a representative range of sources on the human rights role

of the U.N., O.A.S., and C.S.C.E. For a useful summary of regional and international mechanisms, see "Human Rights in the International Community and in U.S. Foreign Policy, 1945–76," prepared for the House Subcommittee on International Organizations by the Foreign Affairs and National Defense Division of the Congressional Research Service of the Library of Congress (July 24, 1977) (Washington, D.C.: U.S. Government Printing Office, 1977).

10. The Genocide Convention, adopted by the U.N. General Assembly in 1948 and entered into force in 1951, provides that genocide is a "crime under international law"—meaning that the individual perpetrator is himself punishable for a grave offense against the entire international community. The International Convention on the Elimination of All Forms of Racial Discrimination, adopted by the U.N. General Assembly in 1965 and entered into force in 1969, prohibits "any distinction, exclusion, restriction or preference based on race, color, descent, or national or ethnic origin." It provides for enforcement by the Committee on the Elimination of Racial Discrimination and adjudication by the International Court of Justice. Impressive as this list of U.N. documents is, it is just the tip of the proverbial iceberg of U.N. conventions and declarations in the field of human rights. For a more comprehensive listing, see Louis B. Sohn and Thomas Buergenthal, *Basic Documents on International Protection of Human Rights* (New York: Bobbs-Merrill, 1973) and Thomas Buergenthal and Judith V. Torney, *International Human Rights and International Education* (Washington, D.C.: U.S. National Commission for UNESCO, 1976).

11. The U.N. Commission on Human Rights was established in 1946 as a subsidiary organ of the U.N. Economic and Social Council (ECOSOC). It has shifted its role, from early focus on drafting human-rights instruments, to the capability to deal with complaints brought by individuals and nongovernmental organizations, provided in ECOSOC Resolution 1503 of 1970. Since the United States has not ratified the two international covenants on human rights, it does not participate in the committee set up under the attendant protocol.

12. The European Convention on Human Rights, drawn up within the framework of the Council of Europe and entered into force in 1953, is generally regarded as the most advanced international system for the protection of human rights. It is by far the most complete regional system, since its institutions, the European Court of Human Rights and the European Commission of Human Rights, have the power to try and decide cases brought by individuals against governments, to award damages, and to order governments to take appropriate remedial action. For more discussion of the human-rights machinery of the O.A.S., see the two texts cited in note 9, as well as Louis B. Sohn and Thomas Buergenthal, *International Protection of Human Rights* (New York: Bobbs-Merrill, 1973). For more specific statements of U.S. policy, see the transcripts of hearings held regularly on the O.A.S. by the House Subcommittee on International Organizations, and speeches made by U.S. officials at the annual meetings of the O.A.S. General Assembly.

13. Quoted in *The New York Times*, July 2, 1978.

14. David Hawk, "Human Rights at Half-Time," *New Republic*, vol. 180, no. 14 (April 7, 1979), 22.

15. White House address, December 6, 1978.

16. For more information on this subject, see David Weissbrodt, "The Role of International Nongovernmental Organizations in the Implementation of Human Rights," *Texas International Law Journal*, vol. 12, nos. 2–3 (Spring/Summer 1977), 293–320.

17. John Stuart Mill, *Dissertations and Discussions: Political, Philosophical, and Historical*, Vol. 3 (Boston: William Spencer, 1865–68), 251–52.

18. From an address at Amherst College, December 9, 1964.

19. Ernst B. Haas, *Global Evangelism Rides Again: How to Protect Human Rights Without Really Trying* (Berkeley, Calif.: Institute of International Studies, 1978), p. 15.

20. Fouad Ajami, "Human Rights and World Order Politics," *Alternatives*, vol. 3, no. 3 (March 1978), 357.

21. Quoted in *The New York Times*, April 16, 1978.

22. Jyotitindra Das Gupta, "A Season of Emergency Regimes and Development Politics in Asia," *Asian Survey*, vol. 18, no. 4 (April 1978), 315–49.

23. For elaboration on another point critical to this discussion—the perennial question of the relation between economic development and democracy—and, indeed, for all matters relating to more strictly economic questions, see Chapter 6. For the domestic counterpart of Chapter 2, see Chapter 4.

24. It is worth pointng out that voting in the Chilean referendum was mandatory, that it was held on what was declared a public holiday, and that the space for a "yes" vote for General Pinochet was placed under a Chilean flag, whereas the space for "no" was under the black flag of anarchism.

25. According to Columbia Law Professor Louis Henkin, "Legal norms . . . are subverted for political ends." Louis Henkin, "The United States and the Crisis in Human Rights," *The Virginia Journal of International Law*, vol. 14, no. 4 (Summer 1974), 662.

26. Bryce Wood, "International Organization and Human Rights with Special Reference to the Organization of American States," Paper prepared for an O.A.S. Seminar with U.S. scholars of Latin American affairs, April 8, 1976.

27. Quoted in *The New York Times*, April 10, 1978.

28. See the semiannual reports submitted to the U.S. Commission on Security and Cooperation in Europe by the Department of State.

29. Ernest W. Lefever, "The Rights Standard," *The New York Times*, January 24, 1977.

30. I am indebted to Professor Norman Graebner, distinguished writer on American diplomatic history, for assistance on the historical backdrop to human-rights diplomacy. This section draws on his writing (published and unpublished) and discussions with him at the Council on Religion and International Affairs. For the domestic counterpart to this discussion, see Chapter 4, "The Politics of Human Rights."

31. George Kennan, *American Diplomacy, 1900–1950* (Chicago: University of Chicago Press, 1951).

32. Hans Morgenthau, *Politics among Nations* (New York: Alfred A. Knopf, 1961), p. 273.

33. Haas, *Global Evangelism*, p. 30.

34. Thomas L. Hughes, "Carter and the Management of Contradictions," *Foreign Policy*, no. 31 (Summer 1978), pp. 34–55.

35. Peter L. Berger, "Are Human Rights Universal?" *Commentary*, vol. 64, no. 3 (September 1977), 61.

36. Quoted by Walter Laqueur, "The Issue of Human Rights," *Commentary*, vol. 64, no. 5 (May 1977), 33.

37. Elio Gaspari, "Carter Si!" *The New York Times*, April 30, 1978.

38. Ajami, *Alternatives*, p. 382.

39. Lefever, "The Rights Standard," *The New York Times*, January 24, 1977.

40. John Stockwell, "A Call for Openness as an Antidote to the C.I.A.'s Secrecy ('Poison')," *The New York Times*, May 17, 1978.

41. Leonard Meeker, address, "Human Rights and Other U.S. National Interests," June 2, 1977, p. 16.

42. White House address, December 6, 1978.

43. Marshall D. Shulman, "On Learning to Live with Authoritarian Regimes," *Foreign Affairs*, vol. 55, no. 2 (January 1977), 337.

44. White House address, December 6, 1978.

45. Louis B. Sohn, "The Human Rights Law of the Charter," *Texas International Law Journal*, Vol. 12, Nos. 2 and 3 (Spring/Summer 1977), 133. Article 103 of the charter provides that obligations under it prevail over "obligations under any other international agreement." Delegates from over a hundred nations at the International Conference on Human Rights, held in Teheran in 1968, proclaimed unanimously that the declaration "states a common understanding of the peoples of the world concerning the inalienable and inviolable rights of all members of the human family and constitutes an obligation for all members of the international community." The General Assembly has invoked the Universal Declaration in resolutions relating to southern Africa. Although the declaration was adopted by fewer than fifty votes (48–0), with some important abstentions (six communist states, Saudi Arabia, and South Africa), 105 states voted for the two main human-rights covenants. Thus, according to Sohn, "although the Covenants apply directly to the states that have ratified them, they are of some importance, at the same time, with respect to the interpretation of the Charter obligations of the non-ratifying states." *Ibid.*, pp. 135–36. For further discussion of the legal status of international documents on human rights, see Buergenthal and Torney, *International Human Rights and International Education* and Sohn and Buergenthal, *International Protection of Human Rights*.

46. I am indebted, for this brief treatment of the complex subject of shared values undergirding international promotion of human rights, to several sources. Among the most concise recent treatments of the subject are: Peter L. Berger, "Are Human Rights Universal?" (cited above); Raúl S. Manglapus, "Human Rights Are Not a Western Discovery," and Raymond D. Gastil, "Pluralist Democracy and the Third World," *Worldview*, vol. 21, no. 10 (October 1978), 4–6 and 37–42, respectively. For a stimulating piece on the historical backdrop to human rights, see Elaine Pagels, "Human Rights: Legitimizing a Recent Concept," *The Annals of the American Academy of Political and Social Science*, vol. 422 (March 1979), 57–62. For more extensive treatment of this subject, I am particularly grateful to the Council on Religion and International Affairs, which invited me to participate in a discussion series entitled "Human Rights: Cultural, Theological, and Philosophical Foundations," and to the Rockefeller Foundation for inviting me to participate in a conference on human rights in developing nations in Bellagio, Italy (June 1979). I also owe much of my education in this area to discussions with representatives from Third World nations at the United Nations and at conferences sponsored by organizations, such as the International Studies Association, and universities, such as Columbia and Notre Dame.

47. Julius K. Nyerere, "America and Southern Africa," *Foreign Affairs*, vol. 55, no. 4 (July 1977), 681.

48. Stanley Hoffmann, "Hell of Good Intentions," *Foreign Policy*, no. 29 (Winter 1977–78), pp. 7–8.

PART II

3

Soviet Union
Exile for Political Protest

Viktor Isaakovich Fainberg was one of seven Soviet citizens arrested in Moscow on August 25, 1968. It was four days after the Soviet invasion of Czechoslovakia when they stood on Red Square with banners that said: "Hands Off Czechoslovakia" and "For Your Freedom and Ours."

Agents for the Soviet secret police rammed Fainberg into a police car. Before he reached the police station, his face was bloody and four teeth had been knocked out. He was charged with "violating public order" and spreading "deliberate fabrications discrediting the Soviet political and social system." In addition, according to Soviet law which lets prosecutors order psychiatric examination of the accused, Fainberg was sent to Serbsky Institute. There doctors recommended that he be committed to the Special Psychiatric Hospital in Leningrad.

Fainberg was not told of the court's decision. Nor was he allowed to take part in the hearing. Some observers believe that Soviet authorities use insane asylums as a means to deal with "antisocial elements" because it is a quiet way to deal with dissidents. There is no need for the kind of public trial required in a criminal case. Once committed to a mental hospital, the accused loses all legal rights and can remain confined indefinitely.

Doctors at the Leningrad hospital-prison told Fainberg that he would be pronounced cured and released if he admitted that he was mentally ill and that he had acted incorrectly. When he refused, he was transferred to a ward for the violent and totally deranged. He shared a cell with other inmates and received meals of watered-down soup and gruel through a small opening in the door. He was allowed visitors for one hour once a month. He was often stripped naked before those sessions to be sure that he had no messages hidden on his body. Even so, he managed, undetected by the orderlies who monitored all visits, to slip notes out of his mouth when he kissed his wife. Eventually, with the help of others, he smuggled out an "Appeal to Human Rights Organizations." Vladimir Bukovsky, who was to become famous later for his meeting with President Carter in early 1977, helped circulate that appeal among Western journalists.

That document described what Fainberg called the "concentration of evil forces" that occurred "under the fig leaf of psychiatry." He stressed the cases of persons who were confined for nothing more than making "disloyal" statements, and the beatings by orderlies sanctioned by the nurses and doctors. He described the use of forms of punishment such as the "roll-up," in which the patient is wrapped in wet canvas bandages that contract when dry and cause agonizing pain, and sulfur injections, which can raise the patient's temperature to as high as 104 degrees Fahrenheit.

In 1971, Fainberg went on two extensive hunger strikes as part of his demand that such practices cease. The result: visitors were forbidden; his books, pencils, and paper were taken away. And, he was given injections of an antipsychotic drug which makes a normal person feel groggy and which can, if given in sufficient quantities, turn him into a human vegetable. When Fainberg's weight dropped to one hundred pounds, he was force-fed—stripped, swathed in a sheet, tied to a cot, and made to swallow life-sustaining liquid through a hose thrust into his mouth.

In November 1973, after five years in the hospital-prison, Fainberg was released, without having recanted and with no reported reason. Soon thereafter, however, he was re-committed because of a hunger strike undertaken in behalf of a group of political prisoners, including Bukovsky, held in labor camps. His health deteriorated rapidly, apparently because of drug injections that were dangerous for someone who had not eaten for weeks. He threatened suicide. That, plus the help of a doctor he had met outside prison, brought an end to the injections and release from the hospital. In early 1974, he received permission to leave the Soviet Union and the customary exit visa for Israel.[1]

*   *   *

The case of Viktor Fainberg could end there. In fact, it does not. After settling in London, Fainberg founded an organization called

"Campaign Against Psychiatric Abuse." His revelations and those of
other exiles dramatize both the particular plight of the Soviet dissident
and the more general problem of the citizen anywhere without political
and civil liberty.

Soviet arrest of Fainberg, like the much-publicized seizure and trial
of Anatoly Shcharansky (1977–78), raises several central questions that
deserve discussion:

« What lies behind the dissident movement in the Soviet Union?
« What explains the behavior of the Soviet Government toward the dis-
    sidents?
« What can or should the United States do in behalf of human rights in the
    Soviet Union?

A look, first, at the Soviet dissidents themselves. Who are they, and
why do some risk torture or death to make their views known?

What scholars call "mainstream dissent" in the U.S.S.R. is relatively
new. It was only in the mid-to-late 1960s that a real human-rights
movement, in which various groups consciously worked with each
other, began to emerge.[2] Although that movement had its roots in reaction to the more general repression of the Soviet system and tsarist rule
before 1917, it sprang up in 1965 because of the arrests of several established dissenters. The seizure of the writers Andrei Sinyavsky and
Yuli Daniel, together with increasing censorship within the Soviet
Union, signaled to some the apparent regeneration of Stalinism and the
need to resist, before a new round of mass purges recurred.

The dissidents were determined to make the point "Never again!"
They received their first widespread attention when supporters for Sinyavsky and Daniel contacted the Western press in 1966 and got their
words played back in Russian via the Voice of America.

The trial of the young intellectuals Galanskov and Ginzburg and the
beginning of the *Chronicle of Current Events* in 1968 made previously
disparate moves more of a movement. That catalogue of dissident activity and underground writing known as *samizdat*[3] also made an explicit
connection between Soviet protest and internationally recognized
human rights. Its origin was tied to the United Nations' designation of
1968 as Human Rights Year. Its masthead featured Article 19 from the
U.N. Universal Declaration: "Everyone has the right to freedom of
opinion and expression. . . ." Soviet Jews soon produced their own version of *Chronicle*. *Exodus* was one way to attract Western attention and
expedite emigration to Israel.

By the late 1960s, the pattern was set for much of the subsequent Soviet dissident movement: its changing cast of characters and diverse
scope of concerns. Those dissidents who received most attention in the
United States—Jews trying to leave the U.S.S.R.—were just one small
part of a movement which was, itself, small (perhaps several thousand
in a population of over a quarter-billion). It included religious believers,
nationalists, and intellectuals. Baptists, Seventh-Day Adventists, Pen-
tecostalists, Lithuanian Catholics, Russian Orthodox Christians, and
others protested the denial of religious freedom and published underground journals. Ethnic or national minorities—such as the
Georgians, Lithuanians, Ukrainians, Tatars, and Germans—struggled
for the preservation of their cultures, languages, and traditions and, in
the case of the Germans, for their right to emigrate. Intellectual protesters ranged in opinion from those, such as Andrei Sakharov, who
seek evolution of a multiparty democratic society, to those such as Aleksandr Solzhenitsyn, who want the spiritual regeneration of "Russia," to
those such as Roy A. Medvedev, who want democratization within the
bounds of the Communist party.

Diverse as the dissident movement was—and is—it drew closer
together in the mid–1970s. The main force for coalescence was the
1975 Helsinki Final Act of the Conference on Security and Cooperation in Europe. It stressed such humanitarian behavior by the thirty-five
signatory governments as provision for reunification of families, increased contact among peoples, and improved flow of information.
With the Final Act as a new catalyst for common cause among Soviet
dissidents, nine activists formed in 1976 the "Public Group Furthering
the Implementation of the Helsinki Agreement in the U.S.S.R." The
"Orlov group"—named after Yuri Orlov, its leading figure—was to
monitor Soviet compliance with the agreement and serve as the model
for scores of "Helsinki watch committees" that sprang up throughout
the Soviet Union and Eastern Europe.

Increased coordination of activities after the Helsinki summit did not,
however, improve the lot of the Soviet dissident. Quite the contrary.
Bukovsky and others reported that prison conditions "tangibly
worsened." The number of threats, beatings, and "accidental" deaths
increased. By late 1976, the heat was indisputably on. Well before
Jimmy Carter took office—and, according to his critics, did more harm
than good for Soviet dissenters—the Soviet government had begun a

severe crackdown. Most members of the Helsinki Watch Group were arrested. Other dissidents, such as Valentin Turchin of the Moscow Section of Amnesty International, were forced to leave or face arrest.

The new Soviet constitution (Basic Law of 1977—although partly an attempt to burnish Soviet credentials for the C.S.C.E. review meeting in Belgrade—left much of the Stalinist constitution of 1936 intact. Unlike the U.S. Constitution, which assumes that citizens are born with rights on which government must not infringe, the Basic Law declares that "the exercise of rights and liberties by citizens must not injure the interests of society and the state."[4] It places greatest emphasis, with regard to human rights, on the fulfillment of economic and social rights. The new constitution undercuts expressed respect for freedom of speech, press, assembly, religion, and privacy by declaring that they are granted only "in conformity with the interests of the working people and for the purpose of strengthening the socialist system."

The result of the crackdown, thus justified by the constitution, was a drastic decimation of dissident ranks. Sharp Soviet reaction against Jimmy Carter's stress on human rights was more of a reflection of prior concerns and a preset course, than a result of the U.S. president's early support for Soviet dissidents. The Soviet authorities seemed determined to contain what little there was of the fledgling movement for human rights in the U.S.S.R.

Why? One editorial in the Soviet newspaper *Pravda* explained treatment of what it called "the little heap of renegades":

> It is necessary, as never before, to display a high degree of political vigilance, to give a timely and effective rebuff to bourgeois propaganda, to fight tirelessly against the political indifference and the lack of ideals that still exist in our midst, and to indoctrinate the Soviet people in the spirit of love for the motherland and of loyalty to the cause of the party and lofty Communist ideals.[5]

In fact, there were probably other reasons for the behavior of the Soviet government.

First, the Helsinki Final Act had taken Soviet leaders by surprise. It had become a rallying point for internal dissension.

Second, growing unrest in Eastern Europe—especially in Poland, the German Democratic Republic (East Germany), and Czechoslovakia—fed chronic Soviet fear of spillover into the U.S.S.R. The perceived domino effect from dissidence had been behind the Soviet invasion of Prague in 1968. Follow-up on the Helsinki Final Act, with Soviet citizens signing statements of support for the "Charter 77" movement in Czechoslovakia, only revived an old nightmare.

Third, the Soviet leaders faced growing economic problems. Those, they feared, might meld with political discontent and pose more serious threats to their authority. Declining prospects for fulfillment of Brezhnev's fifteen-year Economic Plan and rising consumer expectations might make the U.S.S.R. go the way of Poland. Food riots there in the 1970s had put the Gierek Government under increasing political strain.

Fourth, the aging Soviet leadership was conservative and increasingly sensitive to criticism. With all high-ranking members of the Politburo over seventy, an imminent change of leadership was biologically inevitable. That fact did not encourage short-term flexibility on human rights. Detailed decisions about individual dissidents were thus made at the highest political level.

These reasons—together with concern for such external factors as the centrifugal tendencies in the world communist movement (highlighted by criticism of Moscow's rights record by West European communist parties) and the mixed fortunes of Soviet foreign policy—have led to a tough, but pragmatic, stance. The Soviet elite has three general means to maintain control: more of the same, substantial change, or gradual reform. It has chosen the last. According to an apparent compromise between the so-called hard- and soft-liners in the Kremlin, the Soviet leaders have stopped short of Stalinist tactics. The contrast between the 1930s and 1970s is noteworthy. Although his trial in August 1978 was more show than tell, Jewish dissident Anatoly Shcharansky was not shot. The Soviets thus kept the door ajar for needed negotiations and resources in the West, while limiting domestic damage from dissidence.

Moscow's policy on human rights is, as that episode suggests, an effort to reconcile two often competing aims. On the one hand, the Soviet leaders want to control the activity of the dissidents. On the other hand, they wish to contain the foreign-policy costs of that control. In 1978, the first aim was foremost. In 1979, with the negative backlash in public opinion occasioned by the Shcharansky trial and the positive incentive of SALT II and a possible end to U.S. trade restrictions, they let emigration rise to record levels and released several prominent "refuseniks" (so called because of Soviet refusal to grant exit vises to many applicants). They did so, however, while keeping a watchful eye on dissident activities—lest they become too public, attract support from workers, threaten the aging leadership's sense of control, or impinge on security. Should any of the leaders' fundamental interests appear in peril, even the most enticing offers from the West were not apt to deter a crackdown by the Kremlin.

What emerges from the balancing act implicit in Soviet policy is a larger point that applies to both the U.S.S.R. and the United States. Domestic political considerations and calculations of perceived national interest set the course for how each country treats the subject of human rights in the Soviet Union. The dominance of those factors also explains why each plays down the likely reaction of the other. As one Soviet journalist said, "We do not make policy on the basis of the Gallup and Harris polls."[6] One senior U.S. diplomat went further in assessing the Soviets: "They have no comprehension of the American political process; they do not understand how their treatment of their dissidents affects American public attitudes about the Soviet Union in general and thus the ratification process for an arms limitation treaty."

Soviet reaction to dissidence, no matter how modified since the 1930s, is still part of an overriding effort by the Soviet leaders to solidify their power. To do so, they appeal to the patriotism, xenophobia, and, as appropriate, the anti-Semitism of the Soviet people. For example, charging Shcharansky with "treason" touched all these bases and tapped a widespread Russian "love it or leave it" mentality. They bristle at what they consider outside efforts to change Soviet society and undermine their authority. Condemnation of "psychological warfare" from the West by Communist Party General Secretary and President Leonid Brezhnev was representative in that regard.[7] There are also special-interest groups within the Soviet Union, such as the powerful, entrenched police bureaucracy, that press for tighter control of dissident opinion.

Domestic factors are no less important in the formulation of U.S. policy. To a large extent, they have shaped the substance and style of the American approach toward human rights in the Soviet Union. The role of a small but dedicated American Jewish community has often been pivotal. For example, in 1912, American Jews, angry about treatment of their counterparts in Russia, led a move to cancel a long-standing commercial agreement. Abrogation of the Russo-American Treaty of 1832 bore striking resemblance to the Jackson-Vanik Amendment, the provision of the 1974 Trade Reform Act that linked U.S.–Soviet trade to emigration of Soviet Jews. It has often been Jewish leaders—under the umbrella of the National Conference on Soviet Jewry—who have kept the plight of the Jewish "refusenik" before the American public and its political representatives. [8]

A combination of factors—more publicity about the situation of Soviet Jews, genuine concern about their problem, and pressure from the U.S. Jewish community—accounted for important statements and actions in this area during the Nixon-Ford years. During the 1968 presidential campaign, Richard Nixon said, in a speech before the National Conference on Soviet Jewry, "I deplore the discriminatory measures imposed upon the Jews in the Soviet Union." In 1970, Nixon, Kissinger, and then Secretary of State William Rogers appealed to the Soviet Union for leniency toward several Jewish dissidents condemned to death for their attempted hijacking of an airplane for escape from the U.S.S.R. That plea, together with a massive international outcry, apparently persuaded Soviet authorities to commute the death sentences. In both 1970 and 1971, Secretary Rogers handed to Soviet Foreign Minister Gromyko lists of the names of Soviet citizens, mostly Jews, about whom the United States was concerned. State Department spokesmen publicly condemned violations of human rights in the Soviet Union. Soviet leaders responded with protests against outside interference in Soviet internal affairs and efforts to complicate U.S.–Soviet relations. Attorney General John Mitchell used his parole authority in 1971 to provide an open-door policy for the admission of Soviet refugees able to obtain Soviet exit visas. Leonard Garment, a long-time activist on human-rights issues and a representative in U.N. bodies, served as White House liaison with the Jewish community.

However, by 1973, growing U.S. domestic disenchantment with *détente* raised new questions about how to promote human rights in the Soviet Union. President Nixon had tried, after the 1968 low point in U.S.–Soviet relations (when the armies of five Warsaw Pact nations invaded Czechoslovakia and President Lyndon Johnson canceled his official visit to Moscow), to build a new framework for Soviet–American *rapproachement*. Part of that design for *détente* included the 1972 U.S.–Soviet trade agreement, whereby the two nations would enter a new era of economic interdependence. Access to U.S. technology was to give the Kremlin an increased stake in good relations and an incentive to good behavior. Domestic critics balked at that approach. Senator Henry Jackson (Dem.-Wash.) challenged Henry Kissinger head on in an address in Washington. He complained that "we are asked to believe that the prospects for peace are enhanced by the flow of Pepsi-Cola to the Soviet Union and the flow of vodka to the United States." He believed "that we will move much further along the road to a stable peace when we see the free flow of people and ideas across the barriers that divide East from West. . . ."[9]

That debate between Jackson and Kissinger took on a life of its own, with significant implications for both U.S.–Soviet relations and the promotion of human rights. Although Soviet leaders let record numbers of Jews leave the U.S.S.R. in 1973 as part of overall relaxation of relations with the West, they did make that emigration more costly and difficult. Imposing high taxes for exit visas, among other measures, proved to be a disaster in public relations. American Jewish groups were furious about what they considered anti-Semitism. They turned to the Congress for redress. The result was legislation that linked U.S. trade relations with the right to emigrate. The Soviets' reaction against the Jackson-Vanik and Stevenson amendments to the Trade Reform Act of 1974 (signed into law in January, 1975) led to their renunciation in 1975 of the 1972 trade pact. That same year, as previously discussed, critics of the Republican administration condemned Gerald Ford for "selling out" to the Soviets at the Helsinki summit and denounced Henry Kissinger for ignoring dissidents for the sake of *Realpolitik*. During the 1976 Presidential campaign, according to Senator Charles McC. Mathias, Jr. (Rep.-Md.), "Kissinger's strategic idea of *détente* was sacrificed to political expediency."[10] Carter capitalized on Ford's refusal to meet exiled Soviet author Aleksandr Solzhenitsyn. Although Kissinger succeeded behind the scenes in effecting the exchange of Chilean Communist leader Corvalan for Soviet dissident Bukovsky in December 1976, "quiet diplomacy," by its very nature, captured few headlines.

Jimmy Carter came into office in 1977 determined to make human rights a more important part of U.S. foreign policy. The president and the senior members of his administration would have preferred a honeymoon period to sort out priorities and tactics. However, Soviet dissidents moved fast to give Carter his first serious test in the area of human rights. Most high-ranking officials within the Carter administration were to stress later that the president had little choice but to respond promptly and publicly to the letter from Andrei Sakharov, the Soviet nuclear physicist and dissident leader, that reached the White House just eight days after the 1977 inaugural. It was hard, if not impossible, politically for him to ignore that probe of his good faith, after having made such an issue of Ford's refusal to receive Solzhenitsyn. He thus answered Sakharov by saying, in part, "I am always glad to hear from you" and "you may rest assured that the American people and our Government will continue our firm commitment to promote respect for human rights not only in our country but also abroad."

The Soviet response to this presidential correspondence was prompt. Georgi Arbatov, Soviet director of the USA Institute in Moscow, called Carter's emphasis on human rights a calculated anti-Soviet campaign. It could, he warned, bring back the Cold War. His comments called to mind earlier reactions on the same subject. In 1903, spokesmen for tsarist Russia claimed that President Theodore Roosevelt's public references to treatment of Russian Jews constituted "an attempt at interference in her internal affairs."

Carter, by his own admission, was "surprised." He shifted gears by mid-1977—because of pressure from moderates within his administration, concern expressed by important Allied leaders such as West German Chancellor Helmut Schmidt, and the belief that a point, once publicly and forcefully made, need not be repeated at every occasion. He did not, for example, answer a second letter from Sakharov.

That said, political considerations, as well as personal convictions, kept Carter from dropping concern for human rights in the Soviet Union. Expressions of that concern recurred in major speeches on U.S.-Soviet relations, the appointment of Arthur Goldberg to head the U.S. delegation to the C.S.C.E. follow-up meeting in Belgrade, and the president's strong public reaction before and after the Shcharansky trial. Political considerations influenced many of the moves made by Zbigniew Brzezinski in U.S.–Soviet relations. Although he set a comparatively independent course at the National Security Council, he did appreciate domestic sensitivity to *détente* diplomacy. Brzezinski thus made special efforts to confer in this area with White House Chief of Staff Hamilton Jordan.

The general trend of Carter's commitment to human rights in the U.S.S.R. could not, and does not, conceal more fundamental questions. Henry Kissinger, while practicing shuttle politicking during con-

gressional fund-raising events in the late 1970s, criticized President
Carter's confrontation with the U.S.S.R. over human rights. It was, he
said, a venture that only demonstrated "the impotence of the United
States" to affect Soviet domestic policy. Given the dynamics of domestic politics in both the United States and the Soviet Union, what options *are* open to the U.S. to achieve greater respect for all human rights
in the U.S.S.R., and at what cost and benefit?

To sort out those issues requires, first, agreement on American objectives. Does the United States favor comprehensive efforts to foster
human rights for as many Soviet citizens as possible, or a more selective
approach? The record so far suggests the latter. Yet, some scholars argue
that campaigns for a particular political prisoner or in behalf of selected
groups, such as Jews or Baptists, may prejudice the fate of others in similar or worse situations. For example, Soviet leaders may punish some
relatively unknown prisoners more harshly to compensate for the leniency accorded a "celebrity." (On the other hand, to save face, Soviet
leaders may lash out and make an example of a celebrity.) There is the
related question of whether the United States should stress short-term
attention to certain individual victims of human-rights violations or
promotion of longer-term liberalization within the U.S.S.R.—or both.

Second, regardless of the substance of U.S. policy, there is the comparably important point of style. Should U.S. advocacy of human rights
in the Soviet Union be low key or high profile? A hands-off policy
sounds sensible to those who believe that human rights in the Soviet
Union are irrelevant to U.S. interests, that respect for national sovereignty precludes outside "meddling," that U.S. involvement may hurt
the victims of Soviet repression, and/or that U.S. activity in this area
can undercut other American interests, such as prospects for more
trade.

Discreet promotion of human rights means working behind the
scenes so that Soviet leaders can agree more gracefully to such matters
as the reunification of divided families. Statistics on Jewish emigration
from the Soviet Union from 1970 to 1980 suggest some correlation between quiet diplomacy and increases in exit visas.[11] Some experts on
Soviet affairs advocate catering to the modernizers within the Soviet system. (One such expert is Marshall Shulman, special consultant to Secretary Vance and co-chairman of the Interagency Coordinating Committee on U.S.–Soviet Affairs formed in 1977 after the precipitate chill

in Moscow-Washington relations.) Avoiding direct confrontation may best ensure the modification of Soviet official practices that can, over the long term, buttress support for human rights.[12] A corollary to this point is the argument that liberalization inside the Soviet Union, if it is to come at all, must and should come from within. Such change may begin to emerge in the 1980s, as the Soviets themselves recognize that their system is not achieving their own expressed objectives. George Kennan, concerned about both human rights and the overall state of U.S.–Soviet relations, holds, finally, with the wisdom of the whale: you are most likely to get harpooned when on the surface spouting too much.[13]

Yet, an activist policy, albeit heavy on public bombast, has its own rationale. Most Soviet dissidents favor a bright U.S. spotlight on their situation, regardless of the risk to them. Some members of the National Security Council of the Carter administration support an activist approach for that reason, despite admitted personal skepticism about its wisdom. "Who are *we*," one staff member asked, "to say 'no' to *them?*" Zbigniew Brzezinski and others in the administration prefer a course that gives the U.S. what he calls the "ideological offensive" against the Soviet Union. Most proponents of an activist approach deny that it puts *détente* in peril, sets back SALT, and thus pits human liberty against human survival. In addition, they believe that Soviet leaders are, partly because of a long-standing national inferiority complex, sensitive to negative world opinion; they will, especially when it suits their other purposes, respond to it.

Timing, tactics, and motivations vary in all these approaches. Are Americans most interested in sounding or acting tough? That was the conclusion of some critics of the Carter administration, based on the alleged *macho* quality of some of the president's speeches on U.S.–Soviet relations and Brzezinski's decision in 1978, as shown by his trip early in the year to the People's Republic of China and the subsequent move to normalize relations with the P.R.C., to "play the China card." Do Americans feel best expressing the pique of the moment? That seemed the case with some congressmen who responded to Soviet sentencing of Shcharansky with a call to cancel the Helsinki Final Act. Do the protests about the undeniable suffering of Soviet Jews reflect more concern for them or the political gain of U.S. politicians?

Alternatively, are more Americans inclined to look beyond their own immediate sentiments and interests, to set their sights on more distant objectives? "Long-term liberalization" within the Soviet Union lacks the ring of a rallying cry. Further, it is not clear whether such change is possible or likely, or how the United States can affect the process. There is still no definitive answer to the questions raised by the Jackson-Vanik Amendment. Was Congress wise in linking trade and emigration? Has linkage had the desired effect? Are other means more effective in attaining the same ends? How will U.S. legislation affect future prospects for either trade or emigration? With such questions still open and made more timely by U.S. actions to extend Most Favored Nation trade benefits to China, the interim answer is that U.S. leverage in behalf of human rights in the Soviet Union, as elsewhere, may be more limited than most Americans like to admit.

Thus, the seemingly simple effort to help a dissident like Viktor Fainberg can founder on complexity. Moving from description of the ordeal of an individual dissenter, through a more general discussion of Soviet dissidence and official Soviet concerns, to U.S. reactions suggests just *how* complicated the issues are.

Good politics may not mean good policy—and vice versa. Private diplomacy may get some of the best results for victims of violations, but, as Henry Kissinger found, at the cost of lost support for overall U.S. foreign policy. Further, *détente* may carry the seeds of success and setback for both itself and the dissidents. An improved climate for U.S.–Soviet contacts lets dissident dispatches reach the West. When those reports ricochet back on radio broadcasts to the U.S.S.R., the inevitably destabilizing effect of *détente* on the Soviet Union must alarm Kremlin hard-liners and may mean more arrests of dissidents.

Finally, promoting human rights in the Soviet Union can become one way for any U.S. administration to paint itself into a corner. If the president is too tough in behalf of human rights, he risks danger for the dissidents and a deterioration of U.S.-Soviet relations. If too soft, he may lose credibility for his expressed commitment to human rights. The perceived need to assuage both American domestic concern about human rights in the Soviet Union and Soviet sensitivity to alleged intervention in the internal affairs of the U.S.S.R. lay behind Carter's treatment of human rights at the Vienna summit in June 1979. For domestic reasons, he had to be able to say that he had raised the subject. However, for the sake of a Soviet signature on SALT II, he could do so only in his one-on-one conversations with Brezhnev. Since one of Carter's original reasons for stressing human rights was to restore public consensus behind U.S. foreign policy in general and *détente* in particular, increasing reliance on quiet diplomacy seemed to bring the president back to the proverbial square one. In sum, a policy to promote human rights in the Soviet Union—conceived primarily because of U.S. domestic political considerations—can create its own paradox.

Notes

1. Details and quotations for this case study are drawn from a report by Ludmilla Thorne, "Inside Russia's Psychiatric Jails," *The New York Times Magazine*, June 12, 1977, pp. 26–27, 30, 60, 62, 64, 66, 68, 70–71, as well as from portions of the *Chronicle of Current Events* assembled by Peter Reddaway in *Uncensored Russia: Protest and Dissent in the Soviet Union* (New York: American Heritage Press, 1972), pp. 99, 101, 112–14, 126, 236, 247, and 382. For other reports on psychiatric torture, see "Psychiatric Abuse of Political Prisoners in the Soviet Union—Testimony by Leonid Plyushch," Hearing before the Subcommittee on International Organizations of the Committee on International Relations, House of Representatives, March 30, 1976; *Prisoners of Conscience in the USSR: Their Treatment and Conditions*, An Amnesty International Report, November 1975; Sidney Bloch and Peter Reddaway, *Psychiatric Terror: How Soviet Psychiatry Is Abused to Suppress Dissent* (New York: Basic Books, 1977); Walter Reich, "Diagnosing Soviet Dissidents," *Harper's*, August 1978, 31–37; Valery Chalidze, *To Defend These Rights* (New York: Random House, 1974) and numerous issues of the *Chronicle of Current Events*, Kronika Press, New York.

2. Peter Reddaway, "The Development of Dissent in the USSR," *The Soviet Empire: Expansion and Détente*, edited by William E. Griffith, (Lexington, Mass.: Lexington Books, 1976), pp. 57–84. In that collection, see also Griffith's superb essays and Seweryn Bialer's insightful treatment of "The Soviet Political Elite and Internal Developments in the USSR."

3. *Samizdat* was the expressive Russian word for "our own publishing house." It was the vehicle for circulating literature which the Soviet State Publishing House would not print. Typically, an author would type copies of his work which were, in turn, recopied and passed on by others.

4. Chapter Seven, Article 39 of the Soviet Constitution. An English translation of the final text appeared in *The Current Digest of the Soviet Press*, vol. 29, no. 41 (November 9, 1977).

5. Quoted by David K. Shipler, "Soviet Defends Drive on Dissidents," *The New York Times*, February 13, 1977. Shipler's coverage of the human-rights story in the Soviet Union in the late 1970s deserves special attention and commendation.

6. Quoted in *The New York Times*, June 25, 1978.

7. Quoted from a major address before the Supreme Soviet in October 1977 by Soviet Communist Party leader Brezhnev.

8. For a lively discussion of how domestic factors have shaped recent U.S.–Soviet relations, see Paula Stern, *Water's Edge, Domestic Politics and the Making of American Foreign Policy* (Westport, Conn.: Greenwood Press, 1979).

9. Quoted from Jackson's address before the "Pacem in Terris" Conference in Washington, D.C., October 11, 1973.

10. Charles McC. Mathias, Jr., "Our Out-of-Focus Soviet Policy," *The New York Times*, July 12, 1978.

11. The statistical trend shows a high point of 34,933 Jews emigrating in 1973, a low point of 13,459 in 1975, and an increase since then. However, those statistics can be deceptive. How many Jews leave the Soviet Union reflects factors besides official Soviet policy, such as fluctuations in the numbers of those who actually apply for exit visas. Soviet policy, further, depends on more than what the United States may be saying or doing about human rights.

12. For some elaboration on Shulman's views, see "How Shulman Views Soviet Motives and Strategies," *The New York Times*, April 16, 1978; Marshall Shulman, "On Learning to Live with Authoritarian Regimes," *Foreign Affairs*, Vol. 55, No. 2 (January 1977), 325–38; and "Overview of U.S.–Soviet Relations," his statement to the House International Relations Committee, Subcommittee on Europe and the Middle East, September 26, 1978 and October 16, 1979.

13. Kennan is quoted by James Reston, "A Quiet Voice," *The New York Times*, February 11, 1977. Secretary of State Vance voiced comparable caution in a statement before the House Committee on International Relations, June 19, 1978: "To view U.S.–Soviet relations from the perspective of a single dimension is to run the risk of failing to identify our interests carefully and to act accordingly."

4

---•◆•---

Politics of

Human Rights

The United States, as national legend would have it, is more an idea than a geographic entity. No other country so prides itself on a Dream. Central to the so-called American Dream is the belief that individuals have the right to "life, liberty, and the pursuit of happiness." Read: respect for human rights.

And, since that Dream does not stop at the U.S. border, there is a direct correlation between domestic beliefs and American diplomacy. It was no quirk of drafting that the Declaration of Independence invoked universal appeal. Nor was it by chance that Jimmy Carter seized on that sentiment during the 1976 presidential campaign and promised to "make Americans feel proud again."

The politics of human rights—that is, the effect of U.S. domestic politics on the role of human rights in U.S. foreign policy—provides a still-shot of American democracy. It is the *domestic* counterpart to the *foreign* politics or diplomacy of human rights,[1] each being a microcosm of more complex issues. It calls the key U.S. political actors into play: the president, the Congress, the public, and special-interest groups. It serves as many purposes as there are protagonists: from furthering actual respect for human rights to massaging the American ego, from advancing group causes and individual careers to rallying support for larger national objectives. It reflects a selfless enterprise in behalf of victims of repression, as well as an unholy alliance of self-serving interests.

U.S. domestic sensitivity to human rights is thus both a *leitmotif* in American political tradition and a litmus test of prevailing political trends. As such, the politics of human rights constitutes the single most important catalyst to U.S. stress on human rights abroad. It can also—as some response to the situation of the Soviet dissident suggests—reflect a peculiar dynamic of the American political system, one that may be long on commendable sentiment, but short on commensurate insight. A review of the U.S. domestic record on promotion of international human rights pricks some comfortable misconceptions about the American character and raises some uncomfortable questions. But, perhaps most significant, it suggests some new opportunities for positive reaffirmation of human rights at home and abroad. The discussion below will proceed as follows:

« The record behind the rhetoric—a brief survey of the domestic political considerations behind U.S. promotion of human rights (1776–1970)
« The change in the record and the rhetoric—focus on factors and figures responsible for a shift of U.S. policy in the 1970s
« Some conclusions and conjecture for the 1980s

The record behind the rhetoric

U.S. politicians are fond of saying that stress on human rights reflects American tradition. That it does. But, that tradition is more complex than most realize or like to admit.

Americans—whether in their expressed values, ideals, or expectations—defy simplistic typecasting. It *is* true that most U.S. citizens see themselves as part of a unique political experiment. They have a Dream that, they hope, may become the destiny of all. They have gone to war and given many tax dollars to try to fulfill that universal vision. Americans like to think that their nation is different from others. It is, in some respects, because of the origin of the Republic and because Americans continue to make a particular point of espousing the ideals set forth in the Declaration of Independence.

It is also true that there is a darker side to the American Dream. The national character is less distinctive than many Americans acknowledge. Scratching beneath the surface of American tradition, as in other countries, reveals a mix of myths and motivations. There is no simple or enduring domestic consensus behind concern for human rights in U.S. foreign policy—by the executive branch, the Congress, or the

American people. A brief look at the record—with illustrative references only and no pretense at comprehensive coverage—reveals several major themes in American political history. Together, they undercut easy invocation of American tradition as the basis for stressing human rights in U.S. foreign policy.

FREQUENT DISCREPANCY BETWEEN PUBLIC OPINION AND OFFICIAL ACTION. There has been a recurrent gap between public fervor for freedom abroad and the perspective of elected leaders. At various times, U.S. presidents have either ignored public pressure for intervention abroad in order to protect what they considered a larger national interest, or struggled in vain to rouse Americans to respond to abrogation of human rights in other countries.

The first test of domestic commitment to human rights abroad came just ten weeks after the inauguration of George Washington. The Parisian masses stormed the Bastille on July 14, 1789. Many Americans believed that their own actions had helped inspire the French Revolution. They thus greeted the news with a "love-frenzy for France."[2] Jeffersonian Republicans saw France's subsequent declaration of war against Britain in 1793 as a replay and reaffirmation of the American struggle against the tyrannical George III. They battled pro-British Federalists, who opposed the Reign of Terror in France after 1792 and feared that the "moral influenza" might spread to the United States and imperil religion, private property, and all else Americans held dear. Enthusiasts of the French cause gave roaring receptions to Citizen Edmond Genêt, the first minister from the new French republic. John Adams noted later to Thomas Jefferson that "ten thousand people in the streets of Philadelphia, day after day, threatened to drag Washington out of his house and effect a revolution in the government, or compel it to declare war in favor of the French revolution. . . ."

George Washington, however, coolly resisted the public clamor. He was determined to avoid foreign hostilities that would sap the strength of the young Republic. His Proclamation of Neutrality of 1793 quelled the uproar and, reportedly, moved Rudyard Kipling years later to write "If."

Revolutions in Latin America, 1809–10, raised a comparable challenge. Again, most Americans felt flattered that others were apparently emulating their example. Stimulated by stories of Spanish atrocities in Latin America, most U.S. citizens supported democracy south of the border against despotism. New Orleans and Baltimore became bases for privateers backing the Latin American rebels. Henry Clay, with one eye on popular sentiment and the other on higher elective office, proclaimed in the House of Representatives in 1818, "We behold . . . the glorious spectacle of eighteen millions of people, struggling to burst their chains and to be free."[3]

John Quincy Adams, secretary of state in the administration of James Monroe, frowned on such popular fervor for the revolutions. He did not want to jeopardize British and Spanish support for other U.S. interests and thus delayed recognition of the Latin American republics—until after the United States had uncontested title to Florida.

The cool-headed Adams also balked at public pressure in another sphere in order to bolster U.S. self-defense. U.S. "Greek fever" spread across the United States after the Greeks rebelled against Turkish tyranny in 1821. Amidst stories of the Turks' collecting bushels of Greek ears, pro-Greek enthusiasm surfaced in sermons, mass meetings, and congressional resolutions. Adams, refusing to be swayed, talked President Monroe into adjusting his annual message to the Congress in 1823. To strengthen the U.S. hand for the Monroe Doctrine embedded in that message, the president changed his stirring declaration of support for the Greeks to an earnest wish for their success. In return for the hollow act of self-denial in the Greek case, the United States expected European nations to keep their hands off Latin American wars for independence.

Similar detachment from rebellion against repression prevailed in the mid-nineteenth century. Although immense crowds cheered the Hungarian revolutionary Louis Kossuth when he came to the United States in 1851—the poet Henry Wadsworth Longfellow remarked that the throng greeting Kossuth in New York went "clean daft"—the neutrality policy of the Founding Fathers held. Then, as in 1956, there was no direct U.S. support for Hungarian "freedom fighters." Leaders in the American South during the 1850s further assured a neutral stance by the United States. They opposed supporting such human-rights–related causes, for fear U.S. intervention in Europe would open the door to European efforts to free American slaves.

Although the discrepancy between public opinion and official action on human rights often put human rights on the short end of statesmanship appropriate for the first century of the Republic, that changed, to some extent, in the twentieth century. After 1900, it was often the

U.S. president who tried to arouse or channel popular concern for human rights abroad, to limited or belated avail. The momentous national debate over the Treaty of Versailles—including its provision for the liberation of millions of oppressed minorities—was one reflection of that kind of domestic political struggle. President Woodrow Wilson barnstormed the country in 1919 and drove himself to an incapacitating stroke, as he battled against partisan Republicans who wanted Wilson out of the White House.

For the period 1919–41, the nation retreated into isolationism and a "return to normalcy." The public mood of the period contributed to a chain of events on disarmament, debts, and reparations that may have made World War II more likely. Father Charles Coughlin, the demagogic Roman Catholic "radio priest," and Senator Huey Long, who turned Louisiana into his own personal domain, fanned opposition in 1935 to U.S. adherence to the World Court. Although some Americans favored support for anti-Franco Loyalists in the Spanish Civil War, 1936–39, and saw that fight as a battle for democracy, most Americans opposed involvement. There was minimal response to the Nazi extermination of Jews. The general U.S. public response to events in Spain, Ethiopia, Finland, and elsewhere in the 1930s was to embrace and extend U.S. legislation for neutrality. For example, the most that President Franklin Roosevelt was able to do, given congressional sentiment, was to denounce the Soviet invasion of Finland in 1939 as "wanton disregard for law" and call for a moral embargo on the shipment of war materials to the U.S.S.R. The American public, despite overwhelming sympathy for "brave little Finland" and readiness to send agricultural and civilian supplies, was determined to avoid military involvement.

* * *

GAP BETWEEN EXPRESSED AND ACTUAL INTENT. What Americans *say* about human rights has often concealed their real motivations. Latin American leaders saw that the Monroe Doctrine was less for the sake of their freedom than for U.S. interests. Greed for land and growing national pride commingled with idealism in the American Manifest Destiny of the 1840s and 1850s. Hence the references to the "universal Yankee nation" and mandate to embark upon a "civilizing mission" that marked efforts to annex Texas and Mexico.

There were other examples of the gap between real and apparent intent. U.S. security, not concern for liberty, was pre-eminent in American opposition to the French conquest of Mexico in the 1860s. Banishing Russian monarchy from North America was not, as some senators argued, the reason the United States bought Alaska in 1867. Economic, rather than alleged idealistic, motives propelled Secretary of State James G. Blaine's "guano statesmanship" in Latin America in the 1880s. Concerns of American missionaries paled before those of traders, whalers, and Captain A. T. Mahan, high priest of naval power, as the United States moved to absorb Hawaii. In the case of the Philippines, one Protestant clergyman asserted, "Manila stretches out her torn and bleeding hands and we must clasp them and accept our work of redemption, not as a piece of political ambition, but as a mission we have from God."[4] In fact, the decisive outstretched hands were from the American business community, in the person of Mark O. Hanna, senator from Ohio and political confidant of President William McKinley.

Increasing domestic tension over slavery in the United States during the nineteenth century had a significant effect on U.S. promotion of human rights elsewhere. Few Americans then (or now) liked to dwell on the incongruity of Founding Fathers who both owned slaves and asserted that "all men are created equal." Yet, slavery persisted and, to a remarkable extent, helped divert national energy from furthering liberty abroad. President Franklin Pierce tried to divert domestic attention from the increasingly divisive slavery issue by responding to popular pressure to save Cuba from alleged Spanish despotism. James Buchanan won the White House in 1856 because he appealed to southern Democrats who wanted to annex Cuba and thus counter northern territorial gains. Fear that he would lose critical support from slave-owning border states and voters stopped Abraham Lincoln from making freedom for Negroes a major issue in the early years of the Civil War. His Emancipation Proclamation, although exempting Negroes in loyal border states, did indeed lead to heavy losses for the Lincoln administration in the congressional elections of 1862.

* * *

PRINCIPLE AS A POLITICAL PAWN. U.S. politicians have not been above using promotion of human rights for their own political purposes. As will be discussed later in this chapter, President Carter, although genuinely concerned about human rights, did stress morality in American foreign policy as one means to appeal to the prevailing mood of the public. In like manner, earlier in U.S. history, political calculations sometimes lay behind more flattering explanations of America's move beyond its own shores. For example, President William McKinley bowed, reportedly with reluctance, to public fervor fanned by the Hearst press, to declare the "splendid little war" against Spain in 1898. McKinley said that he had turned to prayer as a last resort in deciding what course to take in the Philippines. He concluded that "there was nothing left for us to do but to take them all, and to educate the Filipinos, and uplift and civilize and Christianize them, and by God's grace do the very best we could by them. . . ."[5] Public opinion and the election of 1900 were probably more decisive than Divine Providence in that new imperialist turn to U.S. foreign policy. Teddy Roosevelt's "cowboy diplomacy" in Central America, although based on what he called "a mandate from civilization," had the important political advantage of helping put him before the public eye and, eventually, into the White House.

Domestic political considerations also help explain the early emergence of U.S. concern for Jews in Europe. Teddy Roosevelt instructed John Hay, his Secretary of State, to respond to an outcry from American Jews for intervention against Romanian persecution of Jews. Hay's diplomatic protest reportedly helped the Republicans in the congressional elections of 1902. Hay wrote privately: "The Hebrews—poor dears! all over the country think we are bully boys. . . ."[6] In 1912, after public and congressional protests against massacres of Jews in Russia and Russian discrimination against naturalized U.S. citizens who wanted to return to their native Russia, William Howard Taft placated American Jewish opinion by terminating an old (1832) commercial treaty with Russia. That slap at the tsar did little good for American Jews and hurt American business. Both political and humanitarian interests pushed Harry Truman to help speed the formation of Israel in 1948, on the eve of his uphill campaign for the presidency against Governor Thomas E. Dewey.

* * *

LAPSES IN U.S. PERFORMANCE ABROAD. Most Americans, while often outspoken on the subject of human rights, have sometimes seemed oblivious to U.S. actions that undercut that cause. Although the United

States has frequently helped bolster respect for human rights elsewhere, that commitment has been anything but consistent. For instance, the "sugar conspiracy" of economically-motivated sons of American missionaries in Hawaii led to efforts to depose the native, albeit autocratic, dynasty of Queen Liliuokalani. The United States, spurred by economic interests, imposed financial pressure on Nicaragua in the early twentieth century—despite strong opposition by the Nicaraguans themselves. Much of Woodrow Wilson's "missionary diplomacy" in the Caribbean made a mockery of alleged U.S. dedication to self-determination. After a revolt in Haiti in 1915, American marines landed and shot scores of independence-loving Haitian blacks, while "pacifying" the country. Although defenders of Wilson's policy praised the new era of order and prosperity there, liberals in the United States and abroad condemned the brutality of American intervention. They claimed that the once-free Haitian republic was reduced to a "territory of the National City Bank" of New York. U.S. marines also landed in the Dominican Republic in 1916, to ward off a threat to the Monroe Doctrine. The U.S. Department of the Navy subsequently imposed a six-year military government when the lawful regime in the Dominican Republic refused to accept a treaty imposed by the United States. When the U.S. Marines returned to Nicaragua in 1926 to help quell liberal elements there and, as President Calvin Collidge said, to protect American lives and property, one Democrat in Congress cried: "Oh, Monroe Doctrine, how many crimes have been committed in they name?"

*   *   *

DISREGARD FOR HUMAN RIGHTS AT HOME. Much U.S. advocacy of human rights abroad has been voiced without regard to lapses in American domestic performance. For example, controversy flared between the United States and United Kingdom in the 1840s because the British, who had already abolished slavery in their colonies, wanted to establish the right to search American ships and thus help halt U.S. trade in "black ivory." The United States resisted British efforts to curb slave trade, because U.S. commercial interests wanted protection of their maritime rights and because many southerners feared that England, once cleared to curb transport of slaves, might turn next to end slavery within the United States itself. Later in the nineteenth century, Abraham Lincoln suspended the writ of habeas corpus in the cases of persons detained by military authority, at first as an exercise of his own constitutional power, and, after 1863, with the authority of the Congress. [7]

U.S. reaction to prospective immigrants or those already in the country has often belied the welcome inscribed on the Statue of Liberty: "Give me your tired, your poor, your huddled masses, yearning to breathe free. . . ." Economic and other interests have often meant that the United States is more of a fair-weather haven. Alarmed Californians rallied in the 1870s and 1880s against "the moon-eyed menace" of industrious Chinese who, they thought, threatened their standard of living and prospect for jobs. Author Bret Harte wrote of Chinese stoned to death by "Christian school children" in the streets of San Francisco. With the Irish-born agitator Denis Kearney shouting, "To an American, death is preferable to life on a par with the Chinaman," Congress passed the Act of 1882, suspending Chinese immigration for ten years.

Other actions reflected similar lapses in U.S. domestic respect for human rights. Mob violence against Italians in U.S. cities in the 1890s outraged the Italian government. James G. Blaine, then secretary of state, replied: "I do not recognize the right of any government to tell the United States what it should do." The flareup over "lynching" of Italians—so-called because of the role of a Judge Lynch in that case—led to more domestic calls to restrict immigration from southern Europe. Despite the efforts of President Woodrow Wilson and Secretary of State William Jennings Bryan to avoid antagonizing Japan, the citizens of California, upset by the high birthrate among the Japanese and their energetic acquisitions of U.S. property, passed an alien land law. That law of 1913 forbade aliens ineligible for citizenship, such as the Japanese, to own agricultural land. Political and economic isolationism continued to color many U.S. actions in the 1920s. One manifestation of the national mood was the American Immigration Act of 1924. Afraid of a flood of impoverished Europeans, Congress established quotas for certain nations that drastically reduced the number of new arrivals and completely barred "aliens ineligible to citizenship"—a clause that embraced all Orientals. What may be the most drastic abrogation of civil rights in the United States occurred twenty years later. According to an executive order, ratified by an Act of Congress and upheld by the Supreme Court, Japanese-Americans living on the West Coast were deported or interned during World War II.

Surveys of American public opinion about refugees since the end of World War II indicate often-shallow domestic determination to do something at home to help victims of human-rights violations abroad. Opposition to specific immigrant groups has dominated response. In 1946, there was three-to-one opposition to admitting some of the over 800,000 homeless people in Europe. In 1956, three times as many Americans thought the United States was admitting "too many" Hungarians, as "not enough." According to polls taken in mid-1979—when the mass exodus of "boat people" had become a major story in the American media and catalyst for a United Nations conference—the majority of Americans still opposed, 60 to 40 percent, the large-scale admission of Indochinese to the United States. Therefore, in debating budgetary allocations for Fiscal Year 1980, Congressmen Peter Rodino, Dante Fascell, Lester Wolff, and others stressed the need to limit the intake of refugees since the American people would not put up with ever-increasing immigration.

Finally, U.S. failure to ratify most major U.N. human-rights–related covenants and conventions has made much American espousal of fundamental freedoms suspect abroad. The prolonged consideration of the U.N. Convention on the Prevention and Punishment of the Crime of Genocide stands out in this regard. The United States had played a leading role in developing that convention. Drafted largely in reaction against the Nazi holocaust of Jews, it made genocide an international crime and committed contracting parties to try to prevent and punish it. The U.N. General Assembly adopted the convention unanimously in 1948. President Harry Truman sent it to the Senate for advice and consent to ratification in 1949. There it has remained—for reasons that have thwarted U.S. ratification of most human-rights treaties. In the early 1950s, both opponents and proponents of the Genocide Convention invoked anticommunism. The former considered the convention an opening wedge through which what they called "socialist states or alien ideologies" would ruin the U.S. system of government. The latter urged ratification as a means to pressure the U.S.S.R. in the Cold War. Senator John W. Bricker (Rep.–Ohio) fought for constitutional amendments that would prevent the United States from acceding to treaties under which "any foreign power or any international organization" could "supervise, control, or adjudicate the rights of citizens of the United States within the United States."[8] Accession to the human-rights treaties constituted the "internationalization" of U.S. domestic law and overstepped the authority of the federal government to legislate for the states. Faced with such arguments, John Foster Dulles, secretary of state at the time, reversed his previous support for the Genocide Convention. Thus, during the "Bricker hearings" of 1953, members of the Eisenhower administration sided with prevailing senatorial skepticism about the United Nations and opposed promotion of human rights through international treaties.

Shifting gears on the Genocide Convention has not been easy. Representative Henry Reuss (Dem.–Wis.) and the late Senator Hubert Humphrey (Dem.–Minn.) failed in their attempts during the late 1950s to reverse the malaise of "Brickeritis." However, they did lay the basis for subsequent reconsideration of the convention by the Kennedy and Johnson administrations. Other important congressional advocates would be, among others, Senators Jacob Javits, Hugh Scott, Thomas Dodd, William Proxmire, and Joseph Clark. Together, they helped clear the path for shifts of sentiment within the influential American Bar Association, a letter in 1970 from President Richard Nixon to the Senate renewing the 1949 request for consent to ratification of the convention, and Senate hearings in 1974. However, southern senators, some arguing that ratification of the convention would let Black Panthers and other so-called "extremists" bring charges against the president, prevailed. The early push from the Carter administration foundered in debate within the executive branch over the proper reservations and understandings to be included in U.S. ratification of the Genocide Convention and other human-rights documents. Subsequent movement toward ratification stalled because the administration did not want to antagonize conservative senators by pushing too hard on the convention, and thus lose their support on the close vote in 1978 on the Panama Canal treaty or, later, on the ratification of SALT II. Concern about the "radical" direction of the international human-rights movement makes any move by the executive branch to push for ratification of human-rights treaties a major political effort—since the residue of resistance from the 1950s remains in the 1980s. The United States, like other nations, resists alleged interference in its so-called internal affairs.

The change in the record and the rhetoric

The history of American domestic reaction to human rights at home and abroad helps place national tradition in context, let Americans see themselves more as others do, and put more recent U.S. policy into perspective. Human rights did not spring, first and full-blown, out of the Carter inaugural. President Carter's forceful commitment to the "fate of freedom" did, however, signal the culmination of some important changes in American domestic politics and, perhaps, the beginning of a new era for U.S. advocacy of human rights. A closer look at the period from 1973 to 1980 illustrates how and why American public opinion, the Congress, the executive branch, and pivotal interest groups helped train a global spotlight on millions of once "invisible" victims of human-rights violations. This section below addresses the following issues:

《 Major developments behind the new stress on human rights
《 Role of two key individuals and the interaction between the legislative and executive branches during the Kissinger period
《 Transition from the Ford to the Carter years
《 Relationship between the Carter administration and the Congress on human rights
《 Reasons for continuing political momentum behind human rights
《 Political constraints on promotion of human rights

WHY THE NEW STRESS ON HUMAN RIGHTS? Several factors converged in the early 1970s to help push the issue of human rights to the fore. Among those were domestic backlash against American involvement in Vietnam, spillover from the U.S. civil-rights movement, domestic reaction to particular political events around the world, and changes within the Congress and in relations between the legislative and executive branches of the U.S. government.

Of all those factors, U.S. disenchantment with the Vietnam war was probably pre-eminent. Whether seen as an example of executive excess, a distortion of national interest, or an instance of American moralism run amok, domestic disquiet over the experience set the stage for stress on human rights in U.S. foreign policy.

Reaction against the Vietnam war might have spurred just the opposite effect. Disgust with the distortion of expressed democratic goals in Indochina could have caused more Americans to look inward and resist other efforts to apply their values elsewhere. Instead, that sentiment helped create a moral vacuum and the need to fill it with restored self-respect. As political commentator Ronald Steel observed, "After Kissinger and Nixon, Vietnam and Watergate, there has been a yearning for morality in foreign policy so palpable it could be marketed." [9]

Whatever the marketing, many of the new merchants of morality came from the antiwar movement. They set the tone for the human-rights crusade that might not have been. In fact, one of the more interesting aspects of the human-rights issue is the large number of proponents who were once either activists in the civil-rights movement or opponents of U.S. involvement in Southeast Asia—or both. Representative Tom Harkin (Dem.–Iowa) traces his commitment to human rights to the discovery, while a congressional staff member, of South Vietnam's "tiger cages" for prisoners. Since his election to Congress, Harkin has been a prime mover behind much human-rights legislation. Andrew Maguire (Dem.–N.J., who began his political education by being punched in the mouth during a civil-rights march and who later demonstrated against the Vietnam war, has helped spur U.S. efforts to halt South African *apartheid*. Former Congressman Donald Fraser (Dem.–Minnesota), former U.N. Ambassador Andrew Young, Allard Lowenstein (U.S. representative to the U.N. Human Rights Commission in 1977), Patricia Derian (Assistant Secretary of State for Human Rights and Humanitarian Affairs), David Hawk (former Executive Director of the U.S. Section of Amnesty International), William Goodfellow (Deputy Director of the Washington-based Center for International Policy), and Jacqui Chagnon (Clergy and Laity Concerned and one of the former coordinators of the Human Rights Working Group of the Coalition for a New Foreign and Military Policy) are illustrative graduates of one or both of these movements.

That list suggests the significant spillover, in substance and personnel, from the U.S. civil-rights movement into promotion of internationally recognized human rights. In the 1950s, many American blacks had tried to invoke U.N. declarations on human rights to advance their own efforts to achieve equal rights before the law—much as many Soviet and Eastern European dissidents were to use the Helsinki Accords to help build a legal case for domestic respect for human rights within their societies. By the 1970s, both blacks and whites saw promotion of international human rights as a logical extension of their own work within the United States during the 1960s. Patricia Derian, the highest-ranking political appointee in the Carter administration with the most explicit mandate on human rights, found remarkable overlap between what she had experienced as a civil-rights activist in Mississippi and what she found abroad in nations like Argentina, most notable for their

violations of human rights. Concern with South African *apartheid* became a focal point for U.S. student activism in the 1970s because of the
connection between concern about racial discrimination in both the
United States and the Republic of South Africa. Bayard Rustin, who
helped mobilize the "March on Washington" for civil rights in 1963,
tried to launch the National Conference on Human Rights in 1977.
The idea grew from the belief that the time was ripe for an organization
that might operate in the human-rights area as the Leadership Conference on Civil Rights did on racial change. At the first large meeting in
New York, Rustin made that link by quoting Martin Luther King: "Injustice anywhere is a threat to justice everywhere."

A combination of apparently unrelated political events and developments around the world in the late 1960s and 1970s helped attract even
more attention to the human-rights question and—most to the point of
American political concern—the role of the United States in that repression. Exposés on misconduct by the Central Intelligence Agency, as
well as close U.S. support for dictatorial governments such as those of
Park Chung-hee in South Korea and Ferdinand Marcos in the Philippines, fed a sense of American hypocrisy on human rights. Reaction
grew against the alleged U.S. role in the ouster of Salvador Allende's
Marxist government in Chile and support for the subsequent military
junta; against promotion of *détente*, at the apparent expense of freedom
for Soviet and Eastern European dissidents; against growing U.S. investment in countries such as South Africa; and against official U.S.
programs for training foreign internal-security forces.

Reports on these developments inside and outside the United States
coincided with a related shift within the U.S. government. The pendu-
lum of political power in U.S. foreign policy was beginning to swing
away in the 1970s from the White House to the other end of Pennsylvania Avenue. The nation eased from the era of the Imperial Presidency, to what some called the "Imperial Congress."[10]

Why? From about 1950 to 1970, the president made most U.S.
foreign policy. The Congress went along, lulled into bipartisanship by
the presumed Cold War consensus behind that policy. Vietnam and
Watergate, like thunderclaps on a hot summer night, broke both that
consensus and the mystique of White House omniscience on foreign
policy. Questions about U.S. policy toward the Greek junta, brought to
a head by the Cyprus crisis of 1974; anger about allegedly limited con-

gressional-executive consultations on events in Angola in 1975; and concern about negotiations for bases in Spain and the Philippines were—in addition to revelations already noted—among other developments that fostered congressional disillusionment. More and more members of Congress wondered whether they could trust the executive branch to take effective action on foreign policy.

The mounting conclusion was "no." The Congress thus moved to assume a larger role and increase its oversight in foreign policy. Some specific reflections of this general trend included the War Powers Act of 1973, passed over Richard Nixon's veto, which restrained the power of the president to commit U.S. armed forces abroad; the Clark Amendment of 1975, banning future aid to Angola; and an amendment to the Arms Export Control Act of 1975 that required any sale of military equipment totaling over $7 million to rest sixty days in the Congress before becoming final. To buttress its own authority on foreign policy, the Congress expanded its own staff and access to information. There was a sixfold increase in the size of the congressional staff from 1947 to 1978, including a tripling of the staff for the House International Relations Committee, 1971–78. The Congressional Budget Office, the Congressional Research Service, the General Accounting Office, and the Office of Technological Assessment combined with private research organizations to provide more data.

Stress on human rights was one of the most striking reflections of this expanding congressional muscle in American diplomacy—and the inclination to use it. Emphasis on this issue, as shown by the Jackson-Vanik Amendment to the Trade Act of 1974, let members of the Congress curry constitutent favor, use the power of the purse to participate in more decisions about foreign policy, and hold the executive branch increasingly accountable to the "sense of the Congress."[11]

*   *   *

WHO BROUGHT HUMAN RIGHTS TO THE FORE? Propitious as the times were for espousing human rights, the issue might still have fizzled out without sparking any change in U.S. policy. Action by two individuals in the 1970s proved critical. Henry Kissinger, then secretary of state and a hard-nosed advocate of *Realpolitik*, became the unwitting catalyst for a cause in need of a scapegoat. Donald Fraser, then a little-known congressman from Minnesota, launched the hearings that laid the basis for a challenge to Kissinger's view of U.S. foreign policy and for eventual legislation on human rights.

Two efforts at what both men called "conceptualization" joined the issue in 1973. One was Kissinger's address before the "Pacem in Terris" Conference, October 8. The other was a series of hearings before the House Subcommittee on International Organizations and Movements of the Committee on Foreign Affairs, August 1–December 7.

Kissinger's speech set forth the perspectives on the role of human rights in U.S. foreign policy which were to govern his subsequent actions as secretary and to reappear in later speeches on the subject.[12] His dominant concern in 1973 and thereafter was for the policymaker to strike a "balance between what is desirable and what is possible." After stating that "America cannot be true to itself without moral purpose," Kissinger cautioned:

> When policy becomes excessively moralistic, it may turn quixotic or dangerous. A presumed monopoly on truth obstructs negotiation and accommodation. Good results may be given up in the quest for ever elusive ideal solutions. Policy may fall prey to intellectual posturing or adventuristic crusades.

Referring later to U.S. experience in Vietnam, he was to elaborate on that point in 1977: "It was under the banners of moralistic slogans a decade and a half ago that we launched adventures that divided our country and undermined our international position."

There were several other general arguments that underlay Kissinger's position on human rights. He stated that the legitimate function of foreign policy was to deal, one nation to another, on the basis of external conduct. (Critics would argue that Kissinger's conduct vis-à-vis the Allende government in Chile and elsewhere belied that assertion.) Lapsing into discussion of internal matters could put the United States on a slippery slope, with U.S. spokesmen voicing hollow rhetoric or veering toward intervention. It also posed the dilemma of a double standard, given different U.S. leverage on different situations and the genuine security threat before some nations. Any reference to human rights should be made quietly, since he believed that governments do not respond positively to public assault.

Peace itself was, according to Kissinger, a moral goal. Pursuit of a SALT agreement, resolution of the Mideast crisis, and the "opening to China" were aspects of that effort which the secretary thought might be undercut by a campaign on human rights. He defined a statesman as someone willing to be unpopular and to take the long view, to have a vision of the national interest. That interpretation of the national interest put pre-eminent stress on world order and stability and on security derived from balance among the major global powers.

Focus on geopolitical factors was crucial to Kissinger's view of the world and his mode of operation. Those closest to him—both at the National Security Council and, later, at the Department of State—recognized that fact. Those aides who did raise moral questions with Kissinger discovered that the way to reach him was, as one put it, "to avoid sounding like a bleeding heart." Most efforts to promote human rights had to be couched in the tough terms of the hard-nosed realist. That was, for example, partly how members of his staff presented discussion of U.S. policy options toward the Greek junta.

Stress on strategic considerations was especially critical to Kissinger's belated attention to Africa. While noting the moral reasons for supporting majority rule and peaceful change in southern Africa, those close to the former secretary emphasized other arguments. They asserted, for instance, that stress on human rights could help pre-empt the communists. Kissinger found much of that argument appealing because of his growing concern with expanding Soviet and Cuban activities in Angola and elsewhere in Africa. He thus agreed to deliver a major policy address in Lusaka, Zambia, in April 1976. That speech put a new spotlight on African concerns and helped lay the basis for much subsequent diplomacy by the Carter administration. Whereas Kissinger's advisers had wrapped concern about human rights in geopolitical garb, he did just the opposite for his immediate audience in Lusaka and his more distant listeners in Moscow. He called racial harmony and equality in southern Africa the "moral imperative of our time" and argued that "justice can command by the force of its rightness, instead of by force of arms."

Flexibility for the executive branch was, according to Kissinger, necessary to fulfill national needs and aspirations—whether in dealing with shifting global considerations in Africa or in other parts of the world. As secretary of state, he believed that the Congress should stay out of the day-to-day details of diplomacy. The legislators should not, as one former Kissinger aide described the secretary's view, "hamstring his pursuit of the national interest."

However, it was primarily growing congressional criticism of Kissinger by the mid-1970s—some of which came to a head over human rights—that forced the secretary to pay more attention to the constitutional and political need for a congressional role in U.S. foreign policy. Much of the Hill's human-rights backlash against Kissinger stemmed from the different tack taken by Congressman Fraser. He was concerned by what he considered previously "random" and "unpredictable" congressional attention to human rights. Fraser thus organized, with the help of commitee staff member John Salzberg and others, a series of fifteen hearings in 1973. They were a conscious effort to educate Capitol Hill, the executive branch, and the country on human rights.

The summary report from those hearings struck a tone diametrically opposed to that expressed by Kissinger. It stressed that "the human rights factor is not accorded the high priority it deserves in our country's foreign policy" and that "too often it becomes invisible on the vast foreign policy horizon. . . ." It stated, further, that "an increasingly interdependent world means that disregard for human rights in one country can have repercussions in others." For that reason, Fraser and his staff concluded that "consideration for human rights in foreign policy is both morally imperative and practically necessary."[13]

The conclusions drawn from the Fraser hearings on human rights in 1973 had several implications. They suggested a far different reading of U.S. moral and legal commitments than that usually presented by the executive branch. They reflected a divergent view of how respect for human rights could affect short- and long-term interests of the United States—whether judged by changing U.S. domestic support for American foreign policy or repercussions abroad. And, there was the unspoken assertion that Congress had a particular responsibility to speak out, to adjust the distorted perspective within the executive branch, and thus to reflect the values expressed in the U.S. Constitution and Bill of Rights.

That landmark series of hearings, analogous in some ways to the motivation and effect of those held by former Senator William Fulbright on U.S. policy in Vietnam in the 1960s, accomplished several purposes. It required government officials to re-evaluate their positions on human rights. It built a considerable record of testimony from government spokesmen, representatives of nongovernmental organizations, members of the Congress, and scholars. And it laid the basis for recommendations raising the priority given to human rights in U.S. foreign policy and strengthening the capacity of international organizations to further human rights.

Fraser followed up on those hearings. He supplemented the body of documentation by beginning a barrage of letters to the Department of State on human rights.[14] He was to travel abroad to learn at first hand about violations of human rights. Later, Fraser was to note that such trips as the one he made to South Korea made a powerful impact on his views. There, with the help of the U.S. embassy, he tried to meet with former members of the South Korean National Assembly. The Korean Central Intelligence Agency surrounded their homes so that Fraser and the embassy escort officer had to break through a K.C.I.A. blockade to keep their appointments. After meeting with a former South Korean general who had been tortured by the K.C.I.A., Fraser concluded that "this was not the country American soldiers died for."

Hearings held after the first historic set in 1973 provided, not only a forum for the kinds of concerns Fraser found in his travels, but also a basis for more explicit legislation on human rights.[15] Section 32 of the Foreign Assistance Act of 1973 made a tentative beginning in that direction. For the first time, U.S. legislation declared: "It is the sense of Congress that the President should deny any economic or military assistance to the government of any foreign country which practices the internment or imprisonment of that country's citizens for political purposes." The executive promptly told the Congress that such legislation presented difficulties of definition which, in turn, made implementation impossible. Although that legislation, aimed at the government of South Vietnam, proved impractical, it did lead to the exchange of a series of letters between then Deputy Secretary of State Robert Ingersoll and Thomas Morgan, then Chairman of the House International Relations Committee. In that correspondence, officials at the State Department noted their support for human-rights considerations in foreign policy and began what amounted to institutionalization of this concern within the State Department bureaucracy.[16] On April 4, 1974, the Department of State asked U.S. embassies in sixty-eight countries receiving assistance to report on host-country treatment of political prisoners. Those requests for information were later expanded to include respect for the full range of human rights. Information about the content of Section 32 was brought to the attention of governments in

East Asia and the Pacific region. Kissinger, while opposed to explicit re-
bukes in his own name to foreign governments, would and did clear ca-
bles that conveyed the critical "mood of Congress" on human rights.

Timing worked to the advantage of human-rights advocates. 1974
was a year of growing executive-congressional confrontation over many
issues. The off-year elections brought many antiwar congressmen to
Washington. Some of them, such as thirty-four-year-old Tom Harkin,
were particularly receptive to promotion of international human rights.
Even before the election, members of the Congress had become more
and more troubled by inadequate respect for human rights in countries
receiving U.S. assistance.

Thus, on September 20, 1974, Congressman Fraser delivered to Secretary Kissinger a letter signed by 105 members of Congress. They stated
that their support for future legislation on foreign aid would be influenced by the extent to which U.S. foreign policy showed more concern
for human rights in recipient countries. Since many members of
Congress believed that the executive branch had ignored their concern
about human rights, expressed in 1973, they added a new section to the
Foreign Assistance Act of 1974. Section 502 B stated the sense of the
Congress that, "except in extraordinary circumstances, the President
shall substantially reduce or terminate security assistance to any government which engaged in a consistent pattern of gross violations of internationally recognized human rights." The president was to advise
Congress of extenuating circumstances which might necessitate sending
security assistance to any government engaging in such violations of
human rights.

The State Department had planned to respond by submitting to
Congress country analyses of how prospective aid recipients handled
human rights and why security requirements dictated continued aid.
Although State Department officials knew that Capitol Hill supporters
of human rights welcomed preliminary steps taken in behalf of human
rights within the previous year, they still believed that response to Section 502 B would constitute a critical test of executive branch intent.
Senators Edward Kennedy and Alan Cranston and others had made
clear that they were looking for reduction or elimination of security assistance in serious problem cases and/or persuasive evidence that the
State Department was actively pursuing other measures to foster human
rights.[17]

The executive branch failed that test. Secretary Kissinger decided that making human-rights reports on security-assistance recipients would harm the conduct of U.S. foreign policy. Thus, although the Department of State, under the direction of Carlyle Maw (then the Under Secretary for Security Assistance and personal lawyer for Kissinger), had supervised the preparation of country reports, the department did not submit them to Congress. Instead, it provided what congressional analysts considered "a bland unsigned summary report" to the Senate Foreign Relations Committee. That report stated that neither U.S. security interests nor the cause of human rights would be served by the "public obloquy and impaired relations with security assistance recipient countries" that would follow necessarily subjective determinations on human-rights conditions. It concluded that "quiet but forceful diplomacy" is the best way to further respect for human rights.[18]

Both Senator Cranston and Congressman Fraser disparaged the State Department's contention that no objective means existed to make distinctions among offending nations. Cranston replied, "There may be no objective way to determine the degree of violations, but does the Secretary of State have any subjective feelings about what is going on in Chile, Brazil, Korea, Indonesia, Ethiopia, and the Philippines today?" According to Cranston, the department's report reflected "malignant indifference."[19]

Kissinger seemed to treat Congress as an irrelevant irritant to his own prerogatives on foreign policy. According to his critics, the German-born statesman did not appreciate American values and institutions and reflected that cynical disregard when he thumbed his nose at the U.S. system of checks and balances. Frustration with the "Kissinger administration," augmented by increased congressional concern about specific atrocities committed by the Chilean junta and what Congress considered inadequate executive branch response to more general repression throughout Latin America, thus colored consideration of human-rights legislation in 1975 and 1976. Section 116 of the International Development and Food Assistance Act of 1975—known as the Harkin Amendment, for Congressman Tom Harkin, its main sponsor in the House—had several important provisions. It specified that economic assistance may not be given to any country that consistently violates internationally recognized human rights; required the president to submit to Congress a written report explaining how assistance would directly benefit the people of such a country; and stipulated that, if either house of Congress disagrees with the president's justification, it may take action to terminate economic assistance to that country by a concurrent resolution.

Gone was the loose language reflecting the "sense of the Congress." The legislators were angry at what many considered Kissinger's callous disregard for congressional concerns, and had thus moved to make the *first mandatory* restrictions on U.S. bilateral aid—on human-rights grounds.

Significant as this move was, it did stop short of the possible blanket cutoff sought by Congressman Harkin and Senator James Abourezk (Dem.–S.D.). The 1975 bill carried the proviso that aid might still be given to a repressive regime, *if* that assistance directly benefited the "needy people" in the country in question. What cynics soon tagged the "needy-people loophole" resulted from arguments by the congressional leadership that legislation on security assistance was a more appropriate means for promoting human rights than was development aid. The influential Thomas Morgan, supported by Fraser, helped deflect congressional anger from a course that could have put strong constraints on the program of the Agency for International Development.

Congressional frustration with the executive thus focused on security assistance. The first draft of a security-assistance bill, drawn up in late 1975, reflected a predictably strong position vis-à-vis the executive. Although the State Department tried to work with congressional staff members on a compromise, there was little give on the human-rights language. Fraser held firm, even though, as staff member Salzberg recalls, Morgan "was never enthusiastic about the human-rights legislation." Senators Humphrey, Case, and Javits supported Cranston. When President Ford vetoed the 1976 authorization in May, with the explanation that it raised "fundamental constitutional problems" and "would seriously inhibit my ability to implement a coherent and consistent foreign policy," Congress came back with another version. While more modest than that fashioned in the House, it still held executive branch feet to the fire on human rights.

The result, in fact, was Section 301 on the International Security Assistance and Arms Export Control Act, approved on June 30, 1976. It reflected the draft done in the previous winter of congressional discontent. It established within the State Department the position of the

Coordinator for Human Rights and Humanitarian Affairs, to be appointed by the president with the advice and consent of the Senate, and it required the secretary of state to submit reports every year on the human-rights practices in each country proposed as a recipient of security assistance. The Congress put real teeth into the legislation when it required the executive branch to submit reports on designated countries' performance on human rights, said that security assistance to such countries would cease if the reports were not forthcoming within thirty days, and provided that, in any case, Congress could reduce or end security assistance to violators by adoption of a joint resolution.

This 1976 incarnation of the Foreign Assistance Act was the culmination to a long struggle, marked by increasing congressional frustration with executive-branch resistance—and, sometimes, obstruction—to legislative initiatives on human rights.[20] Therein lay the cause for Kissinger's growing concern. The Congress had enacted provisions targeted at particular countries, including South Korea, Chile, the Soviet Union, and Uruguay. Legislation adopted in mid-1976 required the U.S. executive directors at the Inter-American Development Bank and the African Development Fund to vote against loans to countries where the governments seriously violated human rights.

Fear that such international financial institutions might become what some officials at the Departments of State and the Treasury called "the cutting edge of the human-rights crusade" prompted increased (albeit belated) attention by the Ford Administration to human rights, and consultations with Congress on that subject. Kissinger had already initiated several meetings with Donald Fraser and about fifteen other congressional advocates of human rights. Those sessions helped dispel Kissinger's previous belief that "Fraser was a madman." However, according to one participant in the meetings, of which the verbatim minutes were kept secret, those sessions simply "gave the secretary a chance to expound his own philosophy and left the Hill types empty-handed." Charles W. Robinson, then deputy secretary of state, met with Senator Cranston and Congressman Fraser in July 1976. Briefing materials for the meeting with Robinson suggested that the Department of State had ignored most congressional concerns about human rights and that it was time to reopen channels of communication. Robinson was impressed by his meeting with the congressmen, encouraged by his immediate staff, and prompted by his own personal concern about human rights. He therefore asked the department's policy planning staff to formulate criteria for more thoughtful and consistent implementation of human-rights provisions in existing legislation.

* * *

WHAT TRANSPIRED DURING THE TRANSITION? Time, however, was to run out on that effort—and for the Ford administration. By late 1976, interaction between the executive branch and the Congress on human rights during the Kissinger era had had a twofold effect: a legislatively mandated step forward for U.S. observance of human rights abroad and serious division between the two concerned branches of the U.S. government.

Congress had elicited some grudging executive branch response. It had raised consciousness in the ranks, if not at the highest reaches of the administration. Indeed, even in the latter regard, Congress had had impact. Human rights figured more prominently than before in Kissinger's speeches by 1976. His address before the Synagogue Council of America (October 19, 1976) was honed by appreciation for the sensitivities of the audience, growing congressional interest in human rights, and—it should be noted—the fact that then presidential candidate Jimmy Carter had made a strong human-rights speech before the convention of B'nai B'rith (September 8, 1976). Congressional pressure contributed to the fact that Kissinger—while choosing, against the advice of human-rights advocates, to attend the 1976 General Assembly of the Organization of American States in authoritarian Chile—did make a strong statement in behalf of human rights. He used the occasion, while face to face with members of the Chilean junta in Santiago, to state publicly, "The condition of human rights as assessed by the O.A.S. Human Rights Commission has impaired our relationship with Chile and will continue to do so."[21] And, finally, congressional actions began to have an effect on the bureaucracy. The Department of State established the Office for Human Rights and Humanitarian Affairs and a network of human-rights officers throughout all regional and some functional bureaus and made some effort to take human rights into account in a range of foreign-policy decisions, such as U.S. votes in the Inter-American Development Bank and proposals at the United Nations.

John Brademas, Majority Whip in the House of Representatives, summed up the role of Congress in behalf of human rights by the end of the Nixon-Ford years. Congress had established principles for U.S. foreign policy, it had overseen implementation of that policy, and it had voted or denied money for foreign assistance.[22] The record suggests that it legislated regard for human rights as a last resort. Members of Congress recognized then, as later, that some of their efforts were excessively blunt instruments or that some were downright counterproductive. It was not clear, for example, that requirements to vote "no" in international financial institutions helped human rights more than they hurt the institutions themselves. And the Jackson-Vanik Amendment, by most counts at the end of 1976, had not achieved the goals set by its congressional sponsors.

The transition between the Kissinger era and the Carter administration was thus a time for reconnoitering on human rights within both the executive and legislative branches. Inside the State Department, the bureaucracy wrestled over what to make of pronouncements in the presidential campaign and existing legislation. Draft papers on human rights, prepared at the request of the Carter transition team during December 1976 and January 1977, tended to fuzz over "the problem with Congress." However, officers from several bureaus throughout the State Department (especially Policy Planning, Congressional Relations, the Office of the Legal Adviser, and Human Rights) did question analysis which they believed would either distort the actual situation on the Hill or lack credibility for the new administration. They stressed that congressional insistence on legislation illustrated mistrust of executive branch motives. It would be a mistake, they said, to dismiss the members of the movement—spearheaded by Senators Kennedy and Cranston and Congressmen Fraser, Koch, and Harkin—as a "small band of extremists." They thought that a sizeable majority in Congress believed that the United States should distance itself publicly from repressive regimes to demonstrate disfavor for the violations of human rights. These officials concluded by advocating that the State Department work with, not against, the Congress to find constructive ways to promote human rights.

Just as State Department officials were preparing for a new way to deal with human rights—and the Congress—so were many on Capitol Hill reviewing strategy. Members and those on their staffs gathered frequently in late 1976. Many had been flattered by the attention showered on them earlier in the year by campaigners for Jimmy Carter. The fact that the Carter people had taken time to solicit their views stood in marked contrast to what they considered the "cold shoulder" from the Ford administration. (Such efforts were to lay the basis for much subsequent collaboration between the executive and legislative branches, officially and unofficially, on human rights.) Most acknowledged, according to later interviews, the need to work with the new administration on human rights. Some even conceded the "one-sided" nature of some congressional hearings on human rights and admitted that some legislation was enacted more as a reaction against the "Lone Ranger" style of Henry Kissinger than as the best means to further human rights. Most believed that Kissinger's exit opened the door to a new, more positive attitude at the State Department toward human rights. They welcomed the arrival of a new generation of officials, not molded by the pressures of the Cold War or McCarthyite attacks in the 1950s.

The transition period ended with congressional advocates of human rights wondering about themselves and their prospective counterparts in the executive branch. Could the Congress persuade the other end of Pennsylvania Avenue to take human rights into account when submitting trade legislation or requests for foreign aid? Or would Congress have to keep taking what one staffer on Capitol Hill called "human rights potshots" at the State Department—some of which, he admitted, "miss the target"? And, most troubling for some on the Hill, might the legislators' "over-eagerness" on human rights jeopardize the cause itself for years to come?

*   *   *

HOW CARTER AND CONGRESS ADDRESSED HUMAN RIGHTS. When the new year and new administration arrived, there was prompt word (and some deed) to fulfill campaign pledges on human rights. In his inaugural address on January 20, 1977, the president stressed: "Our moral sense dictates a clearcut preference for those societies which share with us an abiding respect for individual human rights." This section provides detailed description of some early actions by the Carter administration and the Congress—and interaction between the two ends of Pennsylvania Avenue—to illustrate the special domestic political dynamics behind the human-rights issue.

President Carter moved fast to regain executive branch initiative on human rights. Administration officials expressed a commitment to human rights that represented a conscious shift from the position espoused by Kissinger. Both the president and Secretary of State Cyrus Vance stated the firm belief that human rights should be one of the important factors in the formulation and implementation of U.S. foreign policy. Consideration for human rights was to pervade bilateral relations with other nations and such issue areas as arms transfer and the North-South dialogue, a point stressed in the Presidential Review Memoranda of the new administration. In that way, American diplomacy would, as press statements released by the State Department suggested, reflect traditional national values and legal commitments.

To meet one of the immediate problems in this field, the lingering credibility question with the Hill, the State Department's Bureau of Congressional Relations recommended that senior-level officials meet with Hill advocates of human rights. Leaders in the field, such as Fraser and Kennedy, were to be consulted on how to implement the administration's human-rights policy. There was particular concern about reassuring the congressmen on the seriousness of executive branch intent, drawing out their ideas, and discussing the need for certain security assistance programs. That bureau also encouraged the secretary to meet with members of the congressional Black Caucus, in accordance with their request. It did so on the grounds that that group could help the administration develop human-rights criteria, that it could help the administration achieve its objectives in Africa, and that three such meetings held over the previous eighteen months with Kissinger had proved useful.[23]

In addition to such informal meetings with members of Congress, there was a full roster of appearances by senior spokesmen for the Carter administration before congressional committees. Among the first significant statements were those by Secretary Vance before the Senate Appropriations Subcommittee on Foreign Operations on February 24, 1977; by Vance before Congressman Clarence Long's House Appropriations Subcommittee on the overview of the foreign-assistance package on March 2, 1977; and by Deputy Secretary of State Warren Christopher before Senator Hubert Humphrey's Subcommittee on Foreign Assistance on March 7, 1977. Each presentation—the product of weeks of bureaucratic pulling and hauling within the State Department—was considered a crucial early effort to set a new tone, establish *bona fides* on human rights, and meet the Congress more than half way.

The administration moved quickly to complement these statements with actions. There were cuts in security assistance to some repressive governments. [24] More to the point at hand, the administration acted fast in 1977 to test and confirm the sincerity of congressional resolve on human rights. In a notable display of good timing, the White House sought—and got—repeal of the Byrd Amendment. It thus restored a complete boycott of Rhodesian goods, in compliance with U.N. sanctions, just before the president's maiden speech in the United Nations. In that U.N. address on March 17, 1977, Carter announced his intention to seek Senate advice and consent for ratification of major U.N. covenants and conventions on human rights. And the president stressed, in a speech before the Permanent Council of the Organization of American States on April 14, 1977, his intention to seek Senate approval for ratification of the American Convention on Human Rights.

Congress, for its part, responded by pressing promotion of human rights. It did so for several reasons. Mistrust of the executive branch persisted from the Kissinger period. Jimmy Carter, many thought, had yet to establish his credentials on human rights. Other congressional advocates of human rights were jealous when the executive branch *did* show interest in the subject and thus wanted to accelerate their own campaign. And, according to constituent mail and public-opinion polls at the time, the issue of human rights remained popular.

The range of congressional activity on human rights in 1977 was thus extensive. In March, both the House and the Senate—sensitive to massive press play on U.S.–Soviet relations and the role of human rights in that relationship—passed, by lopsided margins, resolutions to convey the interest of the American people in Soviet adherence to the Helsinki Final Act. The Subcommittee on Foreign Assistance of the Senate Foreign Relations Committee, as part of the follow-up on 1976 legislation, made public a State Department "report card" on human-rights conditions in eighty-two nations. Congressman Fraser maintained a brisk pace of hearings that included testimony on respect for human rights in East Timor, Vietnam, Thailand, Cambodia, El Salvador, and Iran and reviews on attention to human rights at the 1977 sessions of the U.N. Human Rights Commission and the O.A.S. General Assembly.

Important as these activities were, action in another quarter provided the most significant index to congressional interest in human rights— and to the relation of the Hill to the White House on this issue. Debate raged throughout much of 1977 over whether to put human-rights restrictions on U.S. participation in *all* international financial institutions. To do so entailed extending the language of the Harkin Amendment, adopted in 1976 for U.S. votes in the Inter-American Development Bank and the African Development Fund, to such major institutions as the World Bank. The human-rights lobby, eager to make legislative purview in the economic sector as complete as possible, pushed for what its member organizations saw as the necessary next step after restrictions on U.S. bilateral aid and some multilateral assistance. A January 1977 report from the Center for International Policy, entitled "Foreign Aid: Evading the Control of Congress," provided much of the grist for a receptive legislative mill. The result was the reincarnation of "Harkin language" in Title VII of House Resolution 5262. That bill authorized increased U.S. capital subscriptions to the International Bank for Reconstruction and Development, the International Development Association, the International Finance Corporation, the Asian Development Bank, and the African Development Fund.

The Carter administration, despite its strong public pitch for human rights, fought hard to resist this bill and, indeed, to repeal Harkin language elsewhere. What one State Department official called "rather tense" discussions ensued between members of the Carter administration and the Congress. The former found themselves in the embarrassing position of arguing for "flexibility," a red flag from the Kissinger era for the Congress. They asked congressional liberals, "Give us time, give us the benefit of the doubt; it's *us* down here now."

Congressional advocates of human rights split over that kind of appeal. One camp preferred to give the "new team" a honeymoon, whereas the other wanted to capitalize on the mounting momentum for what they called "the human-rights cause."

Group One, typified by the human-rights alliance between two Minnesotans (Fraser and Humphrey), chose a vigilant "wait and see" stance. Like-minded colleagues—such as Dante Fascell (Dem.–Fla.), chairman of the "Helsinki Commission" set up to monitor compliance with the C.S.C.E. accords—believed that only executive branch negotiators could finally decide how hard to push in any given case on human rights. Fraser shared that particular view. He wrote at the time that "Congress will welcome a clear declaration of intent by the Executive Branch to stress human rights in its foreign policies. . . ." Further, Fraser said that he and his congressional colleagues "will be ready to accept quiet diplomacy as the most effective way to give expression to the deep-seated desire of the American people that their government be devoted to furthering decency in the conduct of human affairs."[25]

Several of Fraser's allies in the Senate voiced related themes. Humphrey warned against undermining the long-term process of economic development and multilateral cooperation by sporadic intercession on human-rights grounds. Javits counseled caution in behalf of national security in countries such as South Korea where newly-announced withdrawals of U.S. troops might be enough of a destabilizing factor in the Far East.

Group Two, exemplified by Harkin and former Congressman Herman Badillo (Dem.–N.Y.) in the liberal camp to the left of Fraser, refused to take the administration at its word. Spurred in part by the burgeoning of what former congressional staffer Bill Richardson called the new "human-rights industry" on the Hill, they pressed to expand legislative clout on human rights.

With the lines of contention thus drawn, the first round went to human-rights moderates. The administration, after considerable arm-twisting and correspondence from Deputy Secretary of State Warren Christopher and National Security Adviser Zbigniew Brzezinski, agreed to compromise language worked out by Henry Reuss, Chairman of the House Committee on Banking, Currency, and Housing and, traditionally, a strong advocate of human rights. However, Harkin and Badillo led a successful fight on the House floor in April to restore more rigid human-rights restrictions on U.S. participation in international financial institutions. Abourezk, the blunt one-term senator from South Dakota, led the campaign for Harkin-Badillo language in the Senate. In one of his last major legislative efforts, Hubert Humphrey, often using talking points supplied by the State Department, championed the administration's version of the bill. The Abourezk effort surprised Humphrey and the administration. It drew on a rare mix of conservative and liberal support and fell only seven votes short of passage. House and Senate conferees then tangled for weeks to achieve final compromise.

The result of this wrangling was signed into law on October 3, 1977. Title VII of that bill gave some latitude to the executive branch, but not as much as the Carter administration had wanted. The U.S. government was to use "its voice and vote" to advance respect for human rights in international financial institutions. Lest the administration lapse from compliance, the Departments of State and the Treasury were to report to the Congress on their actions. Similar language recurred in the act, signed into law on October 31, 1977, providing appropriations for U.S. capital subscriptions to the multilateral development banks. Throughout 1978, as discussed in Chapter 6, human-rights advocates in Congress continued efforts to extend their legislative mandate into the economic sector and to monitor implementation of language already on the books.

The Carter administration continued to walk a political tightrope. It espoused concern for human rights, while it resisted more congressional restrictions. The longer it was in office the louder it decried decreased flexibility for the executive branch in the pursuit of U.S. foreign policy and the negative effect of some human-rights legislation on other U.S. objectives. Thus, Secretary Vance, while testifying on the Administration's foreign-aid legislation in 1978, said: "I believe that any additional legislative restrictions should be reviewed carefully to insure that they achieve the desired effect of promoting human-rights goals, as well as not undermining the essential functions of multilateral institutions." Unlike his predecessor, Secretary Vance seemed genuinely concerned that the United States find the most effective means to promote human rights. In a letter to House Speaker Thomas O'Neill, Secretary Vance complained that human-rights restrictions on U.S. participation in the international financial institutions would interfere with diplomatic efforts to improve human-rights practices in certain countries.

* * *

WHAT PROPELS PROMOTION OF HUMAN RIGHTS? Pleas for caution from the secretary of state had only limited impact. By the late 1970s, the issue of human rights had a political momentum of its own.

Why? Those factors already outlined, which explained the emergence of the issue in the early 1970s, remained important. They combined with other domestic political considerations to shape the course of the human-rights cause.

Jimmy Carter's victory in the 1976 presidential election provided a decisive boost to promotion of human rights. Placing the power and prestige of the White House behind human rights put a different cast on what had been primarily a congressional cause. It was different because of the greater range of action open to the executive branch and the greater attention the president could command from the media. Further, had Gerald Ford won the 1976 election and continued, as seemed likely, the same substance and style of foreign policy, human rights would probably have remained more of a bone of domestic contention along Pennsylvania Avenue than a subject of international interest.

Jimmy Carter, the man, proved crucial to the new turn to human rights. Although stress on human rights resulted, in part, from the findings of Patrick Caddell, Carter's adviser on public opinion, and the urgings of his campaign staff, the issue was also a natural for him personally. It provided an apt vehicle for his own strong beliefs. He considered it important that political and personal values coincide. Thus, his earnest report to a convention of fellow southern Baptists in 1978: "I have never detected or experienced any conflict between God's will and my political duty." He explained his decision, in June 1979, not to lift economic sanctions against Zimbabwe Rhodesia, largely by saying, "It is the right thing to do." It was, as Andrew Young expressed it, a decision "from the heart." It also reflected a belief—reflected in the president's political autobiography, *Why Not the Best?*—that was to recur in his foreign policy and to contrast with the perspective of Henry Kissinger. Carter felt that U.S. "leadership need not depend on our inherent military force, or economic power or political persuasion," but that "it should derive from the fact we try to be right and honest and truthful and decent."

Whether or not that belief was soft-headed pap or a return to first principles did not emerge clearly before 1980 as a point of national debate. In 1976, Carter was able to translate Americans' yearning for decency into a decisive campaign plus. Astute politician that he was, he seized on that opportunity and translated values into votes. Whether seeking the support of the nation's twenty-six million Baptists or the less numerous Jews (albeit concentrated in several swing states), he made clear during the presidential campaign that the suffering of religious dissidents in the U.S.S.R. "will be very much on my mind when I negotiate with the Soviet Union, and you can depend on that."[26] The issue of human rights appealed to Henry Jackson and others on the right because it applied to the Soviet Union; it attracted liberals because of the opportunity to criticize human-rights violations in Chile and South Korea. Thus, as one campaign adviser who was to join the administration observed, "Human rights was an issue with which you could bracket Kissinger and Ford on both sides."[27]

Advocacy of human rights, while a political *virtue* for Carter during the 1976 campaign, became a political *necessity* for him after he moved into the White House. As the first test case raised by the letter from Soviet dissident Sakharov in early 1977 indicated, Carter sometimes had less latitude than he needed or wanted. All human-rights advocates with a large, visible, or vocal constituency were ready and able to call his bluff. Moreover, Carter was to find subsequently, as one White House aide ruefully admitted, that the president "was damned if he did and damned if he didn't." The American press proclaimed his "retreat on human rights" when the president responded to earlier criticism of what journalists had branded the "open-mouth diplomacy" of Jimmy Carter and Andrew Young, by putting more stress on discreet work behind the scenes.

Developments within the Congress also contributed to the mushrooming movement for more focus on human rights. The issue was as much a boon for political interests on the Hill as it was for Jimmy Carter, and for many of the same reasons. Stress on human rights cut conveniently across the spectrum of congressional concerns. It appealed to both conservatives and liberals. Human rights was thus one of the few issues that could make Jesse Helms, conservative Republican from North Carolina, and James Abourezk, left-wing maverick from South Dakota, vote alike. There was no such thing as a pure vote on human rights, one dictated solely by concern for that issue. Those who rallied around the 1977 human-rights amendment for U.S. participation in the international financial institutions included liberals, dedicated to promotion of human rights; conservatives who opposed any form of foreign aid; those worried about the administration's requests for flexibility; those who wanted to catch Carter on his own campaign rhetoric; those who wanted to strike a pose for the folks back home; a few Democrats who represented districts where organized labor was strong and critical of foreign aid that fostered low-wage imports; those who had not given the issue much thought at all; and those from the South and Southwest who were willing to trade support for human rights for protection against imports of palm oil, sugar, or citrus fruit. It was that last group of supporters for tacking human-rights criteria onto U.S. votes in the multilateral banks that caught the eye of Senator Daniel P. Moynihan (Dem.–N.Y.). Distressed by language linking American concern for freedom with that for sugar cane, he said, with palpable disdain and no little Irish oratorical flourish:

This speaks to the appearance of the integrity of our commitment. How can we stand and ask the rest of the world to follow our example in the field of human rights, and diminish that concern with a proposition having to do with commerce of the most ordinary and everyday type? I ask . . . how would it have been thought if the signers of the Declaration of Independence had concluded that immortal document by stating, 'We mutually pledge to each other our lives, our fortunes and our sacred honor, and further promise to increase the tariffs on soybeans'?[28]

Several other factors peculiar to the U.S. Congress in the 1970s, combined with these interests, objectives, and pressures to fire legislative fervor for human rights. The shift of some important authority on foreign policy from the executive branch to the Congress, described earlier, paralleled a revolution on Capitol Hill itself. There has been a stunning turnover in the membership of Congress. More than half of the national legislators have come to Washington since 1974; few members elected before the early 1960s remain. Most new members, molded by reaction against the Vietnam period, believe that they can do as well as, if not better than, the executive branch on foreign policy. (There is convenient disregard for the fact that Congress concurred with U.S. involvement in Southeast Asia until late in the 1960s.) More members of Congress are interested in foreign policy, because of their growing appreciation for the impact of international events on their constituents or because of their travels and experiences. Thus, those behind the explosion of foreign-policy amendments on the House and Senate floors need not—and often are not—on the congressional committees traditionally charged with foreign affairs. Nor are all in the Senate. The House, once considered the junior partner in foreign policy, has become increasingly outspoken. Donald Fraser's House Subcommittee on international organizations was, in the period from 1973 through 1978, to hold more than 150 hearings on the human rights problems in over forty countries.

In a comment remarkably reminiscent of Henry Kissinger, Zbigniew Brzezinski observed in 1978, "The new-found influence of Congress is not as disturbing as the lack of discipline. . . ." Members report that there is, indeed, no need to "go along to get along." Gone is what some recall as the Golden Age, when Lyndon Baines Johnson could compel legislative cohesion with an iron squeeze of the elbow. Many of the new members of Congress are strong individuals with loose party ties and little personal loyalty to the president. They exhibit pronounced skepticism about traditional political institutions and toward those who advocate a "responsible" approach to foreign policy (read: toeing old lines of bipartisanship and seniority). Many got to Washington by running against it. Stress on human rights is thus a natural issue for the new breed of legislator.

Advocacy of human rights has the added allure, as seen by most members of the Congress, of having few costs. At first blush, it satisfies fiscal conservatives because initiatives on human rights seem to require so little money and often, as in the case of canceled foreign aid, to save some. Since, as one member of a congressional staff notes, it is hard to ignore, question, or limit human rights, it is "the essence of a congressional issue," which "Congress will milk as long as it can."[29] And, Congress can do so, undaunted by its own often-inconsistent approaches to the question. The political dynamics behind U.S. advocacy of human rights are such that there need be no close correlation between the barbarity of violations abroad and the intensity of congressional response. The greatest push for international protest usually reflects the strongest domestic political pressure.

Therein lies the special role of the human-rights lobby. Its work has often been a decisive factor propelling recent U.S. promotion of human rights. That lobby is concentrated on Capitol Hill in Washington and near the United Nations in New York, but backed up by extensive national and international networks. It has grown dramatically since the early 1970s, from a relative handful of groups that had little voice, to over fifty organizations that can and do exercise considerable clout. They achieve much of their impact through providing testimony before Congress, background information for U.S. legislation and U.N. deliberations, pressure on multinational firms, and extensive mailings and educational efforts.[30]

The human-rights lobby has often been able to wield influence disproportionate to its numbers because of its sophisticated appeal to diverse interests on Capitol Hill. It has attracted some supporters for human-rights restrictions because some congressmen are genuinely interested in promoting human rights and think that such restrictions are the most effective means to that end. It has gained backing from conservatives who welcome any excuse to cut foreign aid. It has appealed to the political egos of other legislators who resent programs such as those for the international financial institutions, which escape direct congressional control. Henry Reuss, Chairman of the House Banking Committee, acknowledged the importance of this lobby in 1978 when he said that he accepted a strong human-rights amendment on a bill to contribute $1.7 billion to a special loan program of the International Monetary Fund because "we need the votes of Mr. Harkin and his dogged band of human righters."[31]

Who belongs to this "dogged band"? Representatives from religious groups, labor unions, and internationally known nongovernmental organizations specializing in human rights are most important. Activists such as Edward Snyder of the Friends Committee on National Legislation, and his counterparts from the National Council of Churches, B'nai B'rith International, and the U.S. Catholic Conference are part of what irreverent congressional staff members call the "God squad." They gather information on violations of human rights abroad, spot gaps in U.S. performance at home and abroad, and mount educational campaigns across the country. Although the American labor movement takes a general interest in human rights because of concern about freedom of association for workers, the AFL-CIO stands out for its opposition to communist governments, whereas the United Auto Workers—spurred by their president, Douglas Fraser—are noteworthy for taking strong positions on human rights in regimes of the right and left. Of the nongovernmental organizations, former Congressman Donald Fraser has singled out Amnesty International, the International League for Human Rights, and the International Commission of Jurists for being especially effective. Other organizations that promote respect for human rights include such diverse groups as the Carnegie Endowment for International Peace, the United Nations Association, the Americans for Democratic Action, Clergy and Laity Concerned, the Lawyers Committee for International Human Rights, the American Society of International Law, the American Association for the Advancement of Science, the Federation of American Scientists, the Freedom to Publish Committee of the American Association of Publishers, PEN American Center, and scores of groups focused on specific countries or regions—ranging from the American Committee on Africa, to the Armenian Assembly.

Targets and tactics of those in the human-rights lobby vary. Activists range from those who earn their living by representing corporate clients, to those who see big business as a major culprit behind foreign oppression, and from those who worry about the rights of certain groups, to those who work to secure freedom for particular regions.

William Butler, president of the American Association for the International Commission of Jurists, quips that his corporate clients make it possible for him to spend time on human rights. In fact, there is a professional link between his private practice of law and his work for the commission on the rule of law and role of lawyers. Advocacy of human rights has taken this former staff counsel for the American Civil Liberties Union and the International League for Human Rights to most parts of the world. For example, he met with the Shah of Iran some time before his fall from power and succeeded in getting him to stop beatings of leading Iranian lawyers and to move cases from military to civil courts. He led a mission to Uruguay on behalf of lawyers arrested there. He and his colleagues have helped new states write their constitutions and have had a hand in drafting international covenants and protocols on human rights. Although the commission was established twenty-five years ago with C.I.A. funding, it has no such ties now and instead enjoys open financial support from over twenty countries. It is increasingly active in the Third World, where it holds seminars to help build up indigenous support for an independent judiciary.

What multinational corporations do to promote human rights—especially in South Africa—is the main concern of Timothy Smith. One of his goals, as director of the New York–situated Interfaith Center on Corporate Responsibility, is to "make the issue of *apartheid* a personal one that touches everyone with a bank account." To that end, his center has, among its other activities, prepared a *Shareowners Manual*, which identifies key human-rights issues and campaigns so that its constituent organizations can have a "clean portfolio"—one, that is, without investment in U.S. firms doing business in repressive countries. The center has also sent its representatives to talk with senior officials at leading U.S. banks and major corporations and deployed spokesmen to annual meetings of shareholders.

Working out of a rabbit warren of offices on Capitol Hill, Brewster Rhoads tries to help coordinate Washington's disparate human-rights lobby. The Human Rights Working Group of the Coalition for a New Foreign and Military Policy attempts to focus the efforts of such organizations as the Americans for Democratic Action, Clergy and Laity Concerned, the Institute for Policy Studies, and others. The group has an extensive mailing list to which it sends frequent instructions to "act now," on items ranging from votes on Rhodesian sanctions to attempts to cut security assistance to the Philippines. Rhoads is among those who wage the still-fledgling annual campaign to make transfer of U.S. budgetary resources from defense to nutrition and education part of a larger human-rights objective.

Joseph Eldridge is director of the Washington Office on Latin America—or WOLA. An offshoot of the National Council of Churches, WOLA covers the spectrum of human rights issues in Latin America. He and his small staff have provided key witnesses and documents for congressional hearings on human rights and helped Tom Harkin draft much of the human-rights legislation of this last decade. Because of his work—and that of others—such as Thomas Quigley of the U.S. Catholic Conference; the Reverend William Wipfler, director of the human rights office of the National Council of Churches; and Laurence Birns of the Council of Hemispheric Affairs—Patricia Derian, Assistant Secretary of State for Human Rights and Humanitarian Affairs, says that the Latin American rights lobby "approaches the Jewish community in its effectiveness."

What one Jewish activist calls that community's "extraordinary success story"—over 150,000 Jews gotten out of the U.S.S.R. between 1971 and 1979—merits special mention. William Korey, director of the B'nai B'rith International Council, explains the drive of his colleagues thus: "Only Jews face pogrom." There are other reasons. Many American Jews still harbor a sense of guilt, a belief that they did not do enough for European Jews during Hitler's holocaust. There is also a special sensitivity to the situation of Jews in the Soviet Union since most American Jews have their roots in Russia. As the writing of Saul Bellow, Arthur Miller, and others suggests, the American Jew feels that he is fighting for his parents or grandparents.

The depth of this personal commitment translates into a sophisticated political effort. Leaders of the American Jewish community, whether from the National Conference of Soviet Jewry that serves as the umbrella organization for U.S. Jewish groups or elsewhere, enjoy prompt hearings on their concerns at the highest levels of the U.S. government. They use their leverage, as they put it in describing the economic power of the Jackson-Vanik and Stevenson Amendments, to "buy freedom."

They are impatient. Given what they interpret as increasing anti-Semitism inside the Soviet Union, they say, "We can't wait for long-term liberalization." They pay close attention to proper timing—taking care, as was the case in 1978, not to overreact to the Shcharansky verdict, lest they undermine significant increases in Jewish emigration from the U.S.S.R. They watch carefully for signs of shifts in Soviet sentiment and send some signals of their own, such as those via U.S. congressional delegations visiting in Moscow or through the Romanians.

Indeed, that sensitivity to Soviet sentiments may be crucial to the success of the American Jewish community. Early on, its leaders made the tactical decision to put primary stress on helping Jews, not all dissidents, within the Soviet Union. They did not want to antagonize or seem to threaten the Kremlin. "We decided," as one prominent spokesman said, "to keep our own shirts clean." That decision caused considerable anguish within the Jewish community, where many were concerned about other human-rights issues, and within the human-rights movement as a whole. A delicate *modus operandi* has been effected, whereby Jews, who play a role far disproportionate to their numbers in the U.S. human-rights effort, work for non-Jewish human rights causes under the auspices of other organizations such as Amnesty International. American Jews are also finding that concern for their fellow Jews outside the Soviet Union requires more cooperation with other human-rights advocates. For example, Latin American Jews are often active leaders of the leftist opposition or subject to anti-Semitism in countries such as Argentina. U.S. representatives from B'nai B'rith thus find themselves in closer league now with reformist priests of the Catholic Church who are struggling against repressive military regimes in the Western Hemisphere.

*   *   *

WHAT CONSTRAINS STRESS ON HUMAN RIGHTS? Impressive as the momentum for U.S. emphasis on human rights has been, there are—in addition to the international factors discussed elsewhere—countervailing domestic political forces. Promotion of human rights can have all the idealistic dash of Excalibur or the peril of a double-edged sword.

There is, first, a challenge for the president. Whether the issue of human rights turns from political asset to liability depends on how effectively the chief executive manages the potential contradictions of a foreign policy that stresses promotion of human rights, massages political egos on Capitol Hill and within the executive branch, and communicates the rationale for the policy to the American public. President Carter learned early that politics requires compromise and leaves little room for moral purity. His administration thus had to cave in to early pressure, for example, from Congressman Charles Wilson (Dem.-Tex.), a close friend of former Nicaraguan President Somoza. It approved assistance to Nicaragua in 1978, despite that government's poor performance on human rights, so that Wilson would support the administration's package on foreign aid. (Wilson—together with Representative John Murphy (Dem.-N.Y.), another Somoza ally—subsequently threatened the Administration with "rough treatment" on the bill to carry out the Panama Canal treaty unless Carter scrapped a policy that Wilson said could "turn the largest country in Central America over to the Communists.")[32]

Carter also found, as any U.S. president would, that it is hard to institutionalize official stress on human rights. With or without a president committed to making human rights a major factor in U.S. foreign policy, the idea is sufficiently controversial and complex to invite substantial opposition. Part of the resistance is due to some bureaucratic politics and some honest difference of opinion within the executive branch. For example, in 1978, the Departments of State and Commerce were strongly opposed to the decision, taken by President Carter and favored by Brzezinski and former Secretary of Energy, James Schlesinger, to place all U.S. exports of technology to the Soviet Union under U.S. government control and thus express displeasure with the Soviets' sentencing of the dissident Shcharansky. Predictably, Pentagon officials put more emphasis on the balance of power, and their counterparts at Treasury and Commerce put greater stress on the balance of payments and trade, than on promotion of human rights.

In addition, within the State Department, there has been a strong backlash from some career foreign service officers and some political appointees against what they call the "human-rights freaks." Diplomats are trained to put first priority on maintaining good working relations with their client countries. Without access, they have difficulty doing their job. With acrimonious relations, they can be declared *persona non grata* by an incensed host government and so lose all personal means to convey U.S. concerns about much of anything, including human rights. Thus, when explaining why he did not invite Soviet dissident Sakharov to the embassy's Fourth of July reception in 1978, former U.S. Ambassador Malcolm Toon said, "My job is to get along with the Soviet government."

Second, Congress can cool on promotion of human rights. The fact that the issue prospered politically during much of the 1970s, by means of an often extraordinary alliance of diverse interests, betrays its coincident strength—and weakness. The issue can, as suggested by the vote on human-rights criteria for U.S. decisions in multilateral banks, be all things to all members. It can also be vulnerable to a splintering of support. For example, members of the Black Caucus—blacks in the House of Representatives—often resent attention to human rights abroad, at the apparent expense of U.S. blacks and Hispanics. They also clash with colleagues who are reluctant to impose economic sanctions against South African *apartheid*.

Although often tailor-made for the legislators' political interests, attention to human rights is ultimately a creature of constituency appeal. Voters can turn against a policy they perceive as mismanaged or contrary to their other interests. Played out according to one logical conclusion of statements made by members of both the Congress and the executive branch, stress on human rights could cost more, in terms of lost trade and allies, than most Americans want to pay. Played out according to a more limited scenario, it could be impaled on its own raised expectations. Sole reliance on quiet diplomacy in a few inconspicuous quarters will not have dramatic impact. Most Americans like prompt and positive results from their foreign policy. Since promotion of human rights must be a part of a long-term process, stress on the issue can foster short-term frustration within the American public and thus negative repercussions for some U.S. politicians. Like *détente*, as espoused by Henry Kissinger, the issue of human rights runs the risk of being oversold and promising too much too fast. Should such disillusionment set in, Congress would be inclined to put some brakes on the human-rights bandwagon. With the defeat in the 1978 congressional elections of Senator Dick Clark (Dem.-Iowa) and Congressman Fraser, there are now fewer well-known advocates of human rights to counter such a trend.

Third, American public opinion can and does constrain promotion of human rights. Nationwide polls taken since 1977 indicate that there is comparatively strong popular support for U.S. emphasis on human rights abroad. In most surveys, over twice as many Americans say that the United States should champion human rights as say the contrary. The percentage of support is even higher (about 80 percent versus about 70 percent) among national leaders, compared with the general public.

However, other trends did and do give pause. Americans are increasingly preoccupied with what they see as the diminished world position of the United States. They attribute that change primarily to the declining value of the U.S. dollar and the growing military might of the Soviet Union. There is thus increased support for defense spending. Domestic economic concerns far outweigh interest in foreign policy. There is selectivity in that interest, with, for example, focus on the Mideast and the U.S.S.R. and a disinclination, post-Vietnam, to intervene militarily abroad. Support for foreign aid is down because Americans are more worried about U.S. domestic economic problems, because many fear that giving aid leads to military involvement, and because less than half of the American general public thinks that foreign aid serves U.S. interests.

This latest and heightened American sense of self-interest has direct relevance to U.S. policy on human rights. The main point that emerges from survey data is that Americans support stress on human rights more strongly in principle than in practice. Most favor quiet diplomacy over speaking out vigorously. A strong majority prefers a cautious, case-by-case approach that denies benefits only where such actions get desired results and do not hurt other U.S. objectives. For example, in relations with the Soviet Union, Americans consistently put promotion of human rights below emphasis on arms control. In the case of South Africa, although most Americans oppose *apartheid*, they object to any U.S. policy or action that could result in U.S. military involvement there. Only about one-fourth favor the imposition of economic sanctions to help achieve racial justice in South Africa. Americans rank advocacy of human rights, on a list of national priorities, far below "making sure that the United States is the most powerful country in the world" and their number-one preoccupation, "protecting the jobs of American workers."[33]

That last point, which reflects the perceived clash between U.S. economic interests and humanitarian sentiments, may bear closest watching. Although the human-rights movement of the 1970s and 1980s derives much of its impetus from the civil-rights campaign in the 1960s, there is another aspect to the connection. Many whites a decade or two ago were all for equality of racial opportunity until a black moved next door. Similarly, many Americans today are all for proclamations in behalf of international human rights, but against increasing their taxes to pay for more foreign aid or help refugees.

Citizen support for human rights is, in short, more complex and less firm than it may appear. As with the often-unholy congressional alliance for human rights, the human-rights public consists of many parts. Its very diversity makes solidarity more apparent than real. The participants in a National Foreign Policy Conference on Human Rights held in Washington, D.C. in 1978, although hardly a representative cross-section of the United States, illustrate the kind of political dilemma that may bedevil advocates of human rights. Calls for reform from the five hundred delegates resembled cacophony from a contemporary Tower of Babel. There was little common concern among causes and speakers, and little reflection of the great majority of American citizens, who were not there. Feminists wanted prompt passage of the Equal Rights Amendment, black men asked protection for "America's most endangered species" (themselves), Asian-Americans sought "reparations" for World War II incarceration in California concentration camps, Hispanics condemned U.S. "police brutality," and Indians demanded their treaty rights to resource-rich land. One result of the session for some stunned State Department officials who had arranged the conference: the proposal (since put into action) that U.S. victims of human-rights violations establish their own Helsinki monitoring group.

Several points that were *not* made may have been as important as those that were. There was no indiction of how Americans would react if they were to face terrorism on the scale experienced in Italy or Argentina in the 1970s. Would concern for law and order soon overshadow consideration for human rights? Further, the disparate pleas for protection of human rights came in the context of what amounts to a schizoid citizenry, partly aroused by social issues, but mostly more absorbed by private matters. Ten years after the Kerner Report on urban riots in the 1960s, the United States *is* moving toward two societies—not only one black and one white as then predicted, but one of haves and one of have-nots, separate and unequal. The one rarely sees and thereby understands the other.

The invisible poor of this latter-day "other America," foreseen by Michael Harrington in the early 1960s, are the domestic counterpart of a global phenomenon: one billion people unnoticed below what the United Nations calls "the absolute poverty line." Still others are deprived of basic dignity because of their sex or race. Yet, neither the haves nor the have-nots of the United States seem inclined to make the connection. The American public's line of sight seldom extends from Peoria to Pretoria.

The old issue resurfaces. Whose human rights, and at what cost to whom?

Some conclusions

A look at the U.S. record on human rights can be both illuminating and disillusioning. It suggests what lies behind some American fervor for freedom abroad and what to expect next. Several important points emerge.

Stripped of reference to the law or universal morality, promotion of human rights is a political exercise. At the broadest international level, it is about power: the challenge to the internal political power of an oppressive government and the external imposition of power to change that government or its behavior. Within the United States, promotion of human rights reflects another contest for power: the struggle for pre-eminence by different branches of the government, sectors of public opinion, and vested interests. Values, as U.S. policy toward much of Latin America suggests, can become chameleons in this political context.

Domestic political considerations are thus the decisive determinants of U.S. foreign policy on human rights. They shape *general* mood and *specific* focus: what are the main targets of U.S. concern? What tools will be used? There is no consistent relationship between the severity of the situation abroad and the strength of U.S. reaction. Hence, the coincidence in the 1970s of general U.S. disregard for massive genocide in Cambodia and concentration on relatively few Jewish dissidents in the Soviet Union.

American political history helps put more recent U.S. performance on human rights into perspective. The nation's record is mixed. There has been substantial American sacrifice to make the world a better and freer place. There has also, sometimes, been a self-serving side to U.S. actions. Critics are not all wrong when they condemn some U.S. promotion of human rights as a domestic political gimmick. Further, making human rights a source or surrogate for domestic consensus behind U.S. foreign policy has been, and remains, an exercise in wish fulfillment. Since 1789, U.S. advocacy of human rights has reflected a mass of contradictory impulses at home and actions abroad. The combination of contending forces—ethnic groups, economic interests, regional concerns, political parties, and ambitious individuals—has, on different occasions, led the nation in diametrically opposed directions. During the earliest years of the Republic, leaders such as George Washington and John Quincy Adams realized that the United States could not intervene effectively in behalf of human rights abroad. As far as the United States was concerned, the French Revolution was the right revolution at the wrong time. Dwight Eisenhower made a comparable choice when he mourned, but did not resist, Soviet intervention in Hungary in 1956. Woodrow Wilson reflected another significant facet of U.S. foreign policy in this area. He tried and failed, with the Fourteen Points, to make more Americans look to the longer term and support institutions that might serve both human rights and U.S. national interest. Then, as more recently, Americans got the human-rights policy they thought they wanted and were willing to pay for.

Troubling as some U.S. reactions may be, there has been a general shift in the twentieth century toward a more sophisticated public perception of America's role in the world and the relation of human rights to other U.S. objectives. The contrast between resistance to the Treaty of Versailles and "return to normalcy" in the 1920s and U.S. leadership twenty years later in the United Nations, the Marshall Plan, and the Truman Doctrine is instructive.

At the same time, that shift has created some unexpected problems of its own. Cash for containment of communism had domestic support and diplomatic effect particularly pertinent to the immediate postwar period. However, cultivation of anticommunist allies in the 1950s came to haunt the United States by the 1970s. Nations like South Korea drew belated fire for violations of human rights, often as serious as those which had caused early condemnation of communist governments. Viewed from the perspective of concern for human rights, the fervent anticommunism of the fifties became a partial embarrassment during the seventies, with parts of the executive branch scrambling to redress the alleged imbalance in national security seen by parts of the American public and Congress.

If the past gives pause to complacent invocation of the American Dream, so does the future. Predictions about the coming course of U.S. emphasis on human rights range between two extremes. Critics of an activist policy claim, or hope, that stress on human rights will disappear, like a little-mourned dodo bird of American diplomacy. Proponents see a pro–human-rights policy as the cutting edge of a new definition of national interest.

The likely outcome, as with so much else in American politics, is a little of both. Other issues will replace human rights in press headlines. Indeed, they already have. Presidents without Jimmy Carter's personal commitment and political need for the issue are apt to press for other priorities in U.S. foreign policy. There are practical limits to U.S. advocacy of something that only seems as sacrosanct as motherhood.

That said, focus on fundamental freedoms is not likely to fade away, an ephemera of American foreign policy. It is more than a new cyclical twitch on a traditional trend line. Violations of human rights will continue to impinge on American concerns, be they strictly humanitarian or expressly selfish. If ignored, they will mock Americans' view, however idealized, of themselves. And they will undermine U.S. political and economic interests.

Stress on human rights, for those reasons and others, has a certain self-propulsion. It takes much time and effort to undo U.S. legislation on the subject. According to Congressman Harkin, "We have established a body of law that will be hard to reverse; precedents are set for the State Department and others." It takes even more time to dismantle international machinery. And, it is more difficult still to reverse the flow of world public opinion. In the unlikely event that Americans were to turn silent on the subject, many in other countries would not. There are victims of violations who believe that they have little to lose by speaking out. Soviet exile Valentin Turchin, now in New York, stresses: "Those less known suffer more." There are growing blocs of public opinion on every continent that are forcing their political leaders to pay more attention to human rights. For example, in Canada, large communities of refugees from Eastern Europe and Latin America hold their parliamentarians accountable on this issue. The same is true in Western Europe and elsewhere.

The impact of human rights may be most telling, however, for yet another reason. Its major goals and advocates indicate that it may reflect a longer-term political development inside the United States itself. As political scientists might put it, human rights may be part of a domestic continuum.

U.S. interest in human rights in the 1970s may be a logical culmination of issues raised in the 1960s. And, it may prove to have been the precursor of questions before the nation in the 1980s. Promotion of human rights draws on concerns about political participation, justice, equal opportunity, and free expression that surfaced in student agitation for "participatory democracy," "freedom marches" for voter registration for blacks, the feminist movement, and mass rallies against the Vietnam war. The most zealous members of the human-rights lobby view themselves as part of a political vanguard. Their mission is to raise fundamental questions about what Americans expect of themselves and their nation. It is not by coincidence, nor without good cause, that many who once saw U.S. involvement in Vietnam as reason to rethink old conceptions about national objectives now see promotion of human rights as a related means to the same end. For example, there is growing attention (though not much congressional support) on the part of some human-rights organizations to efforts such as the transfer amendments offered annually by individuals such as Congressman Parren Mitchell and Senator George McGovern. They recommend shifting funds within the federal budget from what they call "wasteful and dangerous military programs" to stress on housing, nutrition, and health care. They are asking for what amounts to a significant shift of U.S. perspectives and priorities. To a large degree, their efforts reflect goals set forth in the U.N. Universal Declaration of Human Rights—particularly those portions devoted to fulfilling economic and social rights.

Old goals in new guise? Perhaps. And with meager prospect for prompt majority support? Probably.

Moving to meet the ideals of the Universal Declaration could require a considerable redistribution of income within the United States and further adjustment in the relationship between government and private enterprise. The traditional conservatism of most U.S. citizens and the current political mood suggest that, for the foreseeable future, most

Americans will balk at too big a price tag on principle and that politicians will take their cue on human rights accordingly.

That said, President Carter has asserted that Americans cannot point fingers abroad without improving their own performance on human rights. Spokesmen for other nations are quick to argue that credibility for U.S. policy on human rights rests on precisely that point. U.S. public-opinion polls confirm a related point: most Americans feel most strongly, when asked about human rights, that "we should set a good example protecting and enlarging human rights here at home."

Thus, despite clear short-term constraints on the pursuit of a full roster of human rights, the ultimate significance of U.S. policy may lie not in promotion of fundamental freedoms abroad, but in domestic impact. The effect could range from more pressure on U.S. multinational corporations to support the sense of the Congress on human rights in their business operations, to closing political and economic gaps for U.S. women, blacks, and Hispanics, to assuring dignity for the elderly and providing reasonably priced health care for all Americans. Over time, as in the past on other issues, more vocal and better organized minorities may challenge the U.S. majority. And, for its part, the majority itself may find promotion of human rights, at home and abroad, to its longer-term interest.

The politics of human rights—the domestic catalyst for part of U.S. foreign policy—may thus come full circle. If so, there may be vindication for the still-small vanguard of human-rights advocates invoking Martin Luther King;

> I have a dream that one day this nation will rise up and live out the true meaning of its creed; 'We hold these truths to be self-evident that all men are created equal.'

Notes

1. For a fuller discussion of the foreign politics of human rights, see Part I.

2. For much of this section, as elsewhere in the book, I am indebted to work on American diplomatic history and literature at Cornell University and the Fletcher School of Law and Diplomacy. Several texts of particular use: Norman A. Graebner, *Ideas and Diplomacy: Readings in the Intellectual Tradition of American Foreign Policy* (New York: Oxford University Press, 1964); Thomas A. Bailey, *A Diplomatic History of the American People* (New York: Appleton-Century-Crofts, 1958); Ruhl Bartlett, *Policy and Power, Two*

Centuries of American Foreign Relations (New York: Hill & Wang, 1963); Samuel Flagg Bemis, A *Diplomatic History of the United States* (New York: Holt, Rinehart and Winston, 1965); and William Appleman Williams, *The Shaping of American Diplomacy* (Chicago: Rand McNally & Company, 1960).

3. Calvin Colton, ed., *The Works of Henry Clay* (Federal edition, New York, 1904), 6:140. This speech was translated into Spanish and read before applauding revolutionary regiments.

4. Quoted from the *New York Herald*, August 22, 1898, by Thomas A. Bailey, A *Diplomatic History of the American People*, p. 472.

5. Quoted from the *Christian Advocate* (New York), January 22, 1903, by Bailey, A *Diplomatic History*, p. 474.

6. *Ibid.*, p. 510.

7. Joseph W. Bishop, Jr., "Can Democracy Defend Itself Against Terrorism?" *Commentary*, vol. 65, no. 5 (May 1978), 60. Bishop has found considerable room for violation of human rights within existing U.S. law. He states that "Congress has armed the President with the broadest imaginable power to do what he thinks necessary, including using the armed forces, in domestic crises. The most sweeping of these statutes, based on the so-called Ku Klux Klan Act of 1871, empowers him 'by using the militia or the armed forces, or both *or by any other means*, [to] take such measures as he considers necessary to suppress, in a state, any insurrection, domestic violence, unlawful combination, or conspiracy' if it so hinders the execution of law that people are being deprived of their legal and constitutional rights (as by being murdered) and the state authorities are unable or unwilling to enforce the law. If that statute, including the words 'or by any other means,' is constitutional, it would seem to authorize every step taken by the British in Northern Ireland, and maybe more. In fact, although Presidents have used it fairly frequently, they have not gone beyond sending in the troops to control riots, in effect as auxiliary police. It has never been tested in the courts, and its extreme reach is still unknown." *Ibid.*, p. 61.

8. U.S. Congress, Committee on the Judiciary, *Treaties and Executive Agreements*, Hearings before subcommittee, Eighty-third Congress, First Session, February–April, 1953, p. 1.

9. Ronald Steel, "Foreign Affairs: So Far, So So," *Politicks*, vol. 1, no. 1 (October 25, 1977), 20.

10. Richard Burt, "On Foreign Policy, Count Congress In—Emphatically," *The New York Times*, May 14, 1978.

11. For more discussion on the general subject of "foreign policy and the democratic process" and the specific shifts in congressional-executive relations, see the three lead articles in the Fall 1978 issue of *Foreign Affairs*—by James Chace, Lee H. Hamilton and Michael H. Van Dusen, and Douglas J. Bennet, Jr.—vol. 57, no. 1, 1–50.

12. For other speeches of particular note, see "The Moral Foundations of Foreign Policy," Minneapolis, July 15, 1975; his address before the Synagogue Council of America, New York, October 19, 1976; and his speech before the New York University Graduate School of Business Administration, New York, September 19, 1977.

13. "Human Rights in the World Community: a Call for U.S. Leadership," Report of the Subcommittee on International Organizations and Movements of the Committee on Foreign Affairs, House of Representatives, March 27, 1974, p. 9.

14. See the exchange of correspondence in the appendix of published hearings "International Protection of Human Rights, the Work of International Organizations and the Role of U.S. Foreign Policy," August 1–December 7, 1973, House Subcommittee on International Organizations and Movements, pp. 804–73.

15. For a listing of those hearings, see the Bibliography.

16. These letters are included in the series *Digest of the United States Practice in International Law, 1974,* Department of State Publication 8809, pp. 145–53. The *Digest,* published annually, provides a superbly comprehensive summary of recent actions and statements made by the Congress and the executive branch on human rights.

17. Senator Alan Cranston (Dem.–Cal.) sent a sharply worded letter to Secretary Kissinger, November 5, 1975.

18. Department of State, "Report to the Congress on the Human Rights Situation in Countries Receiving U.S. Security Assistance," November 14, 1975.

19. From the statement made on the Senate floor by Senator Cranston, November 20, 1975.

20. Two sidelights on this legislation: First, one of the chief sponsors was Senator Hubert Humphrey, faulted by some for being too subject to executive branch pressure on human rights (both with President Ford, 1975–76, and with President Carter). Second, among those staffers most responsible for refining the 502 B language were Bill Richardson (formerly of the State Department's Bureau of Congressional Relations and then with Senator Humphrey's subcommittee), Richard Moose (Senate Foreign Relations Committee staff), and Daniel Spiegel (Humphrey staff). Moose and Spiegel were, subsequently, to assume influential positions at the Department of State under the Carter administration. For a superb summary and assessment of at least part of the politics of human rights during both the Kissinger period and the early portion of the Carter administration, see the study entitled "Human Rights and U.S. Foreign Assistance: Experiences and Issues in Policy Implementation," prepared under the direction of Stanley J. Heginbotham, Chief of the Foreign Affairs and National Defense Division of the Congressional Research Service, at the request of the Senate Committee on Foreign Relations, and made available by the committee in July 1979.

21. From Secretary Kissinger's address, entitled "Human Rights and the Western Hemisphere," before the O.A.S. General Assembly, Santiago, Chile, June 8, 1976. (Available from the Bureau of Public Affairs, Department of State, Washington, D.C. 20520)

22. Drawn from informal remarks made by Congressman Brademas at an international symposium, "Human Rights and American Foreign Policy," held at the University of Notre Dame, April 30, 1977.

23. See the letter from Parren J. Mitchell, chairperson of the Congressional Black Caucus, to Secretary Vance, February 1, 1977.

24. For a more complete discussion of actions taken by the Carter administration, see Chapter 2, "The Diplomacy of Human Rights."

25. Donald M. Fraser, "Freedom and Foreign Policy," *Foreign Policy,* no. 26 (Spring 1977), p. 156.

26. Quoted in *The New York Times,* September 9, 1976.

27. Quoted by Elizabeth Drew, "A Reporter at Large—Human Rights," *New Yorker,* July 18, 1977, p. 38.

28. Quoted by David S. Broder, "Palm Oil, Citrus, Sugar Cane—and Human Rights?" *Washington Post,* July 24, 1977.

29. Robert W. Russell, "Human Rights Provisions in Foreign Economic Policy Legislation," presented at the annual meeting of the International Studies Association/Mid-West Region, May 6, 1978. Russell serves as counsel for the Senate Subcommittee on International Finance, of the Committee on Banking, Housing, and Urban Affairs.

30. One notable example of the communications links among human-rights activists and those interested in the subject is the Human Rights Internet. Laurie S. Wiseberg and Harry M. Scoble took the lead in establishing the Internet in 1976, as a subsection of the

International Studies Association. It was separately incorporated as a private not-for-profit corporation in November 1977. The *Human Rights Internet Newsletter*, published in Washington, D.C., is one of the most useful collections of material available on human rights.

31. Quoted in the *Washington Post*, February 24, 1978.

32. Quoted in *The New York Times*, January 24, 1979.

33. This summary of U.S. public opinion is drawn from "American Public Opinion and U.S. Foreign Policy 1979," edited by John E. Rielly, president of the Chicago Council on Foreign Relations; from data assembled by the Foreign Policy Association's annual "Great Decisions" program; from regular polls conducted by Gallup and Harris and other research organizations; and from discussions with the staff of the State Department's Bureau of Public Affairs.

PART III

5

El Salvador
Existence in Poverty

Rosa Maria Caceres Zeyalandia is tired. She has just returned from a day of planting cotton in the nearby fields, a day that began at dawn. Before the sun sets over the Pacific, just two miles from her thatched shack near the western coast of El Salvador, she must feed and care for her five children.

As she stoops to prepare some salted tortillas, she looks older than her thirty years. And no wonder. Life has not been easy for this typical *campesina* or peasant woman.

She spends six months of the year in her native village, a cluster of huts for several hundred peasants, not far from the seacoast town of Zacatecaluca. The rest of the year, she is out in the fields, planting or harvesting cotton for the *patron* or local overseer for the land owned by a wealthy family in the capital of San Salvador. Home then is a spot under a tree at the edge of the fields, since few landlords provide housing for their workers.

Picking cotton under the hot Salvadorean sun is hard and backbreaking labor for anyone. It is especially hard on peasant women who, like Rosa, are pregnant most of the time. They work the crops regardless. Rosa, for example, has had nine pregnancies, of which two aborted, two were born dead, and five survived. She had her first baby in the fields and worked the next day.

Rose has no husband to help her or the children. She was thirteen when she first became pregnant. Since then, in succeeding harvest seasons, she has had to take in a new migrant worker to get his assistance for her family. She does not know about the rudiments of family planning and would welcome any system offered, including sterilization. Yet, the government of El Salvador lacks the will or means to get assistance to her.

Hard as her work is, Rosa feels lucky to have it. With as many as 50 percent of the peasants unemployed, she at least has some income to help her over the six months when no work is available. She can earn up to $2.50 a day working cotton. Each child over six can join her in the fields and earn an extra dollar. (Those five and six years old babysit the infants.) She would like to get to the coffee-growing area. There the weather is milder, picking is easier (in the shade!), and the wages are better (as much as six or seven dollars a day). But, it is impossible to move her large family so far.

Her children, in fact, are a special problem—again one typical for the Salvadorean *campesina*. Like their mother and everyone else in the coastal lowlands, they suffer from repeated bouts of malaria. Malnutrition has made its mark. All of Rosa's children have parasitic infections, eye diseases, and open sores. Three of her children vomit repeatedly because of poisoning caused by the heavy doses of insecticides dropped by crop-dusting airplanes. The intensity of farming scarce land means that the planes blanket both the village and the fields with lethal pesticides four to six times a year.

Sick as the children are, there is no resident doctor to help. The only medical care is a government health post which opens one day a month. Rosa is reluctant to go, unless one or more of her children is unusually ill. There is a long wait at the clinic and the visit means the loss of an entire day's wages.

Men are conspicuously absent among the clinic's clientele. They rarely assume responsibility for the children they may have fathered or the women with whom they have lived while passing through the coastal community. Nor would any woman ask them to do so. The last time Rosa complained to the worker with her for the summer, he returned, drunk from the drinking bout at which the local men gather every Sunday to spend what is left of their wages, and attacked her with his machete. Peasant women—bruised, beaten, and cut—are usually the first patients to arrive at the health post on Monday mornings.

Rosa sees few ways out of her situation. She has had no schooling, since she went to work in the fields at the age of six. She knows almost nothing about politics, local or national. What she *does* know does not encourage her. Those representatives of "government" she has met have exploited and intimidated her. Once every two years or so, she—or, more to the point, her electoral card—is trucked to a polling place by the local *patron*.

The one unscheduled political event she has witnessed hit closer home. Friends in a neighboring village got into a dispute with a local landowner over what they thought was a field for common usage, about half an acre on which the villagers could grow some beans and maize to supplement their diet. When the landowner persisted in denying them access to the land, they reoccupied the plot. The national guard moved into the village, rounded up all the men they could find, including one who had fathered Rosa's first child. They were taunted with insults, prodded by bayonets, and then hauled away. The next day Rosa learned that all twenty had been found a few miles away—stripped and with their skulls smashed by rifle butts.

That incident confirmed for Rosa the role of the national guard. The nearest post, consisting of two rough enlisted men, is there to suppress peasant attempts to get land or better living conditions. That post, like most, is subsidized by the local landowners. Complaints about failure to pay the minimum wage or to issue mandatory food (five tortillas and beans twice a day) elicit intimidation and retaliation. The courts and legal counsel are beyond the comprehension of the *campesina*—and, in this case, fortunately so. They, like the national guard and local official-dom (ORDEN—the acronym, meaning *order*, for the Organización Democrática Nacionalista), are there to maintain peace among the peasants and control the countryside for the landowners and military junta in San Salvador.

Rosa, for her part, is oblivious to any widespread peasant movement. Indeed, there is a prohibition against forming "unions." Yet, in the mid-1970s, a friend of hers did start a local chapter of the Union Co-munal Salvadorena, a national cooperative movement. When the chapter began to attract more and more disgruntled peasants, the national guard stepped in. They first machine-gunned and later bombed the meeting hall near the market place. The leaders were threatened, then arrested and beaten. The movement, comparatively modest in its demands, collapsed. Rosa heard later that representatives from a more militant peasant organization, accused of kidnapping and killing a land-owner outside San Salvador, were moving into the area.

Rosa herself is more impressed by the nonviolent approach of one priest her sister told her about. Although she calls herself a Catholic, she has seen a priest only a few times. She has never spoken to one herself or heard one speak. She does not connect the Church with politics. The priest described by her sister was well thought of by his rural parishioners. He preached that *campesinos* are human beings and have certain rights. They should, he said, have a decent diet, some shelter, and health care. After several such Sunday sermons, the priest was first threatened and then shot at. About a year ago, the *campesinos* saw him arrested, on unspecified charges, and taken away. They heard later that he had been tortured and gang-raped by members of the national guard. After repeated intercession in his behalf by the U.S. embassy, the president of El Salvador agreed to his release and safe conduct out of the country. He remains in exile and, because of threats against his life, is in hiding.

Rosa has little to say about such events or, for that matter, her own future. She is relieved to survive each day. She sees no way to provide for the day when she can no longer work in the fields or attract a man for seasonal support.

Sometimes she thinks of joining two of her brothers who have migrated to Zacatecaluca. There, despite the filth and poverty of the crowded shantytown, they have found some schools, some medical attention, and some other government services. There, too, in the anonymity of the slum, is some respite from the *patron* and the national guard. However, asked what she will do, Rosa lowers her eyes and says softly, "Perhaps next year will be better."[1]

* * *

Next year is, however, not likely to be better for Rosa Maria Caceres Zeyalandia or any of her counterparts in El Salvador. It may, in fact, be worse. Failure to meet the basic human needs of most Salvadoreans is likely to lead to more unrest among peasants and more oppression from the government. The self-confirming cycle of terrorism and counterterrorism could bring an even more brutal dictatorship of the left or right.

Why, what is to be done, and what role might the United States play?

A look first at El Salvador itself. It is a country with little news appeal, a country that no one seems to notice. And yet it is one of the nations south of the U.S. border most ripe for revolution—a revolution for and about human rights.

Of all countries on the Latin American mainland, El Salvador is the smallest (8,100 square miles, or about the size of New Jersey) and the most densely populated (five hundred people per square mile, compared to the average U.S. population density of about sixty people). It also has the fastest population growth (3.5 percent a year) and the least land for cultivation.

Part of the country's problem revolves around the fact that the people don't fit. Their numbers have increased, but the land has not. At the present rate of growth, the population of El Salvador doubles every seventeen years. Every other person is a child under the age of fifteen. Hunger and malnutrition are common. After Haiti, El Salvador's population has the lowest caloric intake per capita of any in Latin America. Over 50 percent of all deaths occur among children under the age of five years. The increasing mass of landless peasants swells the seasonal labor force, helps keep wages low, and feeds the flow of people to the cities—especially the capital. San Salvador is growing at an estimated rate of 6 percent a year. There the poor, who had not been as conspicuous in the countryside for the nation's leaders, become more obvious. They are concentrated where they can be seen and smelled. Home is the street or a windowless shack with earthen floor, facing an alley that is both passageway and sewer. Few migrants find jobs, since the current program for industrialization is capital-intensive. There is thus a growing army of the unemployed in the inner-city shantytown.

However, overpopulation, even in such situations, is still a relative term. The crucial underlying problem in El Salvador has to do with who owns the land and controls the nation's wealth. Agriculture is the backbone of the economy. Land thus represents the primary source of wealth and, for the majority, the main means of livelihood. But distribution of land is unequal. Four percent of the farms account for over 60 percent of the land area, while 70 percent of all farms account for only 11 percent of the land area. Two percent of the citizens own 60 percent of the land, while most peasants have no land or such small holdings that they must work for the larger landholders to supplement their incomes.

Income distribution reflects this imbalance in land ownership. Less than 10 percent of the population takes over 50 percent of national income. Wealth is in the hands of so few that Salvadoreans themselves say that *los catorce*, or the "fourteen families," run the country. The extremes between wealth and poverty show up in the capital, where the

AMERICAN DREAM/GLOBAL NIGHTMARE

168

rich live in elegant suburban homes surrounded by high walls and guards and the poor make do in packing cases or mud huts along the deep gullies that slice through San Salvador. The same contrast prevails in the countryside, with the juxtaposition of rambling villas with lush gardens and thatch-roofed shanties of *campesinos*. Although the average per-capita income for El Salvador is an estimated $440 per year, in fact the discrepancy between the rich and poor means that the typical peasant gets more like $100 per annum.[2]

The pattern of agricultural production compounds the poverty of the poor majority. El Salvador draws its main revenue from coffee, sugar, and cotton. All three are cash crops, grown primarily on large plantations that demand a substantial labor supply. Labor is plentiful, given the distribution of the land. Because most peasants are desperate to find jobs, owners of the big estates can and do pay meager wages. Even when prices for export crops rise, wages rarely do. At the same time, the use of land for exports denies the peasants the means to raise food for themselves. Much of the "food problem" in El Salvador, as elsewhere, reflects a course of economic development that puts greater priority on overall growth, rather than on individual human needs. Continuing along this path, without true land reform, may—according to demographer J. Mayone Stycos—"mean more belt tightening around already emaciated bellies."[3]

Politics in El Salvador must be seen against this economic backdrop. Government officials have either been baffled by the economic and social problems of the poor majority or opposed to addressing them. The result has been a history of exploitation. The national guard, formed in 1912, repressed peasant "agitators."[4] The *Policia National* has performed a comparable role in the cities. In 1932, the government crushed a massive peasant uprising in the coffee-growing region of western El Salvador. It was the first in the Western Hemisphere in which communists played an active part. An estimated twenty thousand peasants were killed in that *matanza* or slaughter.[5] Since then, there has been a sharp split in the Salvadorean population. Members of the upper class and the military officers supported by them equate communism and peasant organization. They call crushing the *campesinos* "fighting communism." The peasants, for their part, find it hard, if not impossible, to communicate with and trust the governing alliance of generals and gentry. They have had, according to Salvadorean law, no right to organize into trade unions or agrarian leagues. Elections have provided no real recourse for reform. Candidates who sought a greater political voice were, through apparent electoral fraud, denied the presidency in 1972 and 1977.

Concern about radical agitators has become a self-fulfilling prophesy. From 1932 to 1972, there was no clear indication of communist guerrilla activity or violent opposition operating in El Salvador. That situation began to change when the army prevented the election of reformist Christian Democrat José Napoleon Duarte in 1972. With the Christian Democrats intimidated into silence and the army occupying the university, some young leftists began to organize opposition and to kidnap—and kill—members of El Salvador's fourteen families. Peasants in the countryside began to campaign for better living conditions. By late 1975, these groups joined others to form the Popular Revolutionary Bloc.

The reaction of the Salvadorean government was to use repression in order, as one official explained, "to save democracy." A right-wing paramilitary organization was dispatched to harass and kill peasant leaders. The Molina government (1972–77) resorted to increasingly oppressive measures to stay in power. The successor government of Carlos Humberto Romero sank deeper into the morass of violence and oppression. For example, in early May 1979, Salvadorean security forces opened fire, without warning, on peaceful demonstrators standing on the steps of the main cathedral in downtown San Salvador. Thanks to a CBS videotape, Americans watched as some Salvadorean students scrambled for cover and others fell, their bodies bounced about by the volley of bullets. When guerrilla groups retaliated against the death of twenty-three persons that day by killing the minister of education, the government declared a state of siege.

The president of El Salvador was caught in a vise. On the right, the business community and military demanded all-out war against terrorists. On the left, impoverished peasants, encouraged by the success of the Sandinista rebels in Nicaragua and radicalized by growing oppression in El Salvador, joined the Popular Revolutionary Bloc in greatly increasing numbers. In October 1979, an army-backed junta overthrew President Romero.

The Catholic Church was to become one of the main targets of attack by the government. Long a supporter of the oligarchy, the Church shifted its focus to social justice after the conference of Latin American bishops held in Medellin, Colombia, in 1968 and during the aftermath of the Second Vatican Council. President Molina identified the "theology of liberation," allegedly espoused by reformist priests in the Salvadorean countryside, as the ideology of the "subversive" camp. During the period 1974–76, El Salvador's seven bishops, individually and collectively, issued pastoral letters protesting the violation of human rights and the injustice of the country's economic system. Molina's short-lived attempt to introduce land reform in the mid-1970s—launched partly as a response to such expressed grievances—led to counter-reaction from the nation's estate owners and the first open attack on the Church. Bombing of the Catholic University, torture of priests, and the exile of others ensued.

Attacks on the Church intensified after Monsignor Oscar Romero—no relation to the general who came to power in 1977—became Archbishop of San Salvador and accelerated support for *campesino* movements. As a reprisal for the kidnapping and killing of Salvadorean Foreign Minister Mauricio Borgonova by an unidentified guerrilla group in 1977, members of the government-sanctioned right-wing group, called the White Warriors's Union, killed Father Alfonso Navarro, an energetic parish priest who had been working with peasant and labor groups. The right-wing group then issued a press bulletin that accused the Jesuits of following a communist line and gave them one month to leave El Salvador. Although nothing happened then, and no Jesuits fled at that time, activist priests subsequently continued to risk death by telling their rural parishioners that a full Christian life is impossible without human dignity. They tried to raise the political consciousness of the poor, to persuade them that it is *not* God's will that their children die of malnutrition. That challenge to the fatalism of centuries, the control of the Salvadorean elite, and, indeed, to the hierarchical structure of Church authority led to the death of more priests in 1978 and 1979. The political role of the Salvadorean clergy and their Latin American colleagues was a major issue at the Third Conference of Latin American Bishops, opened by Pope John Paul II in Puebla, Mexico, in early 1979. The debate about the Church's role in promoting human rights continues. In Latin America, as in Eastern Europe, this development could eventually have more impact on those in power.[6]

The combination of the entrenched interests of the wealthy elite and the rising discontent of the poor suggests that political turbulence is likely to continue in El Salvador. The state that calls itself the "Savior of the World" is in danger of repeating some of its own history. When members of the fourteen families, many of whom travel in bulletproof cars or have fled to Miami, talk of the *matanza*, it is with one concern in mind. They worry, not about addressing the reasons for peasant unrest, but about suppressing the peasants themselves. According to one conservative Salvadorean lawyer, "The reaction is always to put down the peasants before they get out of control." For that reason, he stated that "the discussion among the rich families now is whether 20,000 or 50,000 or 100,000 peasants should be killed to restore peace."[7]

The Romero government was not able to deal effectively with the economic grievances expressed by the peasants. Spending on social services did not keep pace with the rapid growth in population, the dislocations occasioned by migration from the countryside to the cities, and the sharp rise in prices for basic necessities. At the same time, officials continued to try to keep tight reins on those, such as the reformist priests or members of the Popular Revolutionary Bloc, who might turn the discontent of the poor against the government. Thus, for example, the imposition of the state of siege (February 28–June 30, 1977), with its attendant restrictions on freedom of movement and expression. The "Law of Defense and Guarantee of Public Order" promulgated on November 24, 1977, authorized officials to ban public meetings, break up strikes, and jail anyone who criticized the government—in contravention of El Salvador's own constitution and the American Convention on Human Rights approved by that nation in 1978.

There has been widespread evidence of torture of detainees and the disappearance of hundreds of peasants—corroborated by the International Commission of Jurists, members of U.S. religious organizations, and the Inter-American Commission on Human Rights. A special report by that O.A.S. Commission, made known in 1979, accused the government of El Salvador of "systematically persecuting" the Roman Catholic Church. After listing ninety-nine known "disappeared persons," the commission asserted that its investigators had found five secret cells at the headquarters of the national guard which were "veritable slave prisons," three feet by three feet, without light or ventilation.

Reaction to this situation from within El Salvador is noteworthy. The Romero government's main response to criticism of its practices was either to deny that it violated human rights or to protest against what its representatives considered outside interference in the sovereign affairs of El Salvador. The repressed poor of the country were hurt by the falling world prices for Salvadorean coffee exports that were, in turn, reflected in continuing low wages and the government's inability to put increasingly scarce resources into meeting basic human needs of the poor. Their response speaks for itself. Terrorist groups have grown in number and prospered, with kidnap ransoms for foreign businessmen totaling over $30 million during 1977 and 1978. By 1979, El Salvador had become the principal source of illegal migration to the United States from Central and South America. An estimated 25,000 illegal migrants, in addition to 2,500 legal migrants, depart annually for the United States. With continuing tension in El Salvador, that figure could well increase.

*   *   *

U.S. attention to the deprivation of human rights in general and to economic and social rights in particular in El Salvador did not begin with the Carter administration. Pressures from officials in the Kennedy administration, through the Alliance for Progress, led to some moves in the early 1960s toward greater democracy in El Salvador. Ignazio Lozano, the former U.S. ambassador to that nation first appointed by President Gerald Ford but kept on for the early part of the Carter period, often took the initiative in raising the subject of human rights in discussions with Salvadorean officials. Lozano subsequently stated during congressional hearings that he received little or no support from the Carter administration for his efforts and that his campaign was thus dismissed by host-country officials as a personal vendetta against them.

Some of the strongest criticism against the human-rights situation in El Salvador has come from Congress. Representative Donald Fraser held hearings on June 8–9, 1976; on March 9 and 17, 1977; and on July 21 and 29, 1977. Those held in March focused on the 1977 presidential elections in El Salvador and their implications for U.S. foreign policy. In the view of John Salzberg, who set up most of Fraser's hearings on human rights, those sessions stand out in several respects. They were, reportedly, the first congressional hearings held to review elections in another country.[8] Not only did Fraser call as witnesses non-Americans—one of the most controversial innovations of his Subcommittee—but he also called two men most likely to arouse the ire of the Salvadorean government. They were the 1972 presidential candidate and the 1977 vice presidential candidate of the main opposition party. Fraser included in the testimony tape-recordings of the Salvadorean national guard instructing its units to stuff ballot boxes and arrest poll-watchers. Infuriated by those hearings, the government of El Salvador asked the United States to terminate its military-assistance program.

Increasing threats and reprisals against Catholic priests in El Salvador led to rising concern within the United States—particularly among American Catholics. To help focus U.S. attention on the human-rights situation in El Salvador, Father Timothy S. Healy, president of Georgetown University, went to that country in February 1977 to confer an honorary degree on the besieged Archbishop of San Salvador. Healy was deeply moved by the scene he confronted in the large central cathedral—over ten thousand crying and chanting people filling the sanctuary—and the reports he heard elsewhere of government-sanctioned violations against the peasants. A robust Irishman, Father Healy was to speak with particular poignancy to U.S. Catholics, reared on memories of suffering in Ireland, about the situation in El Salvador. In a speech on Saint Patrick's Day in 1977, he claimed that "the echoes of Ireland are too numerous to deny." He stressed that "we are talking of an agricultural people who starve to death on rich land while they farm it" and "we are talking of distant and absentee landlords who suck the land dry, return nothing to it or the people, and live a safe and protected distance from their oppressed peasants. . . ." And, he concluded, "We are talking of a government tied totally to the power structure and quite content to let the peasants starve if it keeps the rich happy."[9]

Healy's concern, as well as that of such influential leaders and long-time advocates of civil and human rights as Father Theodore Hesburgh, president of the University of Notre Dame, led to high-level meetings with members of the Carter administration. Some of the most important were held with Secretary Vance, who, in turn, communicated U.S. concern to officials in the Salvadorean government.

The outcry from the U.S. Catholic Church converged with growing anxiety within the larger human-rights lobby and both branches of the U.S. government. It came to a head in debate over what to do about a proposed $90-million loan from the Inter-American Development Bank for the building of a large dam in El Salvador. To vote "yes" might suggest that the Carter administration was not serious about its human-rights policy. (The human-rights lobby, led by the Washington Office on Latin America, had identified administration response to El Salvador's allegedly fradulent elections in 1977 as one of the first tests of the new administration's resolve on human rights in Latin America.) A "no" vote risked further angering the Salvadorean government, without getting an improvement in its performance on human rights. The decision was to try to postpone action on the large loan for the San Lorenzo Dam.

For a while, that gesture of disapproval from the highest levels of the U.S. government acted as a deterrent to further extremes of repression by El Salvador's military leaders. They allowed students who once might have been summarily carted off to prison to demonstrate. They agreed to admit an investigative team from the Inter-American Commission on Human Rights.

Those positive actions, together with the continuing argument from the Salvadorean government that leftist guerrillas were the *real* violators of human rights, began to strike a responsive chord in Washington. In addition, many officials in the State Department believed that El Salvador would borrow money in Europe for the San Lorenzo dam if the United States continued to block the loan for that project. In that case, the United States might lose leverage with the Salvadorean government. (Others argued that forcing El Salvador to borrow in Europe at a higher rate of interest would force the Salvadorean government to take the question of human rights more seriously.) The result of that debate within the Carter administration was to choose the carrot over the stick—i.e., reverse the U.S. position on the loan and give the go-ahead for the dam.

It was as if some figurative dam broke. Officials in El Salvador and elsewhere in Latin America interpreted that decision as a new signal of U.S. approval and decreased concern about human rights. Comments made in El Salvador by Terence Todman, then Assistant Secretary of State for Inter-American Affairs, undermined the asserted thrust of the administration's human-rights policy. He stated in early 1978 that "terrorism and subversion are the major problems confronting the people of Latin America" and that the "police are fighting valorously" against those threats. Frank Devine, a career foreign service officer appointed by the Carter administration to head the U.S. embassy in El Salvador, developed a close relationship with Salvadorean President Romero. The pressure, in short, seemed to be off.

The Romero government responded to this apparent reprieve from reprimands on human rights with a massive escalation of repression. It renewed its campaign against opposition groups. Dozens of peasants and workers disappeared or died. The government adopted the sweeping "Law of Defense and Guarantee of Public Order" mentioned previously. Ambassador Devine—reportedly received an advance copy of the law and gave it his blessing. The day after the law was approved, he said in a speech before the American Chamber of Commerce: "We believe any government has the full right and obligation to use all legal means at its disposal to combat terrorism."[10]

Congressman Robert F. Drinan (Dem.–Mass.) visited El Salvador in January 1978. A Catholic priest himself, he had become alarmed by the reports of increased persecution of his fellow Jesuits and the peasants they were trying to help. At a press conference held in Washington on January 13, 1978, he reported that he had heard "at least forty separate stories of the murders, the disappearances, or the jailing of husbands and sons against whom no charge was ever brought." He stressed that "in the countryside, one can literally feel the fear, anguish, and desperation which fill the lives of the peasants."[11]

Despite such statements, spokesmen for the Carter administration remained silent, and support continued for the government of El Salvador. The United States maintained a three-man military group for the alleged purpose of keeping good contacts with the Salvadorean military and provided $10 million in economic assistance. During the massacre of an estimated two hundred protesters after the 1977 election in El Salvador, there were ten U.S. military officers based in the headquarters of the Salvadorean army. To many Salvadorean citizens, the U.S. embassy remained closely linked with the military government. The Catholic Archbishop of San Salvador, dismayed by this turn of events, said: "I feel greatly disappointed because we had hoped the U.S. policy on human rights would be more sincere."

The contradictions in U.S. advocacy of human rights in El Salvador during the Carter administration have reflected several factors. First, there was a sharp split within the bureaucracy of the State Department.

Patricia Derian, Assistant Secretary of State for Human Rights and Humanitarian Affairs, and Mark Schneider—her deputy, who had been a vigorous advocate of human rights in Central and South America on Senator Edward Kennedy's staff and had also been a Peace Corps volunteer in El Salvador—were profoundly concerned about the deterioration of the human-rights situation in El Salvador. They clashed head on with the Bureau of Inter-American Affairs, where many of the officers often seemed more concerned about preserving good relations with their clients than with promoting human rights. A trip to El Salvador in May 1978 by Mark Schneider and Sally Shelton—another political appointee, who was to serve briefly as Deputy Assistant Secretary for the Central American area—was intended to help reaffirm U.S. dedication to human rights.

Second, and more significant, is the confusion felt by senior officials at the State Department. Most do not know what the United States can or should do about the situation in El Salvador. Several believe that the U.S. "lost" El Salvador in the 1950s and 1960s. It had put highest priority then on political stability and economic growth. It had also trained many of the military officers, now in the Salvadorean ruling elite, to consider their main mission fighting communism.

The irony of the present is that this past U.S. policy succeeded so well. Many members of the fourteen families are genuinely puzzled by President Carter's position on human rights and the kind of criticism leveled against El Salvador in reports to the Congress. They believe that they are upholding law and order, helping boost general economic development, and fending off the "communist threat."[12]

By the end of the 1970s, no matter what their views on the human-rights situation in El Salvador, U.S. policymakers diverged over what leverage, if any, could be brought to bear on that tiny country. Some said that, since the United States had no great strategic or economic stake in El Salvador, it had little to lose by pushing the Salvadorean government hard on human rights. After all, if the United States did little or nothing in a situation where it enjoyed unique dominance, where, wondered some skeptics, could it hope to exercise an effective human-rights policy? Others claimed that, with declining U.S. aid to El Salvador (because of U.S. domestic decisions to send limited economic assistance elsewhere) and the move by other countries to fill the growing U.S. military vacuum, Washington had declining influence. The U.S. government could do little but jawbone for social justice.

The debate was most pronounced over how or if to use U.S. economic aid to improve respect for human rights in El Salvador. During the period of the Romero regime some favored total dissociation, including cutting off economic assistance for the poor. They argued that most aid never reached the poor people for whom it was intended, that such funds could become a weapon in the hands of the Salvadorean government, and that the military rulers interpreted grants of U.S. aid as endorsement of their regime. On the other hand, those concerned about meeting the basic human needs of the Salvadorean poor countered with the argument that drastic withdrawal of U.S. aid would punish the oppressed for the sins of their oppressor. Even human-rights advocates outside the U.S. government, such as those from the Washington Office on Latin America, which had influenced congressional legislation in this area, opposed having the United States "opt out of its responsibility for the social and economic needs of the Salvadorean poor."

Debates over degrees of dissociation and pressure for reform focused, finally, on the fundamental question at issue in El Salvador and most of the Third World: how to achieve change. In September 1979, Viron P. Vaky, Assistant Secretary of State for Inter-American Affairs, told a House subcommittee: "The central issue is not whether change is to occur but whether that change is to be violent and radical or peaceful and evolutionary and preserving individual rights and democratic values."

Violations against the security of the person and denial of civil and political liberties in most developing nations may be more important as symptoms of deeper problems. They may reflect refusal by the ruling elite to address the economic and social needs of the majority of their citizens. If so, what can the U.S. government do? To what extent can external pressure—either by the positive incentive of economic aid or the negative inducement of sanctions against, for example, key exports—spur internal reform? What kind of bilateral foreign assistance can be effective in helping meet the basic human needs of the poor? To what extent can any U.S. program that does not reflect a broader multilateral consensus have constructive impact? Will well-intentioned efforts at change prove beneficial? (Some forms of land reform, for instance, may, by breaking up the economies of scale of large plantations, decrease overall production and thus set back more general economic development.) Must not reform come from within the country in question? On the other hand, what prospect is there for that kind of reform if the change must come either from those on the top who have the least to gain in the short term, or from those on the bottom, who have little means to effect it? Must change of such a fundamental nature be violent? If so, is the United States, which prides itself on its revolutionary origin, able to shift from its past adherence to the *status quo* and its present preference for evolution? At what cost to U.S. interests?

This apparent clash between concern for human rights and fear of radical change is one of the most striking dilemmas before U.S. policymakers in the 1980s. They seem trapped. Most military and business elites in nations such as El Salvador blame much of their domestic unrest on U.S. promotion of human rights. Opponents to such oppressive governments argue that the United States resists *real* reform. Leftists claim that the United States does not interfere to any significant degree because the *status quo* serves traditional U.S. interests. In fact, the United States shies away from intervention more out of confusion than conviction. It is not clear how or if it can help and at what geopolitical price.

What *is* clear is official Washington's phobia of "another Cuba." The U.S. approach to El Salvador—much like the belated and often mistaken response to the decline of Nicaraguan dictator Somoza during the late 1970s—suggests that the United States has begun to devote attention to Central America, less because of the underlying problems of that region and more because of the Cuban threat engendered by those problems. U.S. policymakers must now decide: can they deal with fundamental social change or must they remain hostage to the fear of Fidel Castro?

Notes

1. The name, Rosa Maria Caceres Zeyalandia, is fictitious; the situation is not. Details of her life are typical of the Salvadorean *campesina*. For many of these details, I am indebted to William Walker, State Department Fellow at the Council on Foreign Relations (1977–78) and political officer at the U.S. embassy in El Salvador (1974–77); other State Department officials who provided me with information "on background"; Alan Riding, Central American correspondent for *The New York Times*; Cressida McKean and Joseph Eldridge of the Washington Office on Latin America (WOLA); Robert Armstrong, former Peace Corps volunteer in El Salvador and activist in the Committee against Violations of Human Rights in El Salvador; and innumerable publications—most notably, testimony

before Congressman Donald Fraser's House Subcommittee on International Organizations, "El Salvador Reports," and documentation from Amnesty International (especially *El Salvador: General Background*. External Report, AI Index No. AMR/29/18/77), and Report by Donald T. Fox for the International Commission of Jurists ("Mission to El Salvador"—July 1978).

2. Much of this material on economic and social indices is drawn from discussions and documentation provided by officials at the Department of State and the Agency for International Development, participants in a discussion group on Central America held at the Council on Foreign Relations (Spring 1978), and staff members at WOLA. A report by Cressida McKean provides a concise summary of data on economic, social, and political conditions in El Salvador and response by the U.S. government. See *Human Rights Conditions in Selected Countries and the U.S. Response*, prepared for the House Committee on International Relations by the Foreign Affairs and National Defense Division, Congressional Research Service, Library of Congress, July 25, 1978, pp. 80–99.

3. There are few good or up-to-date books on El Salvador. One of those I found most illuminating, particularly on the subject of human rights and human needs, is that by J. Mayone Stycos, director of the Cornell University International Population Program, and photojournalist Cornell Capa, *Margin of Life* (New York: Grossman Publishers, 1974). One of the most provocative accounts is Robert F. Drinan, John J. McAward, and Thomas P. Anderson, "Human Rights in El Salvador—1978, Report of Findings of an Investigating Mission" (Boston, Mass.: Unitarian Universalist Service Committee, 1978).

4. Alastair White, *El Salvador*, (New York: Praeger, 1973), p. 94.

5. For two excellent books on this bloody event, see Thomas P. Anderson, *Matanza: El Salvador's Communist Revolt of 1932* (Lincoln, Nebraska: University of Nebraska Press, 1971) and A. Jones Ogilville, *The Communist Revolt in El Salvador in 1932* (Cambridge, Mass.: Harvard University Press, 1970).

6. For more information on the role of the Catholic Church, see writing by and about Father José Alas, a Salvadorean priest now living in exile in Washington, D.C. (Material available from WOLA). On the more general topic of the role of the Church in Central and South America, I am particularly indebted to conversations with Father Brian H. Smith and his colleagues at the Woodstock Theological Center, Georgetown University, Washington, D.C. For one illuminating treatment of this subject, see the unpublished paper, Brian H. Smith, S.J., "Churches and Human Rights in Latin America: Recent Trends in the Subcontinent," May 1978. See also Alan Riding, "Latin Church in Siege," *The New York Times Magazine* (May 6, 1979), pp. 32–34, 38, 40, and 42–44.

7. *The New York Times*, April 27, 1978.

8. "Human Rights in Nicaragua, Guatemala, and El Salvador: Implications for U.S. Policy," Hearings before the Subcommittee on International Organizations of the Committee on International Relations, House of Representatives, June 8–9, 1976, and "The Recent Presidential Elections in El Salvador: Implications for U.S. Foreign Policy," March 9 and 17, 1977.

9. Quoted by Georgie Anne Geyer, "From Here to Eternity," *Washington Post Magazine*, September 10, 1978, p. 17.

10. Quoted by Alan Riding in *The New York Times*, May 8, 1978.

11. Quoted in "El Salvador Reports," published by the New York Chapter of the Committee against Violations of Human Rights in El Salvador, March 1, 1978. See also Robert F. Drinan, "The Catholic Fight for Freedom," *Commonweal*, March 3, 1978, p. 134.

12. See, for example, "Country Reports on Human Rights Practices," Report Submitted to the Committee on Foreign Relations, U.S. House of Representatives, and Committee on Foreign Relations, U.S. Senate, by the Department of State, February 3, 1978.

Some insight into Salvadorean reaction to such reports and U.S. policy on human rights in El Salvador was gained from discussions in New York with visiting officials of the Salvadorean government. See also the report on El Salvador included in the State Department's "Report on Human Rights Practices in Countries Receiving U.S. Aid," submitted to the Congress, February 8, 1979, pp. 247–55.

6

---◂•••▸---

Economics of

Human Rights

Most Americans would deplore the plight of a poor peasant in rural El Salvador—with no land to farm, little food for the family, and no way out. Few, however, would relate that daily struggle to survive with international emphasis on human rights—or accept the consequences. Therein lies a challenge of conception, capacity, and credibility for U.S. policy.

"Human rights" has a traditional ring for the average American. The term reflects those fundamental freedoms set forth in the U.S. Bill of Rights. It suggests that governments should not permit what the United Nations calls "crimes against the security of person"—that is, officially sanctioned murder, torture, or detention without trial. And traditional interpretations of human rights suggest traditional responses by the U.S. government, such as discreet *démarches* to the dictator in question or public denunciation before the U.N. General Assembly.

That traditional reading of human rights—what they are and what governments should do about them—is, however, only part of the contemporary picture. Eighteenth-century concerns with civil liberty alone may not be wholly appropriate to the twentieth-century problems that put over one billion people on the razor's edge of subsistence. Governments, according to the newer and louder argument from the Third World, should address those economic and social rights essential to survival and well-being. They should reorder priorities to meet such basic human needs as adequate food, shelter, and health care and, to the extent possible, provide for other less urgent economic and social objectives set forth in the U.N. Universal Declaration.

The programmatic counterpart to that normative proposition is that governments must match words with deeds. Oppressive regimes must be open to genuine reform. Governments, like that in the United States, must practice at home what they preach abroad. And, if seriously committed to ending violations of human rights elsewhere, the United States cannot rely only on pleas behind the scenes or public wringing of hands. It must also seek increased respect for human rights through the affirmative appeal of more foreign aid to democratic governments or the punitive sting of sanctions against dictators.

This broader reading of human rights raises important issues. There are *specific* questions about the implementation of U.S. policy on human rights. The U.S. Congress has seized on economic measures to promote human rights. But, are economic "carrots and sticks" apt to help, or hinder, advancement of human rights and other expressed U.S. objectives? There are more *general* questions raised by the clash between the apparent need to give more attention to economic and social rights and the ability to do so.

Adopting a program to meet the basic human needs of the poorest people could be costly. Economists at the Overseas Development Council in Washington have put a speculative price tag of $20 billion per year on this kind of assistance from the developed countries to the less developed countries. Although estimates vary and some costs could be covered by shifting funds from other kinds of economic assistance, U.S. participation in a program of that size would probably require increased allocations for foreign aid. That hike in official development assistance, perhaps paralleled by more spending on U.S. domestic welfare, could require either major changes of priority within the federal budget or large increases in U.S. taxes. Are most Americans prepared to accept a potentially substantial redistribution of income within and away from the United States?

Marshalling a full-scale campaign to fulfill fundamental freedoms could raise new challenges for the U.S. economic system. Laws already on the books, which include human-rights restrictions on many economic activities, have, according to American corporate executives, put more governmental shackles on U.S. business operations abroad and led to lost contracts and investment opportunities. What are the tradeoffs between respect for human rights and pursuit of U.S. economic goals, such as a healthy balance of payments or full domestic employment? Should multinational corporations, because of the alleged contradiction between the profit motive and promotion of human rights, be forced to move out of certain pariah states? Or does a pull-out by U.S. business amount to an American cop-out on the problems of the poor and politically oppressed?

Finally, even if U.S. taxpayers and business firms were to take on the full challenge of human rights, what difference could they make? There is mounting evidence that America's human-rights reach may exceed realistic grasp. For example, government-instigated torture of peasants in El Salvador may be most significant as a symptom of more pervasive problems, problems that strike to the core of who holds power there and why. If so, and if that situation in fact prevails in most nations today, how can any U.S. policy on human rights amount to more than a palliative for a disease with no obvious cure?

Such questions suggest, in short, that there is an unexplored economic underbelly to the corpus of current discussion on human rights. Few political leaders, at either end of Pennsylvania Avenue, have probed the likely consequences of present or projected policy. Thus, although the economics of human rights cannot be detached totally from treatment of the domestic politics or international diplomacy of the issue, it does deserve scrutiny on its own terms. The two major sets of questions posed by the economics of human rights are:

« Promotion of economic and social rights—why bother, why not, and what is the relationship between economic development and denial of human rights?

« Use of economic measures to promote all human rights—how and at what cost or benefit?

Promotion of economic and social rights

Proclaiming concern for human rights signaled a bold beginning by the Carter administration. The president declared in the 1977 inaugural address: "Because we are free, we can never be indifferent to the fate of freedom elsewhere."

That proclamation proved to be bolder than believed at the time. "Freedom," according to subsequent speeches by administration officials, was to include the "right to be free from governmental violation of the integrity of the person" and "the right to enjoy civil and political liberties." It was also—and this was a crucial new departure for U.S. diplomacy—to embrace "the right to the fulfillment of such vital needs as food, shelter, health care, and education."

That increased emphasis on economic and social rights, stated first and most comprehensively in a major policy speech by Secretary of State Cyrus Vance in 1977,[1] made few headlines. There was scant commentary at the time about why the Carter administration had included those rights in its overall policy or what difference they might make for most Americans. The administration itself did not call attention to this new focus of its foreign policy. Indeed, that emphasis on economic and social rights may have emerged more by accident than design. It was a belated addition to the draft text for Vance's initial human-rights speech. The secretary's address, in turn, filled a vacuum in the early months of the Carter administration. The human-rights issue had taken off faster than most administration officials had expected and before they had mapped out a comprehensive policy on human rights.

The triad of rights—security of person, basic needs, and political liberty—spelled out in the Vance speech became, in the absence of other high-level guidance, new policy writ for the foreign-affairs bureaucracy. That formulation of rights acquired the self-perpetuating momentum often peculiar to the bureaucratic process. Its themes were to recur, like a litany, in subsequent speeches, testimony before the Congress, directives to U.S. missions abroad, interagency working groups, and presidential review memoranda and directives.

* * *

WHY BOTHER ABOUT ECONOMIC AND SOCIAL RIGHTS? Whatever the specific stimulus to this policy decision, there were, in fact, fundamental reasons for stressing economic and social rights. It was not solely by chance that Vance advocated a broad interpretation of human rights.

First, there was and is the staggering scope of economic and social needs. Despite the trebling of world output since the late 1940s, roughly one billion people live in chronic poverty. There is what the Overseas Development Council calls a "vicious circle of widespread illiteracy, unemployment or under-employment, malnutrition, hunger, ill health, and short life expectancy."[2] Growth in Gross National Product for many developing countries has not translated into improvements in what the Overseas Development Council calls the Physical Quality of Life Index, which measures such items as life expectancy, infant mortality, and literacy.

Poverty is a problem not only in absolute terms, but in relative measure. The gap between developed and developing nations is large. The average per-capita Gross National Product in high-income countries, like the United States, is almost thirty times that in low-income nations, like Sri Lanka. A baby born in Mali is ten times as likely to die in its first year of life as is one born in the United States. That gap between rich and poor nations may be growing, as is the gap between rich and poor *within* developing nations. The ratio of income received by the top 20 percent of U.S. and British citizens, compared to that received by the bottom 20 percent, is about six to one. In contrast, it is twenty-nine to one in Ecuador, twenty to one in Brazil, and fifteen to one in Mexico.[3]

Second, the persistence of poverty, in the face of some impressive aggregate increases in Gross National Product for the developing countries has fed the growing belief that economic growth alone does not guarantee fulfillment of basic human needs for the poor. Concerned members of the Carter administration thus decided that they needed to sharpen the focus of foreign assistance on the special problems of the poor. (A later section of this chapter will provide further discussion of this issue.)

Third, there are international declarations and covenants that stress concern for economic and social rights. The U.N. Universal Declaration of Human Rights, adopted without any negative votes by the U.N. General Assembly in 1948, devotes considerable attention to the subject, as part of its codification of more general principles present in the U.N. Charter.[4] The emphasis emerges most clearly in Article 22 of the declaration, which states that "everyone, as a member of society, has the right to . . . realization, through national effort and international cooperation and in accordance with the organization and resources of each State, of the economic, social and cultural rights indispensable for his dignity and the free development of his personality." The declaration goes on to detail the individual's right to "equal pay for equal work," and "protection against unemployment" and the right to a "standard of living adequate for the health and well-being of himself and of his family," to education, and other items. The U.N. Covenant on

Economic, Social, and Cultural Rights—formally adopted by the U.N. General Assembly in 1966 and brought into force in 1976 after ratification by the requisite thirty-five states—is the means for making the principles proclaimed in the Universal Declaration binding treaty obligations on ratifying states and for providing international machinery to help enforce guaranteed rights.[5] Other statements—such as the Inter-American Charter of Social Guarantees, adopted by the Organization of American States in 1948, and the Social Charter that makes promotion of economic and social "rights" a matter of treaty obligation for members of the Council of Europe—illustrate further the international basis for the Carter administration's broad reading of human rights.[6]

Fourth, this international concern about economic and social rights reflects growing U.S. sensitivity to the subject. Indeed, the U.N. Universal Declaration drew in part from points in President Franklin D. Roosevelt's "Four Freedoms" of 1941 and in his "second Bill of Rights" (economic and social) in 1944. There had been an important shift of attitudes in the United States and elsewhere after the devastating impact of worldwide economic depression in the 1930s. In the Employment Act of 1946, Congress declared that "it is the continuing policy and responsibility of the Federal Government" to create and maintain useful employment opportunities for those who seek work, and to promote "maximum employment." The sentiment has grown since then. President Lyndon Johnson told Congress in 1968 that its task was "to give reality to the right to earn a living." Presidents Nixon, Ford, and Carter have made comparable statements and thus given increasing domestic legitimacy to claims for economic and social rights.

Fifth, many representatives from the majority of U.N. member states argue that, among human rights, economic and social rights stand paramount. A related manifestation of the more general concern among developing countries about economic equity—albeit for a redistribution of resources from rich to poor nations, rather than from rich to poor individuals within their own societies—is the call for a New International Economic Order. The nonbinding Charter on the Economic Rights and Duties of States, adopted by the U.N. General Assembly in 1974, asserts some sweeping new rights, primarily for the benefit of the Third World.

Spokesmen for the so-called Second World of communist nations put comparable stress on economic and social rights. Their constitutions place highest priority on items such as the right to work. Because they have allegedly eliminated unemployment, they consider themselves a success in human rights and the United States a failure. Communist delegates at the United Nations and those charged with follow-up on the Conference on Security and Cooperation in Europe counter U.S. criticism of Soviet political repression with ripostes against U.S. treatment of America's inner-city blacks or the elderly.

There is a domestic counterpart to these arguments from the Second and Third Worlds. Members of U.S. minority groups—particularly blacks and Hispanics—believe that promotion of internationally recognized human rights should begin at home. Pre-eminent stress should fall on bread-and-butter issues: more jobs, better housing, and decent medical treatment. Vernon E. Jordan, Jr., president of the National Urban League, argued early on that for an administration as concerned with morality in public, as the Carter administration claimed to be, "it is unconscionable to place the burden for balancing budgets and controlling inflation on the backs of the poorest and most deprived in our society."[7] Veteran civil-rights activist Bayard Rustin called President Carter's urban package, unveiled in Spring 1978, a program that leaves a "permanent underclass in the country."

That cry from the underclass, at home and abroad, created a challenge for the Carter administration. If the president were to succeed in making stress on human rights a means to help restore domestic support for U.S. foreign policy and in getting more international respect for human rights, U.S. policy had to reflect the aspirations of more people. Read: emphasis on economic and social rights. Without renewed stress on those rights—which the United States had helped articulate in the drafting of the Universal Declaration but which it had failed to endorse through ratification of the U.N. Covenant on Economic, Social, and Cultural Rights or approval of the Inter-American Charter—the United States would fall short as a *credible* exponent of *any* human rights.

Sixth, most U.S. policymakers believe that political, civil, economic, social, and cultural rights are part of a whole. To deny one is to infringe on another. As Secretary Vance stated in his speech of April 30, 1977, "Our policy is to promote all these rights." Although he admitted that "there may be disagreement on the priorities these rights deserve," he emphasized: "I believe that, with work, all of these rights can become complementary and mutually reinforcing."

Some spokesmen from the Third World agree. In an interview before return to his native Nepal—and jail—former Prime Minister B. P. Koirala argued that "economic development starts from politics." If the priority of economic development is to fulfill the economic and social rights of the people—and not just boost the productive capacity of the state—the citizens should be able to determine the process and goals of development through regular democratic consultations. Moreover, he asserted, it is "insulting the dignity of people of the poor nations, to present the issue as a choice between poverty and democracy."[8] Would Americans ask welfare recipients in the United States to choose between food stamps and the right to vote? The point for the poor in the Third World, as blacks and feminist groups within the U.S. can attest, is that economic advance most often parallels increased political power.

Seventh, progress toward fulfilling economic and social rights abroad can serve U.S. national interest. In the short term, it is true that stress on meeting the basic human needs of the Third World poor may mean higher costs for the United States. Governments of developing countries may require increased concessional transfers as an incentive or means to address basic human needs, and broader distribution of income may initially curtail overall national growth and thus reduce, for example, purchasing power for U.S. goods. In the long run, however, there is substantial reason to believe that the United States would gain from a strategy of growth with equity in the Third World.

Concentrating on basic human needs is far more than a humanitarian or charitable gesture. It may be most important as a way to complement other aspects of economic development. One of the primary goals of a program directed at basic human needs is to increase the productivity and productive income of the poor. That approach should help build a better foundation for self-generating, sustained, and expanding development. For example, providing information on family planning or giving women access to job training can help reduce rates of population explosion that often overwhelm rates of economic growth. By reducing such constraints on growth, while at the same time increasing the skill and productivity of more of its citizens, a developing nation can have far better prospects for economic takeoff.

As more Third World countries adopt increasingly broad-based strategies for economic development, they become more likely to provide expanding economic opportunities for the United States. Such opportunities may have mounting significance for Americans, since the United States, together with much of the industrialized world, faces several developments that could affect its own economic growth. These include higher rates of inflation, protracted unemployment, higher costs for raw materials, reductions in investment, lower gains in productivity and profitability, and continued disequilibria in foreign-exchange markets. Developing countries with healthy and expanding economies could, over the next decade, offer growing markets for U.S. exports (thus creating jobs in export industries) and supply more low-cost consumer goods (thus helping to reduce the inflationary pressure that restricts national growth).

One particularly important area in which there is a clear complementarity between efforts to address basic human needs in the Third World and efforts to serve U.S. national interests is that of food. Most analysts conclude that developing countries must make dramatic increases in food production (or triple their grain imports) if they are to meet the nutritional needs of their growing populations—and if nations such as the United States are to hold down a key factor behind inflation, the soaring cost of food. Economists at the Overseas Development Council and elsewhere argue that "the North American granary cannot provide another 100 million tons of exports for the developing countries, while simultaneously meeting rising demand both in North America and in other developed countries, without sharply increasing prices during the 1980s and 1990s in order to cover rising costs of production."[9]

Whatever happens in fulfilling economic and social rights— especially in developing rural areas and increasing food production in the Third World—will have a significant general impact on the United States and a specific effect on future prices in American supermarkets.[10] Strategies that stress basic human needs can, when combined with other approaches to economic development, help achieve structural change within most national economies and reform in the international economic system. Persistent failure to address the unmet basic human needs of the poor in the Third World can, over time, both place an effective cap on continuing economic expansion and lead to political disturbances that threaten U.S. security interests, disrupt the supply of vital raw materials, and endanger U.S. investments. At the same time, the inability of the poor to achieve a minimum standard of living and/or to find a job will contribute to a continuing flow of economic refugees into the United States.

The link between economic development abroad and U.S. national interest is becoming part of the new conventional wisdom in American diplomacy. Former Secretary of State Henry Kissinger made the point, albeit prompted by the oil embargo of 1973–74, in his watershed speech before the seventh special session of the U.N. General Assembly: "If the advanced nations fail to respond to the winds of change, and if the developing countries choose rhetoric over reality, the great goal of economic development will be submerged in our common failure."[11] That theme has been picked up by spokesmen for the Carter administration, as well as by influential members of the Congress. Just before his death, Senator Hubert Humphrey wrote about the relationship between the economic needs of developing and developed countries. He spoke of the demand for fundamental and radical change—coming like a "gathering storm"—that leaves the United States with a critical choice:

> The question is, will we, by our positive efforts, help to affect and move this global upheaval in a direction consistent with our values and beliefs? Or will we merely resist it? Will we design our future or will we simply resign ourselves to it?[12]

* * *

WHY NOT IGNORE ECONOMIC AND SOCIAL RIGHTS? Compelling as the case for U.S. commitment to economic and social rights may be, it *is* open to challenge. Academics and politicians alike have disputed that broad reading of human rights (as opposed to more narrow focus on crimes against the security of persons or on political and civil rights) and, thereby, the necessary response by the U.S. Government. Put bluntly, there are related problems of conception and implementation.

Critics of the broad interpretation of human rights argue that putting economic and social rights into the same category with political and civil liberties muddies the overall concept of human rights. Maurice Cranston, British writer, faults the U.N. Universal Declaration on just that point. He states that "the effect of a Universal Declaration which is overloaded with affirmation of so-called human rights which are not human rights at all is to push *all* talk of human rights out of the clear realm of the morally compelling into the twilight world of utopian aspiration."[13] Cranston and others assert that there is a difference between absolute *rights* which can be declared and enforced by law and *ideals* which may take time, money, political will, and good fortune to achieve. To speak of a universal right suggests a universal duty. If, for example, all people have a right to live, there is then an obligation on all to respect human life. Cranston perceives no such universal duty in the case of economic and social "rights." Those imply rights to be given something, like a decent income or education. But whose duty is it to give it? Vernon Van Dyke, U.S. writer on human rights, makes much the same point. Van Dyke argues that "most economic, social, and cultural rights differ from civil and political rights in the manner in which they can be implemented." They are, he says, "non-justiciable or program rights" that cannot be flatly guaranteed.[14] Their realization depends on policies and activities that may have to be carried out over a considerable period of time.

Richard Claude, another distinguished academic analyst, has expanded on that distinction between the two so-called sets of rights and talked about what he calls "positive" and "negative" rights. According to him, economic and social rights "are distinguished from political and civil rights as 'positive' rather than 'negative' rights" because "the state enforces the latter by refraining from certain practices that infringe upon individual freedoms and by assuring standards of judicial procedure." On the other hand, he asserts that "positive rights must be promoted by legislative, administrative and executive planning to ensure basic human needs such as jobs, education, shelter, and health care which the individual alone cannot provide."[15] In the United States, most thought has been given traditionally to the negative view of rights. For example, the Bill of Rights is primarily a document setting forth prohibitions *against* the encroachment of government on the indiividual. It does not stress affirmative initiatives by the government *for* the individual. The right to live is defined negatively as the right not to be killed. It is largely in the period since the Great Depression and the New Deal that there has been a significant effort in the United States to address positive fulfillment of economic and social needs.

How the nation state follows up on positive rights is thus, for many Americans, very much open to question. Claude argues that the state must, to guarantee rights, act against those elements whose power and disproportionate share of national resources inhibit state action in behalf of those who would not otherwise enjoy such rights. "Economic and social rights cannot be promoted," he says, "under conditions of laissez-faire capitalism, and the scarcer the resources, the more planning and careful priority setting is likely to be required."[16] Ernst Haas, of Berkeley's Institute of International Studies, warns that asserting the individual's "right" to equal pay for equal work or social security payments amounts to making the Scandinavian welfare state the model for the world. That he dismisses as "beyond the economic and administrative capacity of most states."[17]

In fact, there is a distinction between the two U.N. covenants on human rights that suggests a solution somewhat short of that posed by Claude, Haas, and others. Whereas a state that becomes party to the Covenant on Civil and Political Rights is under an "immediate" legal obligation to comply with its provisions, ratification of the Covenant on Economic, Social, and Cultural Rights merely obligates each State Party "to take steps . . . to the maximum of its available resources, with a view to achieving progressively the full realization of the rights recognized in the present Covenant by all appropriate means. . . ." That language indicates that fulfillment of economic and social needs may be both an immediate ideal and ultimate right—the very point implicit in the program of the Carter administration.

It is comparably important to stress that concern about economic and social rights should focus on the most *basic* needs. Given the absolute depth of deprivation in many societies—indicated, for example, by the starvation and malnutrition of millions every year—and the relative dearth of readily available resources, a realistic human-rights policy need not, and should not, put as much emphasis on provision of social-security payments as it would on provision of minimal daily requirements for caloric intake. Attention to such priorities may well blur the distinction between so-called positive and negative rights. For example, when a government contributes directly to the death of its own citizens through the failure to distribute vital supplies of food to starving people—as happened when Emperor Haile Selassie denied that there was a massive famine in Ethiopia in 1973—it may be as guilty of violating human rights as if it had shot the victims.

Whether most U.S. politicians can or will accept the argument for attention to basic economic and social rights—even with that caveat for priorities—is not clear. The alleged dichotomy between the negative rights expressed in the U.S. Bill of Rights and the positive rights espoused in the Universal Declaration has long aroused bitter debate within the United States. During the 1950s, Senator John W. Bricker (Rep.-Ohio) was appalled by the declaration's reference to economic and social rights. According to him, they were "not rights or freedoms in any true sense. . . . They are not constitutional rights. . . . Our constitution was designed in the belief that mankind's aspirations can best be achieved through individual initiative."[18] Approving the U.N.'s roster of economic and social rights would be tantamount to "socialism by treaty." Such congressional sentiment, together with the long-standing opposition by the influential American Bar Association and others, has meant that the United States has not embraced those documents on economic and social rights of most concern to the majority of U.N. and O.A.S. member states. For instance, the United States did not sign the Covenant on Economic, Social, and Cultural Rights until 1977 and the U.S. Senate has yet to give advice and consent for ratification.

* * *

ARE ECONOMIC AND POLITICAL RIGHTS INSEPARABLE? No matter how politicians and academics decide to define and act on basic human needs, there is another issue in the debate that requires attention. Whether human rights are conceived broadly, as in the Universal Declaration, or more narrowly, as in Anglo-Saxon tradition, there is the question: what relationship exists between economic development and denial of human rights? And, if there is a link, what consequences flow from that connection?

In the mid-1970s, Mahbub ul Haq, noted Pakistani economist at the World Bank, opened his provocative book on economic development in the Third World with the declaration, "A poverty curtain has descended right across the face of our world. . . ." He argued that that curtain divides the globe "materially and philosophically into two different worlds, two separate planets, two unequal humanities—one embarrassingly rich and the other desperately poor." It is an "invisible barrier" that exists within, as well as, among nations. "The struggle to lift this curtain of poverty is," he argues, "the most formidable challenge of our time."[19]

Here is not the place to explore why the "poverty curtain" has fallen or how to lift it. For discussion of economic development *per se*, the reader should turn to the considerable body of contemporary literature on that subject.[20] The question at hand is the relation between that process and the problem of human rights. The point that emerges bears on both.

The struggle against poverty, as Haq and others have argued, is *political*. To reach the poor requires a major change in internal and external structures of power. That fact provides the key to the connection between current efforts to achieve economic growth and campaigns to quash human rights—and the insidious logic to that linkage.

The usual argument, made by many leaders of developing nations and some U.S. academics, is that rapid economic growth requires repression. The assertion holds, with some notable variations, for governments of the right or left. For the latter, the usual pattern of development is pursuit of economic growth and equity, accompanied by disregard of political rights and security of the person. Cambodia under the Khmer Rouge was one extreme example of this totalitarian model of the left. There the rulers rationalized liquidation of entire "categories" of the citizenry for the sake of national self-sufficiency and creation of a new egalitarian, agriculturally based society. For governments of the right, something must give in the quest for quantum leaps forward in Gross National Product. That something is a better life for those on the bottom rung of the economic ladder and political participation by that sector. The pattern of development is one of authoritarianism, in lock step with more poverty for the poor. Leaders in such nations argue that the majority must endure sacrifice and exercise discipline in order that the country as a whole can achieve fast economic growth. They say that growth must precede redistribution of wealth. Before that egalitarian millennium, there are to be no actions by trade unions or political parties, *inter alia*, that could disrupt the stability preferred by many national economic planners and foreign investors.

The result of this rationale for repression is that the ruling elite consistently reaps the greatest reward from what economic development does occur. An eminent Indonesian writer, commenting on economic development in his country, has said: "What has been built serves mainly the needs of the foreign investor and the Government, not the people of Indonesia."[21]

That critique of development in Indonesia applies to much of the Third World. There is a correlation between economic and political interests at the core of the current impasse in economic development.

The elites that now hold power in most developing nations, particularly those of the authoritarian right, have no interest in giving a larger slice of the economic pie to the poor. Their understandable instinct, when the poor make demands, is to suppress those agents for reform. They thus prohibit labor unions; bar demonstrations, political opposition, and freedom of the press; or kill what they call "Marxist agitators."

Nicaragua—the scene of an ascending spiral of popular dissatisfaction with the Somoza government, response by the counter-insurgency corps of the national guard, mobilization of guerrilla attacks, and air-strikes on major urban centers—is a case in point. The Somoza family dominated the political and economic life of that nation for over forty years. Although most headlines about the human-rights situation there focused on national guard action against the Sandinist National Liberation Front, that political conflict reflected an underlying economic problem. According to World Bank statistics in the late 1970s, there was a wide gulf between rich and poor, despite the infusion of foreign economic assistance. The bottom 20 percent received 4.3 percent of total private income, while the top 20 percent received 50 percent. Over half of the children under five suffered from malnutrition.

To deal with this situation, representatives for the Somoza government said that they had an ambitious program to improve the quality of life for the poor. Allocations for the national budget showed significant increases in spending to enhance agricultural production, health care, nutrition, family planning, and education. However, critics charged that most development programs were more conducive to profiteering than to increasing the well-being of the poor. The Somoza family controlled much of the Nicaraguan economy, including the national airline, its shipping line, 20 to 30 percent of arable land, vehicle distribution, and a newspaper and television station. The largest farms continued to grow at the expense of the smallest. Some considered the government's program for rural development a political tool against peasant opposition to Somoza. The Somoza family continued to profit from relief sent after an earthquake leveled downtown Managua in 1972. (General Somoza's Banco de Centroamerica became a funnel for much aid to Nicaragua, including that from the United States, while his new construction companies received most of the government contracts and Somoza's friends cashed in on a real-estate bonanza by building a new Managua on the outskirts of the old capital.)

Change, whether generated externally or internally, invites, at the least, resentment, and, more likely, stiff resistance—particularly when the power of the ruling group itself is at stake. In the Nicaraguan situation, the Somoza family responded with police action against political opposition from the poor to assure what it called "internal security" and with outrage against the United States because of its alleged interference in the domestic affairs of another nation. General Somoza never publicly acknowledged the real reasons for unrest in Nicaragua or showed much inclination to do something constructive about it.

The situation in Nicaragua—similar to that in El Salvador (but for the special role of the Somoza family) and much of the Third World—illustrates a critical point. Although violations of human rights are themselves problems, they are often also symptoms of more fundamental problems. Therein may reside their overarching significance.

Deprivation of freedom often indicates that the political system is not working well for either the rulers or the ruled. For example, peasant leaders in Central America have, for the most part, resorted to terrorism only when all avenues to peaceful reform, such as the opportunity to vote in an honest national election, seem closed. Whether or not they see such terrorism as a last resort in a society with no legitimate outlet for grievances, the conservative oligarchies in Central America treat terrorism as a threat to internal security. Officially sanctioned counter-terrorism and torture of so-called political agitators, while sometimes effective in intimidating the opposition, generally undercut the very sense of security they seek. Thus, the spectacle of leaders afraid to leave home or office without armed guards. At the same time, those protesting against the group in power have little prospect of achieving goals such as land reform, unless and until the elite decides to address their economic needs—or topples from power.

Pursuit of full human rights can thus amount to a frontal assault by the impoverished and disenfranchised majority against entrenched elites. To stop underlying deprivation of economic opportunity may require ending political oppression. This view of the relation between economic and political prerogatives may daunt even the most determined advocates of human rights. Taken to one logical conclusion, it may suggest that an effective human-rights policy, dedicated to fulfillment of all basic rights, must seek the overthrow of repressive governments.

This perspective on the linkage between economic and political rights may also call into question the cherished premise of the free-enterprise system. British economist Barbara Ward is not alone in arguing that the "market system, wholly uncorrected by institutions of justice, sharing, and solidarity, makes the strong stronger and the weak weaker."[22] Reliance on the automatic mechanisms of the free-enterprise system may assure some economic growth, but not equitable distribution of that growth. U.S. political scientist Richard Fagen has thus argued that "facing up to the distributional problem" may mean "taking actions that challenge the basic logic of existing class and market arrangements."[23]

The Salvadorean *campesina* may be one embodiment of that hypothesis. Some analysts of the world agricultural situation argue that the "food crisis" may be more a matter of market mechanisms than of too little food for too many people.[24] Food, so the argument goes, is made available because of economic, not human, demand. In the case of El Salvador, the nation's fourteen families divert land from agricultural production for domestic consumption to cultivation of coffee or other crops for export. They deny an individual peasant, such as Rosa Maria Caceres Zeyalandia, the opportunity to own land, to use that land to feed her family, or to derive a dependable living from it. Without that land, she must depend on the large landowner for her living, or find other means to survive. Without additional training, she has no way to find alternative means to earn money to buy the food she might have grown herself. She becomes part of the growing surplus of landless and unskilled labor and the product of what passes for economic development in much of the Third World. She is, in that sense, one of the expendable people.

It is thus no wonder that many in the Third World are both weary and wary of being told that they must forego political liberty for the sake of economic advance. Economic development at the price of political oppression has not helped the majority in most countries. Even though it is not possible with current data to prove that political democracy inevitably enables economic development, it is at least possible to shift the burden of proof to those who say oppression is essential for that purpose. Robert E. Goodin, British writer, is among those arguing with economists in the latter camp, and in their own economic terms. For example, he challenges the economists' argument that consumption by the poor must be sacrificed to assure capital accumulation. He notes that many development programs are not and should not be capital intensive, that the wealthy do not necessarily have a lower propensity to consume, and that much of their consumption is nonproductive (for new cars and other luxury items) or spent outside the country. He also reminds apologists for repression that their course has economic costs. For instance, policing workers so that they do not organize may well waste more man-hours on surveillance that contributes nothing to national development, than would be lost by striking labor unions.[25]

Much experience to date bears out this sort of argument. The authoritarian political systems of Burma, Pakistan, Bangladesh, Afghanistan, and Nepal have not achieved economic results superior to those in democratic India or Sri Lanka. If Gross National Product and foreign investment are reliable measures of progress—a dubious proposition, admittedly—democratic Brazil under Juscelino Kubitschek enjoyed growth rates that were as high as those achieved under the subsequent dictatorship. The foundation for the so-called economic miracles in South Korea and Singapore was laid during the days of constitutional democracy. And, finally, Raúl S. Manglapus, former foreign minister of the Philippines, suggests that "one might take a long serious look at democratic India's industrial growth, which surpasses that of its neighbor, China, and wonder at the same time if its still largely unrelieved and visible poverty is any worse than the hidden poverty in the regimented shadows of the People's Republic."[26]

Use of economic measures

The overlap between either the economic growth that benefits a rightist elite and authoritarian repression that throttles the poor—or pursuit of state socialism and totalitarian repression of political rights by leftist governments—creates a dilemma of humbling magnitude for the United States. The relationship between abuses of power and violations of freedom may vindicate a broad reading of human rights. According to the foregoing discussion, the political, civil, economic, social, and cultural rights set forth in the U.N. Universal Declaration are often inseparable. The expressed scope of the Carter administration's human-rights policy, while ambitious and unfulfilled, is at least realistic in one respect: it reflects both the causes and effects of the problem. No U.S.

protest against political repression in a country such as El Salvador can have much effect if it ignores the economic roots and ramifications of that repression. And no attention to economic rights can mean much for the poor unless, for example, foreign aid actually gets to them.

The very scope of the human-rights problem may defy hopes for solution. The understandable first inclination of many U.S. policymakers and the American public is to oppose crimes against the security of person, particularly in those countries where the United States has special interest or apparent leverage. Those crimes are most obvious, most odious to the international community, and, seemingly, most readily eradicated. However, limiting a human-rights policy to protests against killing, torturing, or jailing political opponents skirts the reasons for such governmental actions. It treats the symptoms of a deeper problem. It may thus be doomed to disappoint both the victims of violations and their would-be supporters in the United States.

Growing appreciation for this enormity of the human-rights problem helps explain some recent evolution of U.S. policy. It is not by accident that a problem with so many economic causes has often evoked economic responses, and that it will continue to do so. The following discussion explores what economic measures the United States has adopted to help promote respect for human rights, why, with what effect, and what remains to be done.[27]

The Congress assumed the lead within the U.S. government in using economic tools to tackle human rights. That effort took two approaches: what might be called *positive* programs to orient U.S. foreign aid, and *punitive* approaches to withhold economic resources from repressive rulers.

* * *

WHITHER FOREIGN AID? The positive part of congressional initiatives began as a result of a basic re-evaluation of development strategy in the early 1970s. By then, the United States, as well as other nations and multilateral organizations, was taking a fresh look at one of the central questions of economic development in the Third World: how to reach the poor. Some key members of Congress undertook that inquiry just as human rights began, simultaneously, to emerge as an issue. The congruence of events was not by coincidence and may not be without consequence for the 1980s.

During the 1950s and 1960s, the United States had tried to address global poverty through foreign-assistance programs that put primary emphasis on maximizing growth of output. The underlying assumption was that the benefit of expanding Gross National Product would "trickle down" to the poor, in the form of more jobs, food, and services. Programs stressed capital-intensive technology and investments, despite the scarcity of capital and relative abundance of labor in most developing countries.

This approach achieved some success. Gross National Product in the developing countries as a group increased twice as fast as did that in the industrialized nations during a comparable stage in their development. Average life expectancy in the developing nations increased from about thirty-five to fifty years during the period 1950–75. And, in education, the number of pupils in primary schools tripled; the number of students at the elementary and high-school levels increased six fold.[28]

However, overall gains in that period masked other problems. Although some developing nations did achieve dramatic upward jumps in per-capita GNP, others did not. Those average figures concealed wide discrepancies in the degree to which development benefited different groups within Third World nations. In most such countries, the so-called modern sector in the cities and on large farms was the major beneficiary. Most of the urban and rural poor were left behind. That group amounted to nearly one-quarter of the world's population. Although most lived in the low-income nations, many lived in middle- and upper-income countries. For example, millions of inhabitants of northeast Brazil did (and do) live in chronic poverty, despite Brazil's status as an emerging middle power with dramatic overall growth in Gross National Product. In the poor nations of Asia and Africa, living standards for the poorest 20 percent had actually fallen.

In short: most U.S. foreign aid had not trickled down.

Recognition of that fact had begun to surface within the U.S. "development community" during the late 1960s and, eventually, to rouse interest on Capitol Hill. Congressman Donald Fraser was what one key participant in the process called the "sparkplug" for dramatic change in U.S. foreign aid. He—together with other new leaders of the House International Relations Committee, such as Thomas E. Morgan and Lee H. Hamilton—was open to new views because the thirty-year-old U.S. aid program was in deep political trouble. The razor-thin margins of congressional approval for appropriations for the Agency for International Development (A.I.D.) in the early 1970s seemed to indicate that the choice was: Redesign the program—or let it die.

Fraser and his colleagues chose the former. They took their cue from what might be called the Vietnam syndrome. Disgust with funneling sizeable chunks of U.S. foreign aid to the corrupt Thieu government had turned much of the Congress against all American assistance. To sell foreign aid on Capitol Hill, the House leaders sought a substantial overhaul of the whole program. To that end, Fraser got the help of James Grant, Charles Paolillo, and Ted Owens—all affiliated at some point with the Overseas Development Council. Their ideas, together with those percolating in other circles, such as the International Labor Organization, led to a letter from fifteen members of the House International Relations Committee to President Nixon, setting forth major principles for a new approach to aid. When there was no response from the White House, legislators like Fraser decided: "If they won't do it, we will."

The result was the "new directions" legislation of 1973. Zablocki and Fraser marshalled support through breakfast meetings in the House and by mobilizing Hubert Humphrey and others to manage the legislation on the Senate floor. After its passage in December 1973, more U.S. official development assistance was to address integrated rural development and such specific needs as food, population planning, health care, and education for the poor. Less was to line the pockets of rich elites.

According to the general theory behind the new directions of the Agency for International Development, increased U.S. stress on basic human needs was to help the Third World achieve an optimal mix of general growth, more reliance on labor-intensive development, and redistribution of income. Making fuller use of abundant labor and providing larger incomes to the poor was to increase overall effective demand and thus spur more general economic growth. More economic growth was to occur in sectors that stressed the production and supply of goods and services to meet the needs of the poor, not those in relatively high-income brackets.

Such an approach seemed most appropriate for reaching someone like Rosa Maria Caceres Zeyalandia. A peasant woman—exhausted by pregnancy, disease, and malnutrition—can neither work effectively nor learn new skills. She is consigned to a cycle of suffering by her social status and sex. Giving her enough nutritious food, minimal health care, information on family planning, and vocational training could break that cycle. Giving those opportunities to enough peasant women—through the fuller integration of women in the development process and follow-up on the World Population Plan of Action (1974) and the U.N.'s World Plan of Action in the Decade for Women, 1975–85—might be the beginning of the end for overpopulation and poverty in El Salvador and other developing nations.[29]

However, the theory behind A.I.D.'s new directions—refined in strategy papers drafted within the executive branch and in the International Development and Food Assistance Act of 1978—has yet to emerge in much satisfactory practice. The fault lies not necessarily with the theory itself, but in the obstacles to implementation. No matter how development aid is packaged, it has difficulty overcoming existing patterns of economic development.

There are, to begin with, several complications raised by those nations that receive assistance for meeting basic human needs of their people. The problem of entrenched power, noted before, stands out. Bangladesh provides an apt illustration. In a controversial critique of U.S. foreign aid, analysts for the Center for International Policy—located close to Capitol Hill in Washington and directed by Donald L. Ranard, an outspoken former senior officer in the U.S. foreign service—charged that the poverty in that country "is rooted in a social order which benefits a small elite at the expense of the poor majority." According to them, "this elite holds power from the national government down to the village level, and it is through this elite that foreign aid is channeled." The Center's analysts thus concluded that, "under such conditions, Americans can expect their foreign aid dollars to perpetuate, rather than alleviate, poverty. . . ."[30]

In addition to the problem posed by those who siphon off assistance, there are other challenges. Roger Hansen, development economist and an early consultant on Third World issues for the Carter administration, points out—despite his own strong advocacy of a basic human-needs approach—that no one yet knows how to assure the kind of social change that gives the poor a role in establishing and maintaining the services they need, such as health clinics and job-training centers.[31] It is an issue of implementation that plagues broad-based human-rights programs, inside and outside the United States. Nor has anyone resolved what Hansen calls the "intervention issue." When asked about U.S.

proposals for stress on basic human needs in developing nations, one representative spokesman for the Third World at the United Nations reacted sharply. That delegate asserted, "We *do* object to someone from the outside telling us what our priorities should be—particularly when the United States is not willing to change international structures for trade and technology that might help us." That U.N. delegate was not—and is not—alone in believing that emphasis on basic human needs is "anti-growth," that it represents a sort of "international welfare system" designed to keep developing nations dependent on the industrial powers, and that it signals decreased donor-country commitment to foreign aid.

For donor nations, there are also difficult questions. Members of the U.S. Congress know that American taxpayers are understandably loath to pay for programs that may amount to an income transfer from the middle class of America to the upper class of the Third World. On the other hand, targeting aid to those relatively few developing nations that *are* attacking the root causes of poverty also raises popular hackles. There is little political support for assistance to leftist governments, such as that in Cuba, because of ideological or strategic concerns. In nations such as Ethiopia, where, since the 1974 ouster of Emperor Haile Selassie, violent methods have often been used to redress the previous imbalance in economic and social rights, spokesmen argue that the United States is not prepared to reward an equity-oriented program with preferential grants of aid.[32] The result is an A.I.D. program that nibbles at the margin of evolution on the right and eschews support for revolution by the left.

For both recipients and donors of basic human-needs aid, there is the question, Who pays the piper? The economic costs may be large. And there may be significant constraints on capacity to meet those costs—constraints that are both political (because of the resistance to economic change by those with vested interests) and economic. The latter has assumed increased salience because of general shifts in global economic structures and the shakiness of donor-nation economies in particular.

* * *

ADDING THE STICK TO THE CARROT. Economic and social rights will not be fulfilled overnight. Congress's appreciation for that fact, even as it was launching the "new directions" for U.S. aid, combined with increasing distaste for affiliation with dictatorial governments. Legislators therefore joined the issues of economic development and repression in a new way. Those issues emerged under the rubric of human rights—and with a *punitive* twist. The main means available to this end was the power of the purse traditionally held by Congress. Recourse to that power, with all it implied in terms of congressional appropriation and authorization of funds for federal programs, became explicit by 1973. Although there had been earlier expressions of congressional concern about human rights,[33] it was in that year that Congressman Fraser launched his landmark hearings on U.S. policy and human rights and that Congress began a series of legislative initiatives on human rights.

The record of congressional actions since 1973 illustrates how the legislative branch set out to use economic measures (primarily punitive) to help implement a broad human-rights program. The following legislation—some discussed from a different perspective in Chapter 4—suggests the pattern:

《 In 1973, Section 32 of the Foreign Assistance Act (FAA) expressed the sense of Congress that economic and military aid should be withheld from the government of any foreign country practicing internment or imprisonment of its citizens for political purposes.

《 In 1974, Section 502 B of the FAA stated the sense of the Congress that, "except in extraordinary circumstances, the President shall substantially reduce or terminate security assistance to any government which engages in a consistent pattern of gross violation of internationally recognized human rights."

《 In 1975, Section 310 of the International Development and Food Assistance Act moved from a simple expression of the sense of the Congress to the stipulation that economic assistance may not be given to any country which consistently violates internationally recognized human rights; the president must submit to the Congress a written report explaining how assistance would directly benefit the people of such a country; and the Congress may take action to terminate economic assistance to that country by a concurrent resolution if either house of Congress disagrees with the president's justification.

《 In 1976, new legislation required the U.S. executive directors of the Inter-American Development Bank and the African Development Fund "to vote against any loan, any extension of financial assistance, or any technical assistance to any country which engages in a consistent pattern of gross violation of internationally recognized human rights. . . ." Section 502 B of the International Security Assistance and Arms Export Control Act prohibited security assistance to gross violators and required the State Department to prepare annual reports on the human-rights performance of proposed recipient countries.

« In 1977, an amendment to the FAA carried a comparable provision in the area of U.S. bilateral assistance, with the instruction that aid go through in any event if it "will directly benefit the needy people in such country." Other legislation that year charged the U.S government to use its "voice and vote" in *all* the major international financial institutions, including the World Bank, to channel assistance to nations other than those violating human rights.

« In 1978, the International Security Assistance Act amended the FAA so that no security assistance—and specifically, none to "the police, domestic intelligence, or similar law enforcement forces of a country" —should go to gross violators of human rights, "unless the President certifies in writing to the Speaker of the House of Representatives and the chairman of the Committee on Foreign Relations of the Senate that extraordinary circumstances exist warranting provision of such assistance. . . ." Language was added in the International Development and Food Assistance Act that prohibited all aid to Vietnam, Uganda, Cambodia, and Cuba, while doubling funds (up to $1.5 million) for specific promotion of human-rights activities.

That list of human-rights restrictions on U.S. bilateral and multilateral aid indicates the overall direction of largely punitive legislative initiatives on human rights. The main purpose of those laws, according to most sponsors, has been to help distance the United States from the most distasteful regimes. Withholding foreign aid signals American disapproval. It is also a move by the Congress to assure that the executive branch takes human rights into more serious consideration than it has in the past when formulating U.S. foreign policy. At the same time, the legislation reveals a conscious effort to leave some leeway to the executive branch for *positive* action. Funds can still be allocated for "needy people" who happen to live in repressive countries. As Congressman Harkin has explained, "We do not want to absolutely tie the hands of any of our programs or any of the administrators of our programs, . . ." but "we all want the world to know that if the United States stands for anything in the world arena, it stands for upholding basic human rights."[34]

* * *

COMPLIANCE WITH CONGRESSIONAL MANDATES ON HUMAN RIGHTS. How the executive branch translates legislative intent into action has depended on whose view prevailed at its end of Pennsylvania Avenue. In that regard, there has been a clear difference in tone, if not always substance, between the policy of the Nixon-Ford years and that of the Carter period.

Secretary of State Henry Kissinger set the mood of the executive branch on this subject from 1973 through 1976. He opposed making stress on human rights a conspicuous factor in American diplomacy and fought increasing congressional involvement in the formulation of U.S. foreign policy. His position on economic measures to further human rights was what senior officials at the time called "damage limitation": curtailing congressional activity as much as possible and containing negative impact in target countries.

The U.S. decision in June 1976 to oppose a proposed loan from the Inter-American Development Bank to Chile illustrates how Kissinger's stragegy worked. U.S. officials explained to their Chilean counterparts, after the bank decision, that the United States had voted "no" not because the U.S. government found fault with the human-rights situation in Chile or held the Pinochet government to blame for alleged violations but because of congressional pressure. Since Congress had already branded Chile an international pariah, U.S. failure to oppose a loan for an industrial credit institution (i.e., a loan that could not be interpreted as directly benefiting the needy) would only anger the Congress and incite that body to even more restrictive human-rights legislation.

Dodging the issue was another reflection of damage limitation in the Kissinger period. The secretary was such a forceful figure and had made his views on human rights so unmistakable—the secretary rebuked the U.S. ambassador to Chile for "political science lectures" when that official raised the topic of human-rights violations—that most State Department bureaucrats kept quiet. Or, as one foreign service officer explained, "We told the boss what he wanted to hear."

When possible, officials at State and Treasury tried to avoid making the determination, required by U.S. legislation prior to approval for U.S. economic assistance, whether the recipient-country had engaged in a "consistent pattern of gross violation of internationally recognized human rights." Instead, according to congressional critics, they tried to slip through what came to be called the "needy-people loophole." U.S. officials drafted project descriptions so that they contained the favored buzz words on basic human needs, and they interpreted project descriptions as liberally as possible, so that few loans failed to pass muster.

Not until late 1976, when several controversial decisions on multilateral loans brought tension between human-rights advocates and skeptics in the State Department to a head, was there a concerted effort to deal more systematically with the questions raised by human-rights legislation. There had been, for example, no agreed-upon criteria for making the decisions required by U.S. law and no established mechanism for identifying difficult loan decisions for interagency review.

It remained for the new Carter administration to address the more general issues of policy on foreign economic assistance and human rights and the more specific questions of procedure. At the initiative of career officers in the State and Treasury departments, a working-level task force was set up in early 1977. Chaired by an office director from the State Department's Bureau of Economic and Business Affairs, it tried to get from the multilateral banks more advance notice of when loan requests might come due and what proposed projects entailed. At the same time, what was then called the Office of the Coordinator for Human Rights and Humanitarian Affairs assembled material (often scanty, uneven, or inaccurate) on the human-rights situation in proposed recipient nations. When representatives to that lower-level interagency group failed to reach consensus, Action Memoranda were sent to the deputy secretary or secretary of state for decision.

That procedure, while some improvement on prior *ad hoc* arrangements, still left much to be desired. Concerned senior officials at State, Treasury, A.I.D., the National Security Council, and elsewhere had little opportunity to meet and thrash out policy options at first hand. As with any new administration, there was an initial shakedown period in which political appointees were understandably more concerned about getting Senate approval for their appointments and reading into their new responsibilities, than in taking firm action on something as complex as human rights. That fact of political life left career bureaucrats treading water for some months until the administration began to find its course.

By spring 1977, the need for some higher-level mechanism to sort out the questions raised by congressional linkage of human rights and foreign economic assistance became obvious. Thus, the directive on April 1, 1977, from National Security Adviser Zbigniew Brzezinski to establish the Interagency Group on Human Rights and Foreign Assistance. Warren Christopher, deputy secretary of state, became chairman of the committee, predictably dubbed the "Christopher Group." That group did succeed in establishing what the deputy secretary liked to call a "sequential and calibrated" approach to decisions on U.S. bilateral and multilateral economic assistance to developing nations. That meant taking into account two sets of questions:

> « *What is the nature of the case that confronts us?* What kind of violations or deprivations are there? What is their extent? Is there a pattern to the violations? If so, is the trend toward concern for human rights or away from it? What is the degree of control and responsibility of the government involved? Is the government willing to permit independent, outside investigation?
> « *What effective action can be taken?* Will U.S. action be useful in promoting the overall cause of human rights? Will it actually improve the specific conditions at hand? Might it make matters worse? Is the country involved receptive to our interest and efforts? Will others work with us?[35]

After making an assessment based on response to those questions, the Christopher Group has generally proceeded with a strategy that amounts to tactical escalation. To illustrate: If Country X is an undisputed violator of human rights, the U.S. government may first register concern with a call on the host-country foreign ministry by a low-ranking U.S. foreign service officer. If no response is forthcoming, the next move may be a call, still done discreetly and without public fanfare, by the U.S. ambassador. Country X's continuing resistance to reform may then elicit, in ascending sequence, public condemnation (by increasingly senior U.S. officials in increasingly prominent forums), warnings of possible U.S. opposition to loan requests, abstention on such a request, and, finally, a negative U.S. vote in a major multilateral bank.

* * *

CONGRESS AND ITS EXPANDING PURSUIT OF HUMAN RIGHTS. Despite serious efforts by the Carter administration to comply with existing legislation, noted in Chapter 4, Congress was not content. Its initiatives on human rights did not stop with restrictions on U.S. bilateral and multilateral aid. It began, as one member of a Senate subcommittee staff said, to work human rights provisions "into every corner of U.S. law pertaining to international economic transactions."[36]

There was, for example, an amendment to the Export-Import Act of 1945, signed into law on October 26, 1977, which required that the

Board of Directors, in authorizing any loan or guarantee for the Export-Import Bank "take into account, in consultation with the Secretary of State, the observance of and respect for human rights in the country to receive the exports supported by a loan or financial guarantee and the effect such exports may have on human rights in such country."[37] A representative from the bank—sometimes its president—has attended meetings of the Christopher Group so that the status of human rights in a given country can be reviewed before the bank board makes a decision on a direct loan or financial guarantee. Pursuant to discussions at the Christopher Group, the board has turned down transactions, primarily on human-rights grounds, in such countries as Chile, Argentina, and Uruguay. After extensive hearings in 1978, human-rights language was included in Congress's continuing authorization for the Export-Import Bank.

The Overseas Private Investment Corporation (OPIC) Amendments Act of 1978, signed into law on April 24, 1978, amended the Foreign Assistance Act of 1961 so that OPIC would take into account the status of human rights and the effect of its programs on human rights in countries where it operates.[38] Since that time, a representative from OPIC has joined the Christopher Group, where OPIC contracts undergo interagency review. According to an OPIC spokesman, thumbs down from the Christopher Group ends OPIC consideration of a contract. Tough cases, such as a proposed agribusiness project in Central America that would help both the needy people and an oppressive government, are held "under advisement."

The amendment to the Bretton Woods Agreements Act to authorize U.S. participation in the Supplementary Financing Facility of the International Monetary Fund, signed into law on October 10, 1978, carried special provisions on both human rights and human needs.[39] The U.S. executive director on the Fund's executive board is to initiate efforts assuring use of facility resources for "the poor majority." The Departments of State and the Treasury are to prepare annual reports on the status of human rights in countries receiving such funds. That language is not as stringent as that offered initially by Tom Harkin in the House and echoed by Abourezk, Bayh, Hatfield, and Riegle in the Senate. They would have *required* the U.S. executive director to *oppose* fund transactions which contribute to the deprivation of human rights and needs. What did emerge, however, provided a means for *monitor-*

ing executive branch compliance with the implicit sense of the Congress—a process Harkin and others consider vital for implementing U.S. policy on human rights. And the amendment to the Bretton Woods Agreement Act laid the basis for establishing mandatory restrictions, when and if Congress should deem that necessary.

An amendment to the Foreign Assistance Appropriations Act for Fiscal Year 1979 stated that the president shall direct U.S. governors of the International Bank for Reconstruction and Development, the International Finance Corporation, the International Development Association, the Inter-American Development Bank, the Asian Development Bank, and the African Development Fund "to propose and seek adoption of an amendment to the Articles of Agreement for their respective institutions to establish human rights standards to be considered in connection with each application for assistance." This amendment was to help deal with the argument that the charters of the major international financial institutions precluded taking noneconomic factors—such as, according to some, human rights—into consideration when making decisions on proposed loans. As part of follow-up on this legislation, representatives from the Departments of State and Treasury held a series of consultations with their counterparts in Canada, France, Germany, Japan, the Netherlands, Sweden, the United Kingdom, and several developing nations.

There are also numerous restrictions on transactions with specific countries. For example, Congress has placed various curbs on U.S. economic and military assistance to Chile since 1974, because of the alleged violations of human rights by that nation's military junta. The Jackson-Vanik and Stevenson Amendments were designed to use the leverage of U.S. trade and credits to help achieve freer emigration from the Soviet Union and Eastern Europe. Edward Koch, then Democratic Congressman from Manhattan and now mayor of New York City, won Hill approval in 1976 for a cutoff of military assistance and training for Uruguay. Legislation in 1977 and 1978 prohibited bilateral U.S. economic assistance to such nations as Cambodia and Cuba. Senator Edward Kennedy spearheaded successful efforts to cut off arms transfers ιo Argentina by October 1978. The list can and does go on. It may grow.

The Congress is increasingly inclined to stress country-specific approaches on human rights—for several reasons. First, the legislators have attempted or succeeded in adding human-rights language for most general legislation on foreign economic policy. Many now prefer to see how that legislation works, before making further changes or additions. Others believe, moreover, that putting human-rights restrictions on some multilateral institutions, such as the International Monetary Fund, may not be the most effective means to promote human rights. Even though testimony before congressional committees has reflected concern that the fund often imposes conditions which place disproportionate burdens on the poor, most legislators believe that the fund is designed to deal with balance-of-payments problems and should not be diverted to tasks, such as the promotion of human rights, that seem peripheral to that purpose. Second, more and more members of Congress, confident that they have established their general *bona fides* on human rights, think that it is time to refine implementation of U.S. policy. For example, many, in partial response to pressure from the U.S. business community and because of increasing consternation about the declining competitiveness of U.S. exports, want to back off from proposals, such as that advocating blanket human-rights restrictions on operations of the Export-Import Bank. That, they suspect, may be "too blunt an instrument," one that hurts U.S. business, without alleviating the human-rights problems of most concern to most Americans. There has thus been a trend toward identifying those countries where, in the view of the Congress, the human-rights situation is most objectionable and/or, where the United States can do something about it or should, at the least, make its opposition known. Two countries have stood out in that regard, Uganda and the Republic of South Africa.

There was growing congressional attention to the human-rights situation in Uganda, on two counts. First, former President Idi Amin Dada, the one-time heavyweight boxer and drill sergeant once described in the Western press as the "gentle giant," turned his nation into a slaughterhouse. From the time he seized control in 1971 until he was toppled from power in 1979, he had an estimated three hundred thousand Ugandans killed. Reports at the time revealed grisly evidence of skull-smashing and forced cannibalism. Second, the industrialized nations (especially the United States, United Kingdom, the Federal Republic of Germany, France, Italy, Japan, and the Netherlands) appeared to have the economic means to help oust Amin. Uganda depended on those nations to buy its coffee, that country's only significant export and source of foreign exchange. For such reasons—and despite the objection from the congressional Black Caucus that there should be no sanctions against black Uganda without comparable action against white-ruled South Africa—efforts to impose a trade embargo prevailed in 1978. Language attached to legislation on the Supplementary Financing Facility of the International Monetary Fund prohibited further trade with Uganda "until the President determines and certifies to the Congress that the Government of Uganda is no longer committing a consistent pattern of gross violations of human rights." (Restrictions against Uganda were removed after the fall of Amin.)

South Africa attracted even more attention than did Uganda. It did so—and continues to do so—for several reasons. The Republic of South Africa is *sui generis,* the only nation in the world to practice institutionalized racism. Under "grand *apartheid,*" the country is divided into white areas, which account for 87 percent of the country and where 4.3 million whites have exclusive political rights, and black areas, called homelands or bantustans, where the 18.6 million blacks have self-rule. "Petty *apartheid*" refers to the web of social and economic restrictions which maintain white privilege. Pass laws restrict freedom of movement for blacks. Lest too many blacks congregate in or near white areas, black laborers are forced to leave their families in distant homelands or have them live illegally in makeshift shantytowns. Scores of South African blacks have been tortured and have died, for implausible or undisclosed causes, while held by the South African police.

Given the apparent intransigence of the Afrikaners and special U.S. sensitivity to racial discrimination, Congress has begun efforts to add more stringent economic sanctions to the other restrictions (such as the U.N. mandatory arms embargo) already in effect. Language attached in 1978 to the continuing authorization for operations by the Export-Import Bank prohibits, for example, guarantees from that Bank for exports to the South African Government and its agencies and provides financing to private companies only if they adhere to a code of principles intended to help eliminate *apartheid.* Attempts, so far unsuccessful, such as those to prohibit all new investment in South Africa by U.S. multinational corporations or to deny tax credits to U.S. companies doing business in South Africa, are likely to resurface.

*   *   *

CAUSES AND CONSEQUENCES OF CONGRESSIONAL ACTION. This expanding congressional use of economic measures to promote human rights has been significant in several respects. There has been a marked trend to employ as much of the economic sector as possible. There has thus been a move from concentrating on instruments concerned with economic development *per se*—such as U.S. foreign aid or the international financial institutions—to complementing those approaches with restrictions on institutions with far different functions—such as the International Monetary Fund. In addition, there has been a consistent move from sole focus on official programming, such as appropriations for U.S. security assistance, to activities that impinge more directly on American private business, such as human-rights restrictions on transactions by the Export–Import Bank.

The result of these two trends has been a considerable shift in U.S. policy. It has moved away from Congressman Fraser's original efforts to make most U.S. initiatives on human rights revolve around efforts to cut off official aid and thereby dissociate the United States from dictators. More recent congressional actions on human rights blur distinctions between either aid and trade or operations in the public and private sectors.

What lies behind this continuing metamorphosis in congressional methods? First, the motive that emerges most often from congressional hearings and discussion with members of the Congress and their staffs is the strong desire to reflect concern about human rights. As Congresswoman Millicent Fenwick (Rep.–N.J.) asserted, "Anything that we do with a U.S. Government agency . . . must reflect what the people of this country want, which is a clear policy on human rights."[40]

Second, having gone on record for human rights, most members of Congress want to be effective, to make an impact. During the last decade, many have become convinced that words, while important, can be cheap. They may also not accomplish much. Repressive regimes can slough off reprimands by the U.S. ambassador or denunciations in the United Nations. They have more trouble ignoring the delay or rejection of a loan request—or the threat of it. Such action can force the applicant country to reorder its own programs and, often, suffer other setbacks. Rejection of a major loan request by the World Bank can and does scare off new private investment.

Third, regardless of what the executive branch says and does about human rights, the Congress believes that the legislative branch must assure follow-through. Agitation by the members of the congressional Black Caucus and the *ad hoc* monitoring group on human rights in

South Africa is a case in point. During consideration of human-rights restrictions during the 1978 hearings on the Export–Import Bank, Charles C. Diggs, Jr. (Dem.–Mich.) blamed the White House for its "seeming ambivalence towards adopting measures regarding South Africa that go beyond verbal condemnation and support for the mandatory United Nations arms embargo against Pretoria." He concluded that "it is up to the Congress to move decisively to give concrete expression to our policy pronouncements."[41]

Fourth, the more Congress has probed the human-rights question and tried to establish effective legislative control, the more concerned it has become about the role of U.S. private business in this area. Part of this concern reflects more general skepticism about the behavior of U.S.-based multinational corporations. Revelations about the alleged efforts of the International Telephone and Telegraph Corporation to help topple the Allende government in Chile and the $22 million in bribes paid in Japan, Turkey, Italy, and Holland by the Lockheed Aircraft Corporation revived old suspicions about "Big Business." Part of the congressional concern reflects the power of the multinationals. The economic impact and magnitude of their activity in any one developing country can, and most often does, dwarf even the most ambitious U.S. foreign-aid program. Some argue that the multinational corporations are unaccountable to national governments and that they turn workers, whether in the United States or abroad, into powerless pawns. Thus, many congressmen believe that putting human-rights restrictions on official development assistance, while leaving large corporations free to support repressive regimes, may mock the motivation and undercut the effect of their legislative initiatives.

The discrepancy between professed official U.S. policy and U.S. business practice is most conspicuous, according to some congressmen, in the case of South Africa. Former Senator Dick Clark (Dem.–Iowa) has stated that U.S. corporate interests have strengthened the economic and military *status quo* in South Africa and thus undermined U.S. foreign policy, which aims at a "progressive transformation of South African society." According to data assembled by the Senate subcommittee chaired by Clark, U.S. direct investment, attracted by large profits made possible in part by cheap black labor in South Africa, grew from $105 million in 1947 to $1.7 billion by 1978. Representatives of most U.S. companies operating in South Africa argue that they are helping that nation's blacks by staying there. They provide jobs and training and work quietly to lessen racial discrimination. Developments of the last decade, however, cast doubt on that contention. For example, despite record economic growth in South Africa during the 1960s and early 1970s, the wage gap between South Africa's blacks and whites grew. Further, white repression of the black majority increased—from the Sharpeville massacre of 1960 to the killing in 1977 of Stephen Biko, influential young black leader. Against that backdrop, noted U.S. authorities on the South African situation argue that "only a combination of serious international and domestic pressures will bring home to white South Africans the necessity of moving *now* rather than waiting until it is too late for any form of peaceful settlement."[42] Further, many members of Congress argue that the very presence of U.S. companies creates a major U.S. economic interest in the continuation of Afrikaner rule and helps legitimize *apartheid*.[43]

Some U.S. firms are, in light of such charges, adjusting their stance in South Africa. Some American banks have responded to mounting international pressure against the Pretoria government, increased political instability and declining profit margins inside South Africa, and vocal campaigns by U.S. student and church groups by distancing themselves somewhat from the South African government. The Chase Manhattan Corporation, for example, has established a policy of not providing loans to the South African government, its statutory corporations, the homelands, border industries, or to Namibia (South–West Africa).[44] Specific language in "Chase's Policy on South Africa" was worked out by officers in Chase's international division and Timothy Smith of the Interfaith Center on Corporate Responsibility and given specific endorsement by David Rockefeller. In addition, many firms are responding to the appeal from the Reverend Leon Sullivan, of Philadelphia's Zion Baptist Church, to adopt a set of principles that would require American employers in South Africa to seek out black employees, provide them with education and opportunities for advancement to managerial positions, and help them get better housing, health, and other social improvements outside their places of business.

On the other hand, some U.S. firms have acted or are acting at apparent variance with official policy. In 1968, the United States joined all U.N. member states except Switzerland and South Africa in agreeing to mandatory sanctions against Rhodesia because of the refusal of the white-minority government there to honor the human rights of the black majority. In theory, that U.N. move against the Ian Smith Government meant that Rhodesia would have no supplies, among other items, of oil, except from oil refineries in South Africa. Three of the four South African refineries were wholly owned by Western companies: Mobil, Caltex, and Shell/British Petroleum (BP). According to testimony before U.S. Senate subcommittees, the South African subsidiaries of these refineries managed to circumvent U.N. sanctions against Rhodesia. According to charges made against Mobil on the basis of alleged internal company documents, that company and others succeeded in oil "sanctions busting" through what Mobil officials called a "paper chase" that obscured the connection between Mobil (South Africa) and Mobil (Rhodesia). Officials at Mobil, while not denying that central allegation, argued that South African law prevents them from finding out what its South African subsidiary does or stopping its activities. An investigation by the U.S. Department of the Treasury was inconclusive. (An analogous inquiry into British oil subsidiaries in South Africa by the government of the United Kingdom, reported in 1978, indicated that sanctions busting did take place, with the full knowledge of senior British officials.)[45]

There have been other examples, outside South Africa, of the contrast between the public policy of the U.S. government and the private actions of the U.S. business sector. While Chile's Supreme Court was refusing in late 1979 to extradite to the United States three army officers accused of planning the political assassination of Chile's former ambassador in Washington, Anaconda was signing a contract to invest up to $1.5 billion in a new copper mine in Chile. And, while the Carter Administration was calling the former head of the Chilean secret police a "terrorist" and summoning the U.S. ambassador to Chile home for a critical review of relations with the Chilean junta, the Chase Manhattan Bank was preparing to move into the new offices of its first branch in Chile. Large increases in loans to Chile by U.S. banks in the 1970s—an estimated $2 billion—ran counter to suspensions of U.S. economic aid and to Congressional directives for U.S. participation in international financial institutions. Senator Edward Kennedy condemned this "back-door economic support" and said that such "shocking banking behavior" should "be stopped by the Congress if it were not ended voluntarily by the banks." He thus promised to "co-sponsor legislation to require full bank disclosure of all loans to countries, including Chile, where our foreign aid has been cut off for human rights reasons."[46] Admitted political contributions to the Republic of Korea by Gulf Oil, justified by company management as assistance "in the democratic process," seemed out of phase with U.S. government concern about the suppression of human rights there. The operation of Gulf and Western Industries in the Dominican Republic illustrated how some U.S. multinationals help promote general increases in Gross National Product at the alleged expense of the poor and thus, indirectly, contravene the objectives of the U.S. government's stress on meeting basic human needs in poor nations. Human-rights activists have charged that Gulf and Western controls a disproportionate share of the Dominican economy, thwarts land reform for the poor, and uses physical intimidation to break up unions.[47]

The human-rights lobby has helped prod the Congress on the question of corporate responsibility for human rights. For example, representatives from the Coalition for a New Foreign and Military Policy have sought the abolition of the Overseas Private Investment Corporation (OPIC) because it "insures multinational corporate investment in Third World countries, particularly those with consistent human rights violations."[48] Other human-rights activists have viewed re-evaluation of OPIC as an opportunity to highlight the alleged connection between U.S. private investment abroad and inequitable economic development and denial of human rights in poor countries. William Goodfellow, deputy director of the Center for International Policy, asserted during congressional testimony that the kind of development encouraged by OPIC is guided by the profit motive and not by what reaches needy people. In considering the role of the multinational company in the Third World—and, in turn, official assistance for that role—Goodfellow stated that "the problem comes when maximization of profit and development priorities do not coincide. . . ."[49]

Pro-rights lobbyists have marshaled related arguments in their effort to tie human-rights strings to operations of the International Monetary Fund. They have claimed that, to qualify for a loan from the fund, a country often has to use draconian means to put its economy in shape and regain a good credit rating. The cure—chiefly for the benefit of the large corporations, according to the lobbyists—is worse than the disease. The poor often bear a disproportionate part of the burden imposed by the fund's conditions. Popular resistance to stringent economic conditions often leads to greater political repression.[50] Future debate within the Congress and the executive branch may suggest how or whether the International Monetary Fund should try to treat both balance of payments and issues of social equity—and thus more clearly complement bilateral aid programs and those of the multilateral development banks.

* * *

RESISTANCE TO CONGRESSIONAL PROMOTION OF HUMAN RIGHTS. Whatever the motivation for expanding congressional purview, those efforts have met strong opposition, first from the executive branch and, belatedly, from the U.S. business community. The Carter administration has found itself in an awkward position: espousing human rights in general, but opposing the further extension of congressional initiatives into the economic sector. Critics have pointed out that the administration's objections have sounded remarkably like those raised by Henry Kissinger: the executive branch needs "flexibility;" "quiet diplomacy" works best. In all cases, spokesmen for the Carter administration have argued that the organization in question is not the proper vehicle for promoting human rights and that attempting to turn that organization into a tool for reform would either undercut the primary purpose of that organization or set back other U.S. objectives. They have stated, for example, that the International Monetary Fund is concerned only with balance-of-payments problems and that there should therefore be no human-rights restrictions on U.S. participation in the fund. The Department of the Treasury and the State Department's Bureau of Economic and Business Affairs—as opposed to some other offices within the State Department—have fought making their clients what they see as the "cutting edge" of American moralism. Raising human rights in the multilateral development banks, they charge, politicizes them (even more than they already have been politicized), complicates long-standing U.S. efforts to encourage more multilateral assistance for economic development, and establishes precedents that might harm U.S. interests later.[51]

Even in cases where no one institution seems endangered, the Carter Administration has opposed congressional human-rights action. It withheld support for a coffee embargo against Uganda partly because of the implications for free trade. The Assistant Secretary of State, Douglas J.

Bennet, Jr., wrote Congressman Donald J. Pease (Dem.-Ohio) in 1977: "Boycott actions are not consistent with the principles of the General Agreement on Tariffs and Trade, to which the United States is committed as the basis for international commercial relations." The United States opposed full economic sanctions against South Africa so that Washington might court Pretoria's help on a peaceful settlement of the Rhodesian situation.

If the executive branch has been unhappy with Capitol Hill's broader human-rights reach into the economic sector, the U.S. business community has been even less pleased. There are several reasons. First, to no one's surprise, executives stress that they are in business to make money, not remake the world in America's image. In some representative testimony during hearings on human-rights criteria for operations by the Export-Import Bank, spokesmen for the Machinery and Allied Products Institute stressed that "we live in the real world and not one which is completely dominated by so-called moral concepts."[52] Second, many business executives say that they do not understand where the administration or the Congress really stands on human rights. Many statements and actions appear contradictory; decisions taken on human-rights grounds seem arbitrary and follow no clear pattern. Further, those who think they *do* understand current policy do not accept its general premise (the conviction of some, such as State Department official Patricia Derian, that the United States must use its economic power to pry improved human-rights performance out of repressive regimes) or its application in specific cases. For example, on the question of ending U.S. investment in South Africa, William Norris, chairman of the board of Control Data, has argued that "the withdrawal of U.S. companies, imposition of economic sanctions, or other means of slowing economic activity in South Africa would deepen the poverty of the underprivileged." If carried far enough, he predicted, such measures would "eventually force an uprising" and lead to "many millions of people needlessly killed."[53]

However, what is really uppermost in the minds of U.S. business executives is their belief that "excessive zeal" in behalf of human rights hurts the U.S. economy in general and their firms in particular. Adding human-rights conditions to U.S. arms sales, economic assistance, and international financing means a dulled competitive edge for American companies. That problem has particular urgency during a time of record-breaking U.S. trade deficits. There is, according to some representatives of U.S. business and to commercial attachés at American embassies, a short-term problem of lost contracts. For 1978, an estimated $800 million of U.S. contracts were lost, on human-rights grounds, in Argentina alone. Partly because of its human-rights policy, the United States has surrendered its traditional role as the main arms merchant throughout Latin America. According to press reports—confirmed by officials in the U.S. government—nations such as France, the Federal Republic of Germany, Italy, and Israel are largely unconcerned about political considerations and have thus stepped in where Washington would not tread. Further, Brazil and Argentina are building up a small-arms industry with the Latin American market the target.[54] Reducing U.S. arms sales abroad, for human-rights or other reasons, has significant economic implications. At stake within the United States are 700,000 jobs, including those of employees of large aerospace and arms producers, subcontractors, and support businesses.[55]

U.S. business representatives argue that, in addition to such short-term losses, using economic measures to promote human rights raises some longer-term concerns. They claim that countries with alleged human-rights problems view the United States, increasingly, as an unreliable supplier. Repressive regimes are not sure that they can count on U.S. firms to fulfill commitments, at least not without often embarrassing scrutiny of their human-rights record. They thus prefer to deal with firms from countries that do not mix business with moral judgments. William Verity, co-chairman of the U.S.–U.S.S.R. Trade and Economic Council, has thus criticized U.S. opposition, on human-rights grounds, to selling equipment to help the Soviet Union develop its oil and gas reserves. He claims that such opposition ignores the fact that 95 percent of this technology is available outside the United States. "Our loss," he says, "is a foreign trader's gain, so support for our 'uncompromising stand' may be accompanied overseas by a barely concealed snicker."[56] Further, our businessmen note that delay or cancellation on a major contract on something like a communication system means, not just one lost sale, but "twenty years down the drain" because of the ensuing sequence of follow-up purchases and repairs.

Given such objections to use of economic measures to promote human rights, the U.S. business community has begun, as one government official put it, to "raise Hell all over Washington with those that count." That campaign switched into high gear, following the mid-1978 denial of credit by the Export-Import Bank to Allis-Chalmers, the Milwaukee-based manufacturer of electric equipment, for the $270-million sale of turbines for a new hydroelectric dam on the Parana River between Argentina and Paraguay. The reason: the initial determination by the State Department that the Argentine government remained guilty of serious violations of human rights.

Since mid-1978, there have been more reported exceptions to holding up loans or sales on human-rights grounds. For example, a call to a senior official at the State Department from Speaker of the House O'Neill, when a delayed contract hurts his Massachusetts constituents, can and does expedite approval for loans vulnerable to a human-rights veto. Calls from senators to the White House, where there has been mounting concern about meager business-community confidence in the Carter administration, have translated into new signals to the State Department and corresponding relaxation on some human-rights decisions. Pressure by the U.S. business community and the well-financed public-relations representatives of nations such as Argentina, coincided with the completion of a Commerce Department report to the president on beefing up U.S. exports. The thrust of that report, reflected in a reported cable at the same time (August 1978) from then U.N. Ambassador Andrew Young to National Security Adviser Brzezinski: the importance of human rights in U.S. foreign policy must be weighed against their cost in terms of U.S. jobs and the U.S. competitive position in world trade.

Officials at the State Department sense that U.S. policy on human rights could buckle further because of the backlash from the business (and labor) community. They have thus begun to address that alleged clash of interests. For example, the Bureau of Human Rights and Humanitarian Affairs, together with the Council of the Americas, organized a meeting for business representatives in March 1979. Corporate executives aired their grievances. Mark Schneider and Robert Hormats, both deputy assistant secretaries at the State Department at that time, joined with Donald Bonker, chairman of the main House subcommittee dealing with human rights, and Gale McGee, U.S. ambassador to the Organization of American States, to clarify the actual impact of U.S. human-rights policy on U.S. exports. They pointed out that concern about human rights is only one of several criteria used to screen export licenses—and one of those with the least negative effect on sales. Citing statistics from 1978, they noted that fewer than 350 out of 50,000 applications for exports were denied, that only 23 of the 1,000 license applications reviewed for human-rights concerns were refused, and that credits from the Export-Import Bank were limited or delayed in only four of the 169 countries where the Bank operated.

*   *   *

IMPLEMENTING THE ECONOMICS OF HUMAN RIGHTS. The clash of views over congressional use of economic tools to promote human rights has special importance. It reflects a predictable tug of political power between two branches of the U.S. government and tension among diverse interest groups. But, most significant, the debate over the economics of human rights reveals continuing problems of implementation for U.S. policy.

Inconsistency is a recurrent charge. The ambiguity of much of the legislation, pronounced divisions of opinion within the legislative and executive branches, and the decision by the Carter administration (as with its predecessor) to proceed on a case-by-case basis lead to some puzzling decisions—at least in the eyes of outside observers. For example, the executive branch may approve an A.I.D. grant for a health clinic for the rural poor in El Salvador the same week it votes against a loan from the Inter-American Development Bank for an industrial project in downtown San Salvador. Such a decision by the Interagency Group on Human Rights reflects detailed deliberations. (Assistant secretaries of state find themselves scrutinizing the minutiae of proposed highway routes to see, for example, if they go into an area that would benefit the rural poor.) It may also reflect what U.S. officials consider a sophisticated and finely shaded distinction between helping the poor and slapping authoritarian wrists. However, such distinctions are often lost on the country in question and on others, since decisions are announced without full public explanation of the reasoning behind them. The result is the widespread impression, according to one baffled executive director of a major multilateral bank, that "Uncle Sam is running a kangaroo court."

Congress can and does sound comparably contradictory in its promotion of human rights. Many, as the 1978 hearings on the Export-Import

Bank illustrated, favor restricting financing for South Africa, on human-rights grounds, at the same time they advocate expanding facilities for the People's Republic of China, despite the violations of human rights there. Members of Congress have raised the issue of inconsistency themselves. Les AuCoin (Dem.-Ore.) challenged his colleague Andrew Maguire (Dem.-N.J.), on the latter's position on credits from the Export-Import Bank for South Africa. He asserted, "You are willing to assist, by government action, Federal Government action, trade with a country such as Romania but you are applying a totally different rationale on the question of South Africa."[57] Henry J. Hyde (Rep.-Ill.) condemned what he called "selective self-righteousness." Worried that U.S. actions were motivated more by efforts to "take political advantage" than to advance human rights, he noted that "the day that we condemned Chile for their vote that they had down there, which was loaded and one-sided, but it was a vote, was the very day we handed the Crown of St. Stephen back to the Communists in Hungary."[58]

Some inconsistency in U.S. attitudes has had an ironic twist. For instance, according to testimony before the Congress, some representatives of U.S. labor favor cutting credits to South Africa because of "slave labor" conditions there. Spokesmen for U.S. business, on the other hand, oppose restrictions there because of the alleged concern for laborers—jobs for blacks in South Africa and the United States.

Although some inconsistency is inevitable and perhaps useful in the implementation of U.S. policy on human rights,[59] some indicates deeper problems in the formulation of that policy. U.S. advocacy of human rights may turn into a crusade out of control because of the failure of all concerned parties to do better homework on which economic means can promote human rights most effectively, at the greatest benefit and with least cost to all.

There are three areas that deserve priority attention in this regard—by the executive branch, the Congress, and relevant interest groups (business, labor, farm, and human-rights lobbies). These are the role of international financial institutions, the imposition of country-specific sanctions, and the role of the private sector.

INTERNATIONAL FINANCIAL INSTITUTIONS. Using the major multilateral development banks, as dictated by current U.S. legislation, does underscore the seriousness with which the United States views human rights, does help broaden the base for effective reform (by raising the issue in a multilateral forum), and does create a ripple effect for private transactions. On the other hand, using them for these purposes may put the United States on thin legal ice. Representatives from most developing nations argue that U.S. law conflicts with the bank charters, and U.S. stands on human rights at the board meetings antagonize most other nations without leading to demonstrable changes in their performance on human rights. Since most other donors do not believe that institutions like the World Bank should be used to register disapproval for human-rights performance, most do not vote with the United States. Repressive regimes, anticipating that the United States is likely to be making a unilateral stand and that it has no veto over most loans, can discount a U.S. negative vote or abstention as no more than a minor irritant.

If the United States is to continue using this economic means to human-rights reform, it must deal more seriously with several issues.

First, what are the criteria for making a determination of a "consistent pattern of gross violation of internationally recognized human rights" and for making an allowance for "basic human needs"? Without a clearer articulation of what those terms mean and on which bases judgment is made, decisions by the U.S. government will be unnecessarily arbitrary and misunderstood.

Second, what information is used, and how might more reliable data be found and made widely available? Strictly U.S. sources, particularly when others do not know what they are, lack credibility. So do general U.S. perceptions of human rights if they are not related more clearly and explicitly to international standards. There is thus need to rethink indices for human-rights performance that might be more broadly applicable and acceptable to more nations.[60] There is also a need for a different means of collecting, collating, and presenting information on human-rights violations and trends of performance. The multilateral development banks now lack a reliable and credible source for such data.

Third, what changes might be necessary, possible, or useful within the banks themselves to assure fuller consideration of human rights? Some U.S. officials suggest amendment of the bank charters or changes in the bank management and staff, while others recommend reconsideration of the concept of human rights itself. Current U.S. interpretations of human rights and practices do put most stress, regardless of what the Carter administration says, on crimes against security of person and give otherwise oppressive governments little compensatory credit for fulfilling economic and social rights.[61]

Fourth, what of the debate over whether performance on human rights is a legitimate factor to consider in deciding on a loan? Severe repression of human rights can either guarantee the stability and economic advantages on which investment thrives, at least in the short run—or flag instability that can, over the long term, prevent full return on investment and significant forward movement on broader economic development.

Fifth, what further consultations are needed to strengthen support for U.S. use of the international financial institutions to promote human rights? Regardless of how appropriate it may be to use the banks to promote human rights, that course, once set in U.S. law, requires more advance work (such as identifying difficult loan decisions well before the final vote), wider consultations with developed and developing nations, and clearer public explanation of decisions *ex post*—if U.S. policy is to acquire greater support and, thereby, greater effect. The record of U.S. interventions on human rights so far in the Inter-American Development Bank suggests that there is little economic leverage to be had with repressive Latin American governments until the United States can persuade a majority of the bank's executive directors to vote "no" on human-rights grounds.

* * *

COUNTRY-SPECIFIC SANCTIONS. The Congress has turned increasingly to economic sanctions against certain repressive regimes. It has done so because of outrage at egregious violations, pressure from domestic constituents, and frustration with the diffuse or belated impact of other measures. Hence the previously mentioned Jackson-Vanik and Stevenson amendments against communist nations, a U.S. trade embargo to help end Idi Amin's butchery in Uganda, the flurry of congressional initiatives vis-à-vis South Africa, and the rejection or delay of economic assistance to repressive governments in Latin America.

Tempting as this turn to sanctions may be, it is neither new nor, if one judges from extensive U.S. experience, likely to succeed. The American colonists tried to no avail to use boycotts on imports and embargoes on exports as a means to force the British government to grant them home rule. The United States failed during the Napoleonic struggles in Europe, from 1807 to 1812 to impose liberal conceptions of neutral rights on Great Britain and France. Efforts of southern advocates of slavery to gain English support for their cause in the 1850s, by holding the British textile industry hostage to what they called "King Cotton," came to naught. The British simply used their backlog of raw cotton, while developing alternative sources of supply in Egypt and elsewhere. President Franklin Roosevelt's attempts to deter Japanese aggression in East Asia did not work: embargoes on trade in strategic materials and abrogation of trade agreements incited the Japanese government to further aggression, rather than deterring it. Later economic blockades against Cuba and Rhodesia did not significantly affect the decisions of Fidel Castro or Ian Smith. Despite the U.S. embargo imposed on Uganda in 1978, business proceeded more or less as usual—with much trade coordinated at Uganda's posh U.N. mission in New York.

Several points emerge from this brief assessment of sanctions. Unilaterally imposed economic sanctions are not likely to be effective, when used by themselves, in coercing sovereign nations into a different course of action—particularly when the leaders of those countries believe that there are vital national interests at stake. Indeed, the foregoing examples suggest that targets of economic sanctions can withstand even severe economic hardship; that they often find alternatives to foreclosed trade, investment, or capital; that the private sector often does not cooperate with official efforts to apply sanctions and thus undermines the effort; that the United States cannot use economic sanctions against another country unless it has a significant economic relationship with it (if then); and that the use of sanctions may have exactly the opposite of the intended effect. In the case of Latin America, Bryce Wood has concluded that "a policy of halting or limiting either economic or military aid or both is likely to have little or no effect in itself on the amelioration of human rights of Latin American nationals."[62] There is little leverage, since U.S. aid to the area is too small, since Latin American governments can and do get their arms elsewhere, and since the military rulers regard repression as vital to their nations' internal security and economic development.

Given both past U.S. experience with sanctions and current domestic and international pressure on the subject, prompt and sober reflection should precede precipitate action. Here, as in the case of the international financial institutions, the primary issue is implementation: how can sanctions be applied effectively, if at all, to achieve their intended goal without incurring excessive cost? There can be no overall rule of thumb on sanctions, since each situation is *sui generis*. The cases of Uganda and South Africa illustrate the different kinds of questions and prospects for success in different situations and, thereby, the issues that must be faced before trying to apply sanctions for the sake of human rights in countries ranging from El Salvador (where U.S. leverage may appear to be great) to the Soviet Union (where it varies) to Cambodia (where it is negligible).[63] For those countries that are already or are likely to become prime targets for the imposition of sanctions, there should be immediate, in-depth studies by the executive branch and the Congress. Those studies should address how much actual leverage the U.S. has on the prospective target, in what areas and for how long, with what effect (short- and long-term) on victims of human-rights violations, with what effect on the United States (particular interest groups, other national objectives, etc.), and to what degree effective U.S. action requires co-operation from other nations.

ROLE OF PRIVATE SECTOR. Discussion of the international financial institutions and country-specific sanctions, as well as other economic measures, suggests that American private business firms can play a decisive role in the promotion of human rights. Previous discussion suggests why some believe that U.S. firms can either support or sabotage U.S. policy. When the latter occurs—or just as important, *seems* to occur—hostility mounts on Capitol Hill against U.S. business. More restrictions on the private sector then become likely. Current efforts by U.S. firms to circumvent the sense of Congress by, for example, undertaking more operations through foreign subsidiaries foster congressional efforts to impose broader limits on all U.S. export licenses and codes of conduct for multinational corporations.

The question of the relationship between promotion of human rights and practices by private business came up during President Carter's visit to Brazil in March 1978. Journalists pursued the point at a press conference. Carter responded that "it would be inconceivable to me that any act of Congress would try to restrict the lending of money by American private banks . . . under any circumstances" and that there is "no conflict between human rights . . . and the free-enterprise system." Agitation from the human-rights lobby and warnings from Congress suggest otherwise. The legal framework is already in place for far broader human-rights restrictions on U.S. business than now exist. Before further steps are taken by any of the concerned parties, there should be serious discussion of several issues.

First, there is the question of what U.S. business firms do to help promote human rights. What general objectives should they pursue, and what specific goals in specific countries? Conversely, is any legislatively mandated human-rights role for business appropriate, given the assumed function of business to make money? What goals are realistic for specific U.S. firms, given their size, their resources, their relationship with official and unofficial groups in the host country, and other factors? To what extent can competing firms in other countries be expected to adopt more active human-rights policies, and how might such a trend be encouraged?

There is also the question of consequences. What is the likely effect of a more active role by U.S. business on human-rights performance? What have these effects been so far? Would human-rights restrictions on U.S. trade and foreign investment discourage U.S. business involvement abroad and thus cut back on the resources available for the fulfillment of economic and social rights in poor nations? At what point do human-rights restrictions on U.S. business cease to provide leverage, if they ever had any at all, with the target regime? What are the likely consequences of promoting human rights for the U.S. business firms themselves—in terms of loss or gain of jobs, opportunities for sales and investment, or impact on corporate planning? What effect might a more pronounced human-rights role by U.S. private business have on the entire American economy? Would it decrease the competitive strength of U.S. firms and thus contribute to a worsening of the U.S. balance of trade? Would it, through lost sales and investment opportunities, lead to lost jobs for U.S. workers and higher prices for American consumers? Should the U.S. government consider compensating U.S. firms through, for example, human-rights subsidies, for business lost to foreign firms operating under less stringent human-rights constraints? And, finally, what would be the effect of increased attention to human rights on the international economic system? Are adjustments needed for global arrangements for trade and finance or for response to the New International Economic Order?

* * *

Conclusion

Questions raised by the use of economic measures to promote human rights bring discussion back to the rationale for a broad interpretation of fundamental freedoms. The economics of human rights suggests that there can be no neat breakdown of considerations, whether in the definition of human rights or in the implementation of U.S. policy. One so-called set of rights (economic and social) overlaps with another (political and civil). Violations of political rights for the Salvadorean peasant both thwart and reflect efforts to escape poverty. In like manner, aid and trade—no matter how different in primary concern—are part of a continuum, all of which affects promotion of human rights. In consequence, there is a connection between what a U.S. government committee on foreign assistance decides about the human-rights situation in Argentina and whether an American firm receives financing from the Export-Import Bank.

Thus, just as Jimmy Carter's inaugural proclamation on human rights may have been bolder than believed at the time, so has the United States backed into an issue that is bigger than once thought. There are more questions than answers—and challenges of conception, capacity, and credibility for U.S. policy on human rights.

Although all U.N. member states pay lip service to the Universal Declaration, they use and interpret it differently. Delegates from the Second and Third Worlds argue that the First World is using traditional Anglo-Saxon conceptions of human rights to sabotage their societies or set back economic development. Representatives from the First World, including those from the United States, believe that their counterparts from communist and developing nations employ talk about economic and social rights more to deflect criticism of their political oppression than to meet the basic human needs of their poorest citizens.

In fact, both have a point. It may be unrealistic to expect a starving peasant to worry as much about freedom of the press as where to find the next meal. In like manner, most leaders from developing countries, whatever their intentions, are not apt to enter into a serious discussion of political rights until representatives of developed nations really try to meet economic needs in the Third World. On the other hand, the argument that puts full stomachs ahead of civil liberties, as if there were a choice, fails because there *is* no ultimate tradeoff. The experience of countries ranging from Vietnam to Zaire indicates that states that reduce freedom in the name of development often fail as well to develop or meet the needs of their citizens. A reliable structure of political and civil freedoms—for example, one that lets labor unions operate fully in Chile or Romania—would provide more justice for more people than they now have.

No matter which side of this debate one takes, the underlying premise is open to question. Those who advocate repression and those who espouse freedom as alternative paths to economic development assume the potential for change. But there is little in the record of the Third World during the last thirty years, when most new nations became independent, to justify optimism on that score. Some contend that revolution is the only course in countries where regimes resist reform. Yet, the case of Cambodia, extreme as it has been, suggests that agents of revolution often do little more than rationalize new repression in the name of revolution. Others argue that meaningful change must come from within a nation and over time. Yet, the cases of both the Soviet Union and El Salvador suggest that there is scant prospect for peaceful, internally generated reform of a significant sort for the foreseeable future. And evolution, too, has its price. As Barrington Moore once observed, "The costs of moderation have been at least as atrocious as those of revolution, perhaps a great deal more."[64] Whether change is sought through revolution or evolution, however, or from within the country or without, there is no clear answer to what Denis Goulet calls the "major ethical question" of contemporary history: "how to achieve development's authentic benefits without destroying, in the process, men's capacity to act freely."[65]

Exploring the economics of human rights reveals not only how hard it is to achieve change within developing nations, but also how little some U.S. institutions may help. There is, for example, not much evidence to validate the traditional American view that free enterprise will always lead, at least in the short run, to the greatest good for the greatest number. Indeed, there is an apparent conflict between the profit motive—understandably uppermost in the minds of business executives—and the promotion of human rights, which may entail short-run financial loss, or more fundamentally, a redistribution of resources. That conflict casts doubt on any easy merger between merchants and moralists. The Catholic bishops of El Salvador, impressed by their work with unemployed slum-dwellers, landless peasants, and impoverished Indians, have thus declared: "The Church condemns Marxism-Communism, which by ideology and revolutionary practice denies God and all spiritual values, but with the same forcefulness, the Church condemns the liberal capitalist system which, although it confesses God, nevertheless in practice denies Him by putting faith in profit as the key motive for human progress."[66] Capitalism may not be incompatible with the ultimate promotion of human rights, but it does raise troubling questions. Perhaps even more troubling is the paucity of palatable choices.

Quandary over the route to reform raises another issue: is there the making of what Harlan Cleveland, of the Aspen Institute, calls a "planetary bargain"? Mahbub ul Haq of the World Bank has argued that there is an important complementarity between fulfillment of basic human needs and furtherance of the New International Economic Order. Whereas the former requires a redistribution of resources *within* nations, the latter presupposes a redistribution of wealth *among* nations. There is a new kind of bargain that might be struck because of the relation between the two, despite current resistance by developed and developing nations. If the government of a poor nation were to try to meet the minimal needs of its people and to decide that it required international assistance to do so, the developed countries could be expected to ask what needs have been identified and how they are to be met. At the same time, the developing nation might demand a comparably challenging *quid* from the donor-nation for its *quo* of internal reform. Just as developed nations are increasingly inclined to look more closely at where their aid goes, so, too, are recipients more inclined to blame part of their plight on waste and overconsumption in the rich nations from which that aid comes. Many representatives from the Third World and elsewhere insist that there be an "ethic of fairness" between rich and poor, North and South. There should be, so the argument goes, both a limit to poverty or a minimum entitlement to human needs and a limit to the share which the most affluent person can take from the pool of global resources.[67]

That ethic of fairness assumes a political will and economic means within the United States and other industrialized nations to follow up on expressed concern about human rights. In that respect, there may be a crisis of capacity. The most recent figures available on official development assistance from the industrialized countries indicate that aid, as a percentage of their Gross National Product, is the second lowest since statistics on aid were first gathered in the mid-1950s.[68]

Near-record lows in foreign aid and other developments not only raise doubts about how enough external assistance can address economic and social rights; they also reflect what may be an extraordinary piece of historical bad luck. New economic realities are adding to the moral dilemma of the industrialized democracies and their relationship with the developing world. In the United States, there is little prospect, for the foreseeable future, for a substantial expansion in foreign aid—no matter how big the gap between rich and poor nations—given the shaky state of the U.S. economy, increased American concerns about lost military superiority over the U.S.S.R., and an expanding taxpayer revolt. Furthermore, although countries such as the United States remain committed to building up the economic strength of poorer nations by helping them industrialize and export into Western markets, they find it hard, at a time of high unemployment and serious structural problems in their own economies, to accept the torrent of cheap manufactured goods, like steel, which developing nations are now exporting. There is mounting pressure to cut back or adjust the flow of aid to poor countries so that they will not create even more factories to compete with Western plants. For example—with some irony, during the presidency of Jimmy Carter—American peanut farmers, afraid of lower prices for their products, have sought a ban on aid to rival ground-nut producers in Africa.

The point: some U.S. foreign aid is beginning to pay off just when many Americans think that the United States can least afford the adjustment which that aid has always implied. If anything, given rising prices for energy, this dilemma is apt to deepen. World Bank statistics indicate that the developing nations need new exporting industries to help deal with the demands of rising population and to repay burgeoning debts. Can the United States, in good conscience, stop importing goods produced by industries that it helped create in poor countries that desperately need export earnings?[69] So far, the United States reflects no coherent approach to this problem. A tendency toward increased trade protectionism—combined with attempted application of sanctions on human-rights grounds and emphasis on meeting basic human needs (more than on capital investment in infrastructure)—could curtail industrial growth in the Third World.[70] That, certainly, is what worries many leaders in developing nations.

Fear on that count and others feeds a related crisis of credibility for U.S. policy on human rights. In many countries, including the United States, the politics of scarcity in the 1980s puts highest priority on lower expectations and on limits to what government can or should do, especially for the poor and powerless. Critics from the Third World say that they are most concerned about their citizens' economic and social needs. They argue that U.S. failure to address *their* rights reveals the hypocrisy of American invocation of human rights. The ultimate irony of the human-rights movement and the related North-South dialogue between developed and developing nations may be the coincidence of the revolution of rising expectations in the South and the revelation of falling economic indicators in the North.

The economics of human rights may therefore come down to two basic considerations: the need to demonstrate political will and the need to help the world's poor. The challenge inherent in the broad scope of human rights lies in making a connection between the two. The case of El Salvador helps illustrate why economic development can no longer be measured solely in terms of per-capita GNP. It must encompass larger concern for the quality of life of people—whether in extending life expectancy or in providing participation by the individual in the affairs of the community. Experts at the World Bank have concluded that it *is* possible to change the pattern of distribution that leaves the world's poorest people largely untouched by economic growth. But to do so will require a "considerable re-ordering of social priorities."[71] Developing nations must demonstrate good faith in behalf of their citizens. And Americans must believe that such change is possible, that it serves their own interests, and that it is worth the price. Until that time, advocacy of human rights can achieve only limited, albeit worthy, results. It may alleviate the symptoms, but not address the underlying challenges. Thus, the continuing tragedy for the Salvadorean peasant—and the fundamental dilemma before U.S. foreign policy.

Notes

1. For important expressions of the scope of the Carter administration's human-rights policy, see: "Human Rights Policy," delivered by Secretary Vance in Athens, Georgia, April 20, 1977, and "The Diplomacy of Human Rights: the First Year," delivered by Deputy Secretary of State Warren Christopher before the American Bar Association in

New Orleans, February 13, 1978 (available from the Bureau of Public Affairs, Department of State, Washington, D.C. 20520).

2. John W. Sewell and the Staff of the Overseas Development Council, *The United States and World Development Agenda 1977* (New York: Praeger Publishers, 1977), p. 5. For a comprehensive assessment of the state of global economic developments, see the *World Development Report* for 1978 and 1979, prepared by the World Bank.

3. Sewall, *Agenda*, p. 5.

4. See the Appendix for relevant portions of the Universal Declaration of Human Rights (especially articles 22–29).

5. Although the Universal Declaration itself is, technically, a nonbinding resolution, it is now widely interpreted as constituting "an obligation for the members of the international community." This was the conclusion, subsequently reaffirmed in and by the United Nations, in the "Proclamation of Teheran," adopted at the U.N.-convened International Conference of Human Rights, which met in Teheran in 1968 and which was attended by representatives of about a hundred governments.

6. For more discussion on international reflections of concern about economic and social rights, see Vernon Van Dyke, *Human Rights, the United States, and World Community* (New York: Oxford University Press, 1970), pp. 52–76.

7. Vernon E. Jordan, Jr., "Has Carter Forgotten Black Needs?" *Washington Post*, August 14, 1977.

8. Stated by Koirala in an interview with Theodore Jacqueney, "We Are Abandoned," *Worldview*, vol. 21, nos. 1–2 (January–February 1978), 24.

9. Martin M. McLaughlin and O.D.C. Staff, *The United States and World Development Agenda 1979* (New York: Praeger Publishers, 1979), p. 66.

10. Developing nations are the fastest-growing market for U.S. products. Between the early 1970s and 1977, sales of U.S. goods to less developed countries (L.D.C.s) grew by 22 percent per year, compared with 15 percent for sales to the developed countries. Of the thirty-five countries in 1977 that imported U.S. goods worth over $400 million, L.D.C.s occupied the first 12 places, when ranked by growth rate of U.S. imports. In 1977, L.D.C.s bought 35 percent of total U.S. exports. The U.S. now sells more manufactures to the L.D.C.s than to Western Europe, Japan, and the communist countries combined. Over 45 percent of all U.S. imports come from the L.D.C.s. Those nations provide over 25 percent of U.S. raw material imports and 50 percent of U.S. food imports. The United States depends on L.D.C.s for over two-thirds of its bauxite, tin, natural rubber, and other strategic materials. Nearly half of total U.S. receipts from foreign investment, loans, military services, travel and fares, shipping, construction and engineering, insurance, and other services came from the L.D.C.s in 1977. Two million U.S. jobs now depend on exports to the Third World. By the mid-1980s, the World Bank expects economic growth in the more advanced L.D.C.s to have a significant, positive impact on the growth rates of developed nations like the United States. For more data on this subject, see State Department *Gist*, "U.S. Prosperity and the Developing Countries," August 1978.

11. Henry A. Kissinger, "Global Consensus and Economic Development," United Nations, New York, September 1, 1975.

12. Included in Humphrey's introductory statement to the International Development Cooperation Act of 1978.

13. Maurice Cranston, *What Are Human Rights?* (New York: Taplinger Publishing Company, 1973), p. 68.

14. Van Dyke, *Human Rights*, pp. 62–63.

15. Richard Pierre Claude, "The Western Tradition of Human Rights in Comparative Perspective," *Comparative Juridical Review*, vol. 14 (1977), 3–66.

16. *Ibid.*

17. Ernst B. Haas, *Global Evangelism Rides Again: How to Protect Human Rights without Really Trying* (Berkeley, Calif.: Institute of International Studies, 1978), p. 8.

18. *Congressional Record*, vol. 57, pt. 6 (July 17, 1951), 8257.

19. Mahbub ul Haq, *The Poverty Curtain: Choices for the Third World* (New York: Columbia University Press, 1976), p. xv.

20. Among the texts I have found most useful, in addition to *The Poverty Curtain*, the annual "agendas" published by the Overseas Development Council, and other items already cited, are: Albert Fishlow, Carlos F. Diaz-Alejandro, Richard R. Fagen, and Roger D. Hansen, *Rich and Poor Nations in the World Economy* (New York: McGraw-Hill, 1978); Catherine Gwin, W. Howard Wriggins, and Gunnar Adler-Karlsson, *Reducing Global Inequities* (New York: McGraw-Hill, 1978); Roger D. Hansen, *Beyond the North-South Stalemate* (New York: McGraw-Hill, 1978) Harlan Cleveland, *The Third Try at World Order* (New York: Aspen Institute for Humanistic Studies, 1977); Hollis Chenery, Montek S. Ahluwalia, C. L. G. Bell, John H. Duloy, and Richard Jolly, *Redistribution with Growth* (London: Oxford University Press, 1974); Robert W. Tucker, *The Inequality of Nations* (New York: Basic Books, 1977); Denis Goulet, *The Cruel Choice: A New Concept in the Theory of Development* (New York: Atheneum, 1971); Arthur M. Okun, *Equity and Efficiency: The Big Tradeoff* (Washington, D.C.: The Brookings Institution, 1975); Robert L. Heilbroner, *An Inquiry into the Human Prospect* (New York: W. W. Norton, 1975); John W. Mellor, *The New Economics of Growth* (Ithaca, N.Y.: Cornell University Press, 1976); John McHale and Magda Cordell McHale, *Basic Human Needs: A Framework for Action* (New Brunswick, N.J.: Transaction Books, 1978); International Labor Organization, *Employment, Growth and Basic Needs* (Geneva: ILO, 1976); and E. F. Schumacher, *Small Is Beautiful: A Study of Economics As If People Mattered* (New York: Harper & Row, 1976). In addition to learning from these texts, I am indebted to colleagues at the Department of State, the Agency for International Development, the Council on Foreign Relations, and staffs of various congressional committees, as well as to representatives of many Third World countries at the United Nations for discussion of these issues. I owe a particular debt to Catherine Gwin, executive director of the 1980s Project at the Council on Foreign Relations, for her own probing insight into the questions raised by "basic human needs" and that afforded by the Council's study group on that subject.

21. Quoted by Henry Kamm, "Indonesia's Oil Fails to Wash Away the Blight of Poverty," *The New York Times*, April 27, 1978.

22. Barbara Ward, foreword to Haq, *Poverty Curtain*, p. xii.

23. From the chapter by Richard Fagen, "Equity in the South in the Context of North-South Relations," *Rich and Poor Nations in the World Economy*, p. 193.

24. See the argumentation and extensive bibliography marshaled by Frances Moore Lappé and Joseph Collins in *Food First: Beyond the Myth of Scarcity* (Boston: Houghton Mifflin Company, 1977).

25. Robert E. Goodin, "The Development-Rights Tradeoff: Some Unwarranted Economic and Political Assumptions," *Universal Human Rights*, vol. 1, no. 2 (April–June 1979), 31–42.

26. Raúl S. Manglapus, "Human Rights Are Not a Western Discovery," *Worldview*, vol. 21, no. 10 (October 1978), 6.

27. See Chapter Two, "The Diplomacy of Human Rights," for discussion of the noneconomic measures used to promote human rights.

28. Data drawn from the "Foreign Assistance Study," assembled by the Development Coordination Committee, chaired by the Administrator of the Agency for International Development (A.I.D.), October 1977.

29. For more material on the connection between women's rights and human rights,

see Irene Tinker and Michele Bo Bramsen, eds., *Women and World Development* (Washington, D.C.: Overseas Development Council, 1976) and May Rihani, *Development As If Women Mattered: An Annotated Bibliography with a Third World Focus* (Washington, D.C.: Secretariat for Women in Development of the New TransCentury Foundation, Occasional Paper No. 10, April 1978). For many of the concerns that lurk between the lines of this section, I am indebted to discussions with colleagues at the Council on Foreign Relations and the Overseas Development Council, as well as to talks with Arvonne Fraser in A.I.D.'s Office for Women in Development and Judith Bruce at the Population Council.

30. Betsy Hartmann and James Boyce, "Bangladesh: Aid to the Needy?" *International Policy Report*, published by the Center for International Policy, May 1978, p. 1.

31. See Hansen's essay "The Political Economy of North-South Relations: An Overview and an Alternative Approach," in Fishlow, Diaz-Alejandro, Fagen, and Hansen, *Rich and Poor Nations in the World Economy*, pp. 217–54.

32. U.S. reaction to Soviet activity in the Horn of Africa was probably a more compelling factor behind American decisions on aid to Ethiopia in the later 1970s.

33. The first direct reflection of recent congressional determination to consider human rights in the implementation of U.S. foreign policy came in the "Reuss amendment" to the Foreign Military Sales Act Amendments of 1971 (PL 91-672, signed into law on January 12, 1971). Introduced by Representative Henry S. Reuss (Dem.–Wis.), that provision expressed the sense of the Congress that the United States should make no military sales which had the effect of arming dictators who are denying the growth of fundamental rights or social progress to their people.

34. 121 *Congressional Record*, H 12053, daily edition, November 9, 1975.

35. Again, the significance of the 1977 Vance speech emerged. Those questions were first set forth in that address and subsequently used as part of a general framework for decision making within the Carter administration.

36. Robert W. Russell, Counsel, Subcommittee on International Finance, Senate Committee on Banking, Housing, and Urban Affairs, "Human Rights Provisions in Foreign Economic Policy Legislation," presented at the Annual Meeting of the International Studies Association/Midwest Region, Northern Illinois University, DeKalb, Illinois, May 6, 1978.

37. Established in 1934, the Export-Import Bank—or *Exim*—is a multibillion-dollar, wholly-owned U.S. government corporation that supports U.S. exports abroad. According to the current president and chairman of the bank, its statutory purpose is "to aid in financing and to facilitate exports" on terms "which are competitive with the government-supported rates and terms" available in the world's major exporting countries.

38. In 1971, the Overseas Private Investment Corporation (OPIC) is supposed to mobilize and facilitate the participation of U.S. private capital and skills in the economic and social development of less developed countries. It achieves this objective primarily by selectively insuring private U.S. investments in about eighty countries against the risks of expropriation; inconvertibility of currency; and loss due to war, revolution and insurrection. OPIC also helps identify suitable investment opportunities, provides project financing where adequate private financing is not available on appropriate terms, and furnishes expert counseling to other U.S. government agencies and to private U.S. investors.

39. The legislation was to authorize a $1.7-billion U.S. contribution to a Supplementary Financing Facility in the International Monetary Fund. The facility would provide approximately $10 billion to enable the I.M.F. to make larger, longer-terms loans to countries with especially severe problems in adjusting balance of payments.

40. Quoted from the hearings held before the Subcommittee on International Trade,

Investment and Monetary Policy of the Committee on Banking, Finance and Urban Affairs of the House of Representatives on March 13, 15, 16, and 17, 1978, on the subject of whether "to amend and extend the Export-Import Bank Act of 1945" (Washington, D.C.: U.S. Government Printing Office, 1978), p. 134.

41. Quoted from hearings held before the same committee on the subject "Export-Import Bank and Trade with South Africa," February 9, 1978, p. 28.

42. Clyde Ferguson and William R. Cotter, "South Africa—What Is to Be Done," *Foreign Affairs*, vol. 6, no. 2 (January 1978), 267. In mid-1978, the South African Council of Churches, an ecumenical body that claims to represent more than half of South Africa's 26 million people, stated that "foreign investments and loans have largely been used to support the prevailing patterns of power and privilege" in South Africa, and declared: "We urgently call on foreign countries and organizations, for the sake of justice, to revise radically their investment policies and employment practices in regard to South Africa, in such a way as to benefit the total population." Quoted in *The New York Times*, July 13, 1978.

43. "U.S. Corporate Interests in South Africa," Report to the Committee on Foreign Relations, United States Senate, by Senator Dick Clark, Chairman, Subcommittee on African Affairs of the Committee on Foreign Relations, United States Senate (Washington, D.C.: U.S. Government Printing Office, 1978), January, 1978. In an extract from that report published in *The New York Times* (February 21, 1978), Senator Clark concluded that "financial support of *apartheid* should no longer be tolerated." He advocated a shift in U.S. official policy from alleged neutrality (neither encouraging nor discouraging foreign investment in South Africa) to a stance of "active discouragement"—i.e., prohibiting U.S. government facilities from being used to promote the flow of capital or credit to South Africa, denying tax credits to those firms paying taxes to South Africa that extend loans to or invest in operations of the South African government or its agencies, and withholding endorsement of private groups or associations, such as the U.S. Chamber of Commerce, which organize in defense of U.S. corporate investment in South Africa.

44. In the Chase Code of Ethics, adopted in 1977 and repeated in a document ("Chase's Policy on South Africa," April 18, 1978), that corporation stated: "Strict attention should be given to the legal, moral, and social implications of all loan and investment decisions on a global basis. We should seek to avoid business with identifiably harmful results and assure that we always carefully evaluate the long-term, as well as the short-term meaning of our decisions." In the spirit of the Hippocratic Oath—"Above all, not knowingly to do harm"—Chase foreswore dealings with the public sector in South Africa, but decided "to continue to be willing to consider the financing of private sector needs." The reasoning: "We believe that our involvement with the private sector is a constructive force for stimulating positive changes in that country."

45. For fuller documentation of these charges, see Bernard Rivers, "Mobil and Rhodesia," Corporate Information Center Brief, October 1977, and his testimony before the House Subcommittee on Africa, "Political Developments in Southern Rhodesia, Fall 1977," October 4, 1977. Rivers, a British economist at York University, subsequently completed a six-month study on an oil embargo against South Africa, for the United Nations Center against Apartheid (reported in *The New York Times*, June 18, 1978). For coverage of the U.K. investigation or so-called "Bingham Report," see "Sanctimonious Sanctions-busters," *The Economist* vol. 268, no. 7044 (September 2, 1978), 20.

46. Edward Kennedy, "Challenges to Human Rights in Chile," *Congressional Record*, vol. 124, no. 64 (May 4, 1978). Kennedy cited as documentation two studies: "Human Rights, Economic Aid and Private Banks: the Case of Chile," by Isabel Letelier and Michael Moffitt of the Transnational Institute; and "U.S. Steel Equips Chile's

Military—despite Embargo," by Cynthia Arnson and Michael Klare of the Institute of Policy Studies. Both institutes are located in Washington, D.C.

47. For more discussion of this case, see the documentation compiled by the New York–based Interfaith Center on Corporate Responsibility and the Washington-based Investor Responsibility Research Center, and the response prepared by Gulf and Western, "Gulf and Western in the Dominican Republic," Report no. 3, May 1978.

48. Coalition for a New Foreign and Military Policy, "Up Date," February 1978. (All material prepared by the Coalition is available from its main office located at 120 Maryland Avenue, N.E., Washington, D.C. 20002.)

49. Quoted from Goodfellow's testimony during "Extension and Revision of Overseas Private Investment Corporation Programs," Hearings and Markup before the Subcommittee on International Economic Policy and Trade of the Committee on International Relations, House of Representatives, Ninety-fifth Congress, First Session, June 21, 23; July 19, 20, 21; September 8, 12, and 16, 1977 (Washington: U.S. Government Printing Office, 1977), pp. 143–59. OPIC officials with whom I spoke countered the criticism from Goodfellow and others. They claimed that L.D.C. leaders wanted U.S. private investment and, indeed, most wanted investment in projects like luxury hotels that would attract foreign currency and more investment. Who were *we* to tell *them* what they wanted or needed? Big, furthermore, was not necessarily bad. It was the large multinational corporations that had the capital and expertise to operate abroad. How could OPIC tell Brazil that it could *not* have investment by a Fortune 500 firm? Should OPIC, out of frustration with some admitted problems in its programs, opt out of its stated mission? OPIC officials stressed that the United States should not "leave poor people in the lurch." Pushing too hard on human rights, via restrictions on OPIC, might mean that the "U.S. picked up its investment marbles and went home." Some help on development was better than none. To argue otherwise was to miss the real point of U.S. responsibility for economic development in the Third World. In addition, as long as there were to be political and economic constraints on increased U.S. foreign aid (as seemed likely), U.S. private investment would be all the more important for economic development in the L.D.C.s.

50. For a provocative treatment of this subject, see Patricia Weiss Fagen, "The Links between Human Rights and Basic Needs," *Background*, Center for International Policy, Spring 1978.

51. World Bank President Robert McNamara has concurred with many of those points and raised some of his own:

"The bank perhaps more than any other institution in the world, is helping large numbers of . . . people move out of absolute poverty toward a more decent life. What we are not capable of is action directly related to civil rights. Such action is prohibited by our charter, it would require information and competence which we lack, and there is no agreement among our member governments on acceptable standards of civil rights in a wide variety of political circumstances found in developing countries.

"Many governments, both developed and developing, resent the efforts of the United States to force its own values and its own standards of conduct on other states through international institutions which by tradition have operated on the basis of consensus. Even more, they resent being asked to apply those standards except when the United States decides that its own security interests or other national interests dictate otherwise." Quoted by Leonard Silk, "McNamara on the Largest Issue: World Economy," *The New York Times*, April 2, 1978.

52. For the full text of the M.A.P.I. position, see: "To Amend and Extend the Export-Import Bank Act of 1945," Hearings before the Subcommittee on International Trade,

Investment and Monetary Policy of the House Committee on Banking, Finance, and Urban Affairs, March 13, 15, 16, and 17, 1978 (Washington, D.C.: U.S. Government Printing Office, 1978), pp. 556–69.

53. "Export-Import Bank and Trade with South Africa," Hearing before the Subcommittee on International Trade, Investment, and Monetary Policy of the Committee on Banking, Finance and Urban Affairs, House of Representatives, February 9, 1978 (Washington, D.C.: U.S. Government Printing Office, 1978), p. 5.

54. Alan Riding, "Latin America Turning Away from U.S. Military Guidance," *The New York Times*, July 1, 1978.

55. Bernard Weintraub, "The U.S. Policy on Arms Has a Life of Its Own," *The New York Times*, September 18, 1977.

56. William Verity, "Taking Politics Out of Trade with the Soviet," *The New York Times*, January 2, 1979.

57. Exim Hearings, February 1978, p. 34.

58. *Ibid.*, p. 89.

59. For discussion of this point, see Part I and the Conclusion.

60. Harvard Professor Jorge I. Dominguez, in a paper done for publication by the "1980s Project" at the Council on Foreign Relations, has proposed a "comprehensive index on human rights." His "framework,"—drawn from work by Kenneth Boulding, Karl Deutsch, Richard Snyder, Charles Hermann, and Harold Lasswell—tries to incorporate attention to economic and social rights (since that has not been done in most more traditional formulations of human rights) and, thereby, to provide a schema with more validity across cultures and ideologies.

61. U.S. abstention on two multilateral loans to Ethiopia in early 1977 reflected U.S. concern about ruthless repression of political opposition by the Ethiopian Provisional Military Government that had come to power in 1974. It did not reflect appreciation or approval for the fact that the new government had achieved, albeit through sometimes violent means, the kind of land reform that A.I.D. had long advocated, and that the majority of Ethiopians reportedly enjoyed far fuller attention to their economic and social rights than had been the case under the autocratic regime of Emperor Hailie Selassie. As suggested previously, the new Ethiopian government, as well as others, saw the U.S. votes as evidence of Washington's opposition to the social and economic goals of their revolution and, indeed, of U.S. inability to deal constructively with revolutionary change at all.

62. Bryce Wood, "Human Rights Issues in Latin America," prepared as part of the 1980s Project for the Council on Foreign Relations.

63. For discussion on the pros and cons of sanctions against Uganda, see Richard H. Ullman, "Human Rights and Economic Power: the United States versus Idi Amin," *Foreign Affairs*, vol. 56. no. 3 (April 1978), 529–43; John de St. Jorre, "The Ugandan Connection," *The New York Times Magazine*, April 9, 1978, pp. 27–28, 82, 84, 86, 88; Ernst Haas, *Global Evangelism Rides Again*, pp. 42–45; "United States–Uganda Relations," Hearings before the Subcommittees on Africa, International Organizations, and International Economic Policy and Trade of the House Committee on International Relations, February 1,2, 9, 22; April 6 and 26, 1978 (Washington, D.C.: U.S. Government Printing Office, 1978); and the State Department *Gist*, "Uganda: U.S. Policy," July 1978. In several of the above, there are instructive comparisons with the case of South Africa. For discussion on South Africa itself, see the above-mentioned article in *Foreign Affairs* (January 1978); George Ball, "Asking for Trouble in South Africa," *Atlantic Monthly*, October 1977, pp. 43–51; and any of a burgeoning number of books on the subject. For a concise analysis of the pros and cons of applying economic sanctions against the U.S.S.R., see Richard Burt, "Trade and Foreign Policy: Will Export Controls

Influence Moscow?" *The New York Times*, July 24, 1978. There have been no comparable studies, to my knowledge, on El Salvador or Cambodia.

64. Barrington Moore, Jr., *Social Origins of Dictatorship and Democracy* (Boston: Beacon Press, 1966), p. 505.

65. Goulet, *The Cruel Choice*, p. 330.

66. Quoted in *The New York Times*, January 21, 1979.

67. Cleveland, *The Third Try at World Order*, p. 28.

68. In 1977, official development assistance from the donor nations of the Organization of Economic Cooperation and Development (O.E.C.D.) was only 0.31 percent of their Gross National Product, according to an O.E.C.D. estimate published in the *IMF Survey*, vol. 7, no. 3 (July 8, 1978).

69. For elaboration on these arguments, see Paul Lewis, "Moral Dilemma for the West," *The New York Times*, November 13, 1977. Robert S. McNamara, president of the World Bank, stressed the role of trade in development and the costs of protectionism for both developed and developing nations in his address before the United Nations Conference on Trade and Development, Manila, the Philippines, May 10, 1979.

70. One senior official from the Kissinger era remarked, a year after leaving the State Department, that economics constitutes *the* major issue of U.S.–Latin American relations. There is thus "potential incoherence in stress on human rights and the capacity to cooperate on the important economic problems of the Western Hemisphere. U.S. sanctions on human rights, he claimed, are being imposed on the very items, such as access to markets and loans, that go to the heart of development."

71. Montek S. Ahluwalia, Nicholas G. Carter, and Hollis B. Chenery, Development Policy Staff, World Bank, "Growth and Poverty in Developing Countries," World Bank Staff Working Paper No. 309 (revised), May 1979, p. 50.

Conclusion

Owl kept his head and told us that the opposite of an Introduction, my dear Pooh, was a Contradiction.

A. A. Milne,
The World of Pooh

Promoting human rights may sound like a simple proposition. Jimmy
Carter won the presidency partly because he promised to stress human
rights and thus "make Americans proud again." All members of the
United Nations have agreed to uphold an international bill of human
rights. Who, after all, can oppose fundamental freedoms?

The answer, at some point, can be "almost anybody." Definition and
defense of human rights can deteriorate fast into a contradiction in
terms. Policy, probed to its origins or consequences, can dissolve in
paradox.

Dictators' disdain for democracy and its sundry trappings comes as no
surprise. Many sanction torture, not because they *like* pulling out toe-
nails, but because they think such tactics help keep them in power.
South African practitioners of *apartheid* see their efforts as part of a
struggle for survival, their own and that of "the whole structure of Western civilization, threatened by Russian-backed terrorism." Spokesmen
for the Soviet Union stress the prerogatives of the state and society over
those of the individual.

The mercurial will of nations such as the United States to advocate
human rights is less expected. Yet, a look at the role of human rights in
U.S. policy leads to some instructive revelations. The historical record
is as mixed as it is impressive. Few nations have done more than the
United States for the sake of human rights. Since World War II alone,
the United States has taken the lead in drafting international documents
on human rights and setting up machinery to implement them. Its citizens have contributed lives and dollars for the preservation of freedom.
On the other hand, some U.S. actions have worked *against* protection

of human rights abroad. It was the United States, after all, that helped put the Somoza family into power in Nicaragua. It is thus the United States that must bear part of the blame for the death of fifteen thousand Nicaraguans and the devastation of that country during the battle between the national guard and the Sandinist rebels, not to mention the sequel to those events. U.S. advocacy of human rights can also ring hollow because of some poor performance at home. The United States is the nation where blacks have only recently achieved what Father Theodore M. Hesburgh, president of the University of Notre Dame, calls "the legal abandonment of more than three centuries of *apartheid*." The rights of women and native Americans are still not constitutionally guaranteed and enforced.

Principle, it appears, exacts a price. Many, often understandably, balk at the cost—whether it is financial, political, strategic, or personal. American corporate, labor, and farm leaders often object when human-rights restrictions in U.S. legislation contribute to lost markets and jobs. Policymakers question the wisdom of promoting human rights at some peril to other expressed U.S. goals, such as *détente*. Individual citizens applaud advocacy of human rights until their ox is, as the case may be, gored or ignored.

A final look at the three representative victims of repression and U.S. response helps summarize the discrepancy between what Americans say and what they do—and why.

《 Ly Linn, twenty-five-year-old widow, has risked execution to escape from her native Cambodia. Frightened by the genocide there and forced now to remain in a refugee camp, she is a woman with no country and an unpromising future. President Carter called Cambodia "the worst violator of human rights in the world today." Yet, he had no direct means to change the government from which Ly Linn fled. More to the point, many Americans, upset by high taxes and unemployment, are not sure how wide to open U.S. doors for Cambodian refugees. They are torn between the spectacle of children with their bellies bloated by starvation and the spectre of an endless flow of homeless Indochinese to U.S. shores. Most do not want Los Angeles to become the Ellis Island of the 1980s.

《 Viktor Isaakovich Fainberg has endured psychiatric torture to demonstrate his right to free speech in the Soviet Union. He won release from an insane asylum, largely because of the international outcry in his behalf. U.S. political leaders have consistently spoken out against the plight of Jews in the Soviet Union. According to recent emigration figures, some significant success has been achieved. At the same time, some U.S. proponents of human rights in the Soviet Union have paid little apparent attention to the implications of their actions, short- and long-term, for Jewish dissidents, the many other targets of Soviet oppression, political change within the U.S.S.R., and other objectives of U.S. policy. A case can be made for the contention that what little leverage the United States has for improved Soviet respect for human rights works more often to the advantage of some U.S. politicians than for most victims of violations.

« Rosa Maria Caceres Zeyalandia, is, unlike either the Cambodian refugee or the Soviet dissident, one of the relatively invisible victims of repression. Few Americans know or think about someone in her situation. An impoverished *campesina* in rural El Salvador, she works, sleeps, and gives birth to her children in the cotton fields. She lacks access to such basic needs as decent food, shelter, and health care and to the political means to make her needs known. The U.S. government has endorsed "new directions" for its foreign aid in order to help just such people. But it has not allocated enough money to make that possible. American foreign assistance ranks, as a percent of Gross National Product, in the bottom 25 percent of all non-communist-country programs. Since Americans spend more on pet food at home than on food aid abroad, more may be at issue than economics.

These three cases reveal not only some discrepancies in American actions and attitudes, but also some reasons, appealing and appalling, for them. They also reveal the main corresponding strands of U.S. policy. There is an identifiable diplomacy of human rights—with special instruments of U.S. foreign policy brought to bear on brutality abroad. There is a distinct politics of human rights—through which domestic actors from both ends of Pennsylvania Avenue shape the style and substance of U.S. policy. And there is an economics of human rights— which defines whether human rights begin with breakfast and what economic clout the United States can wield when advocacy of human rights lapses into lip service.

* * *

Diplomacy of human rights

The international area is the most obvious arena for promotion of human rights. It is there—in forums such as the United Nations, the Organization of American States, and the Conference on Security and Cooperation in Europe—that nation states have professed adherence to fundamental freedoms. It is there that they have agreed to hold each other accountable to certain standards. It is there, as elsewhere, that some progress is being made.

It is also in diplomacy that, according to U.S. policymakers, Washington can draw on a rich mix of tools to tackle human rights. The Carter administration moved early to use many of the means at its disposal. Current U.S. diplomacy of human rights is thus—depending on the situation—private or public, bilateral or multilateral, positive or punitive.

What that rich mix can accomplish is another matter. The preliminary returns are themselves mixed. On the one hand, having Jimmy Carter espouse human rights from the world's biggest bully pulpit has helped raise global consciousness on the subject and achieve some concrete results. Partly because of U.S. efforts, thousands of political prisoners have been released and scores of elections held since early 1977. Emigration has increased from the U.S.S.R.; El Salvador agreed to a visit by the Inter-American Commission on Human Rights; and some Cambodian opening to outside contact suggested how even the most bestial regime may respond to global outrage. Opponents of authoritarian governments, from the Philippines to Brazil, report that, while repression has not stopped, more officials at least act as if they must take reaction from the U.S. and others into account. Veteran observers of the human-rights scene take some comfort from the fact that now many student activists are jailed, not peremptorily shot. In short, emphasis on human rights can and does achieve some positive results. And because the scope of action and awareness is increasingly international, the impact may be more lasting.

That said, massive hurdles block any leap into the millennium—even for the most agile Baptist! For several reasons, U.S. advocates of human rights face huge challenges.

Repression is rampant and is assuming more sinister form. In many countries of Eastern Europe, dissidents are now confined to mental asylums, where they have few opportunities to defend themselves. In several Asian nations, rulers use emergency laws to "legalize" the preventive detention of political opponents—often holding them incommunicado and without trial for years.[1] Governments that once openly arrested and tortured opponents now operate more subtly. There is a marked increase in so-called "disappearances." Violations in one country, like Chile, spill over into another, like Argentina, as terrorists and counter-terrorists pursue each other in a self-perpetuating parody of cops and robbers. Intelligence agents in South America have set up computerized information systems and intergovernmental collaboration. As one Argentine general explained his assistance to the Chilean secret police, "Of course we have to cooperate and coordinate across borders; the guerrillas do."[2]

The nation state, outraged target for international acrimony when its leaders run amok, is at once the perpetrator of the problem and the obstacle to its solution. For many new nations in the Third World, the priority of leaders is the prestige of the state, not the protection of the individual. The doctrine of national security is stretched in countries such as Brazil to serve the purposes of the powerful and rationalize sacrifice by the powerless. Leaders violate human rights because they consider such violations in their own personal interest or that of the state, with the two often synonymous in their minds. Such leaders do not take kindly to criticism of their "internal affairs." For example, spokesmen for the Soviet Union, while eager to point fingers at the authoritarian junta in Chile or at alleged injustice against the black defendants of the "Wilmington Ten" in the United States, reject criticism of their crackdown on Jewish dissidents as "psychological warfare." However, since the first duty of a government is to protect its own citizens, a government that sanctions arbitrary violence against them undermines its own legitimacy. Focus on human rights thus exposes the frequent tensions between the rights of the individual and those of the state. Most to the point for policymakers, it underscores the need to strengthen regional and international mechanisms that provide a court of apolitical appeal and means of redress for the individual denied dignity by his or her own government.

Attention to human rights also underscores the clash between the competing claims of the nation state and the international community. To what extent can the state be the agent of change, and to what degree must it stand for the status quo? The nature of violations of human rights suggests that it is decreasingly appropriate for the prerogative of the state to prevail. For instance, those denied access to adequate nutrition are part of a larger world food problem, which defies any wholly national solution. Further, some driven to desperation by oppression turn terrorist. International terrorism often feeds on human-rights grievances within nations at the same time that it fosters tension among them. Human rights is thus a global issue, like the environment or nuclear proliferation. It deserves to be treated as such.

*   *   *

Politics of human rights

U.S. diplomats may either take hope from the diverse tools of their trade, or despair over the obstacles before them. Whatever they do, however, depends largely on those domestic forces American diplomacy reflects.

A cynic might argue that, to serve any higher purpose, the politician must first serve himself. Much in American history suggests that Jimmy Carter is neither the first, nor likely the last, to invoke human rights partly for political advantage. Domestic considerations accounted for much of why the issue of human rights moved to the fore in the 1970s. Congress took the lead, largely to help redress the imbalance of the executive branch excess during the Vietnam period and to provide the international counterpart to the domestic civil-rights movement of the 1960s. The advent of the Carter administration meant that the White House simply continued what Capitol Hill had begun, albeit by shifting the relative position of the two branches of the government on this subject. Instead of consistently resisting congressional pressure, the Carter administration sometimes initiated activities, built on congressional leadership, and moved beyond congressional directives.

Domestic politics also explains some of the self-propelling thrust behind recent U.S. emphasis on human rights. President Carter has staked so much of his political reputation on promotion of human rights that some believe he has become hostage to his own hyperbole. He risks lost stature and votes if he retreats. On Capitol Hill, there are different, though often no less compelling, causes for continuing commitment to human rights. The issue cuts across ideologies and regions. Further, even as its costs become more apparent, many members of Congress find human rights a "motherhood issue," one that they oppose at great political peril.

Nevertheless, some domestic political considerations do constrain U.S. promotion of human rights. Just as conservative congressmen led by Senator John Bricker ripped the domestic rug out from under U.S. leadership on human rights at the United Nations during the 1950s, so may a different brand of conservatism and skepticism undercut American efforts to pursue a credible human-rights policy in the 1980s. Representative Tom Harkin sensed by 1978 a "disheartening change of attitude" toward human rights in some parts of the Congress. He was discouraged by the defeat of some of his own proposals to extend human-rights language further into the economic sector and the reluctance of many legislators to make a closer connection between the promotion of human rights at home and abroad. That congressional resistance he attributed to an attitude he described as, "I've got mine and the Hell with you." Such sentiment, plus the fear that the "loss" of Iran and Nicaragua reflects waning world power for the United States, suggests that—if stress on human rights is mismanaged or misunderstood—there could be a stunning backlash against the Carter administration's policy.

The pre-eminent role of politics in U.S. human-rights policy gives some predictability to that policy. The concerned observer of the human-rights question—whether a foreign diplomat, an American business executive, or the average citizen—can detect the likely direction of much U.S. policy. The key indices lie in public-opinion polls, the composition of the Congress, and the occupant of the White House. The main questions revolve around who stands to gain or lose by promotion of human rights.

The very predictability of much U.S. policy on human rights also reveals a disconcerting catch for those most concerned. No victim of violations can assume that the delicate balance between U.S. domestic political needs and American action on human rights abroad will tip in his or her favor. Several congressmen have admitted, off the record, that legislative restrictions against countries violating human rights may be a better index to happenstance—information on violations abroad and expressions of U.S. public interest at home that *happen* to come to light on Capitol Hill—than to the actual severity of repression. There can also be a self-serving side to the domestic impetus behind U.S. policy on human rights. Too many Americans tend to save their own souls first and ask questions later—if at all.

*   *   *

Economics of human rights

There is an important economic dimension to diplomacy and domestic politics. Senior spokesmen for the Carter administration say that they are for all human rights set forth in the U.N. Universal Declaration. Those rights include protection for the security of person, promotion of economic and social rights, and provision of political and civil liberties. In practice, the Administration has accorded highest priority to the first category and thus concentrated its protests against officially sanctioned murder, torture, and detention without trial.

Economic and social rights have received relatively short shrift, for several reasons. Most Americans do not associate them with their own traditional roster of rights. Some say there is an important difference between absolute rights that can be enforced and ideals which may take time, money, political will, and good luck to achieve. Still others say that the efforts to meet basic human needs will either cost too much or not work, no matter how much money is "thrown" at the problem.

Those *for* stressing economic and social rights marshal another array of arguments. They say that the staggering toll taken by poverty, particularly in the Third World, underscores the need to do something. The fact that hunger and malnutrition contribute to the death of over ten million people a year helps explain why many international documents on human rights give as much weight to economic and social rights as for other rights. Many spokesmen for the Carter Administration believe that there can be no lasting credibility for a human-rights policy that ignores that broad range of concerns. Those rights are complementary and mutually reinforcing. The Salvadorean *campesina* lacks decent food, in part because she has no recognized right to speak out or organize campaigns for land reform. In cases where a government keeps available resources from otherwise helpless citizens, there is no practical or moral difference between a leader who shoots the people and one who starves them. Finally, promoting fulfillment of basic economic and social rights is not a simple matter of charity. It serves long-term U.S. self-interest by defusing tensions between rich and poor and expanding access to markets and resources.

Despite such arguments, those in the Carter administration and their successors who continue the commitment to a broad reading of human rights will face substantial opposition. Arguments pitched to future payoff put most Americans in mind of the Keynesian long run, when we are all dead. It is hard for politicians to expend precious political capital and exact short-term sacrifice from taxpayers for long-term return—especially a return that must sometimes be accepted on faith.

The key to fulfilling economic and social rights in the Third World is political will. It must come, in the first place, from the leaders of developing nations. Although foreign assistance can be a catalyst or complement to indigenous economic development, it cannot be a substitute for it and certainly not when Third World leaders themselves sabotage significant economic advance. U.S. taxpayers questioned, with good reason, foreign aid given to former Nicaraguan President Somoza—when he had amassed a personal fortune of over one hundred million dollars, while the average Nicaraguan peasant earned less than one hundred dollars a year. At the same time, some significant help on meeting the basic human needs of poor people must come from the wealthy industrialized nations. Serious promotion of all human rights implies shifts of power and resources not only within nations but among them. Neither developing nor developed nations have dealt successfully with that part of the human-rights problem.

The debate so far goes thus. Spokesmen for Third World governments clamor for a transfer of resources from rich to poor nations. They seek more foreign aid from donor nations in the Organization for Economic Cooperation and Development. Many interpret the efforts of donor nations to stress the basic human needs of the poorest citizens in developing nations as a threat to their own power and a gimmick to thwart the overall economic development of their nations. For their part, leaders from countries such as the United States distrust the motives of those who want rich nations' resources, without making serious efforts to help the poor. The net effect of much U.S. foreign aid, without reform in the Third World, can be a transfer of funds from the hard-pressed U.S. taxpayer to the Swiss bank account of a greedy dictator. Elite from the North and South thus talk past each other, like characters in a Chekhov play. Victims of human-rights violations pay the price. Should that phenomenon continue, there could be a "Catch-22" for any projected bargain between developing and developed nations. If Third World leaders fail to convince the American public and its representatives of their good faith in behalf of economic and social rights, there is likely to be no *quid pro quo* between emphasis on basic human needs and the New International Economic Order. The United States may try, simply, to bow out of Third World development.

Further, the positive part of U.S. policy on human rights will probably continue to take a back seat to punitive measures. That negative tilt will prevail even though members of the Carter administration—not to mention representatives from the Third World and elsewhere—believe that rewarding respect for human rights is more effective. Most Americans are too skeptical about the prospects for promoting economic and social rights abroad to accept that argument and Congress reflects that view. Frustrated by the slow pace of economic development in the Third World and convinced that it should back its words on human rights with deeds, the Congress is using its power of the purse with parsimonious impact. The recent legislative trend has been three fold: to add increasingly specific and mandatory human-rights restrictions to U.S. bilateral and multilateral aid programs; to hold executive branch feet closer to the fire in this regard; and, more and more, to view aid and trade and the public and private sectors as part of a whole.

Such punitive measures to promote human rights abroad raise some obvious problems. A recent study of the effect of U.S. human-rights legislation concludes that "the record on direct and explicit use of foreign assistance as leverage to bring about specific improvements in human-rights conditions is hardly encouraging."[3] In doing its survey, the staff at the Library of Congress found that most interviewees in the executive branch thought that the results do not compensate for the setbacks in U.S. relations with target countries, the costs in time and conflict within the bureaucracy, and the interruptions in foreign-aid programs. (Others, however, maintained that the furor in the bureaucracy and bilateral relations had subsided after 1977, that growing consensus within the State Department on how to implement the legislation enabled continuity in A.I.D. programming, and that it was too soon to know the real effect of a comparatively new approach.)

Even though the executive branch gives mixed reviews to U.S. legislation on human rights, others do not. World Bank President Robert McNamara is among those strongly opposed to putting human-rights conditions on U.S. participation in the international financial institutions. He claims that such action "is prohibited by our charter," that it "would require information and competence which we lack," and that "there is no agreement among our member governments on acceptable standards of civil rights."⁴ The United States cannot veto loans from the multilateral development banks, except in the case of a few highly concessional loans from the Inter-American Development Bank. Its negative votes thus antagonize nations such as Argentina, Brazil, and Chile, without gaining the voting support necessary to block dispatch of funds.

Impressive as McNamara's arguments are, however, they beg the question of the real role of the large international financial institutions. The World Bank, as a specialized agency of the United Nations, has an obligation not to undercut, as it now does, promotion of human rights. Some of its biggest borrowers are among the world's most repressive regimes. McNamara himself emphasizes the need for the bank to promote "human development" that goes beyond "the simple limits of economic growth" and reaches the poor. Such development rarely occurs in societies where the poor lack access to the political process. Bank spokesmen contend that the issue of human rights is wholly a matter of internal concern for member states. That position runs counter to the prevailing interpretation of U.N. documents and, more to the point, U.N. actions. Nor are human rights only "political" issues, as bank officials argue. The flight of private capital from situations of instability reflecting violations of human rights—such as that in the Republic of South Africa—suggests that a country's human-rights record has clear economic implications. The World Bank and other multilateral development institutions should thus revise their position on human rights and devise policies to promote collective action more consonant with their stated objectives.

In the private sector, representatives of American business complain that current human-rights restrictions tie their hands, complicate corporate planning, give the edge to foreign competitors, and "make the United States an unreliable supplier." Preliminary data on the question of corporate responsibility and risk in this regard indicate that both human-rights advocates and corporate skeptics have a point. Some U.S. business activity, such as that by Gulf and Western in the Dominican Republic and Mobil Oil in southern Africa, has undercut the spirit or letter of U.S. law. On the other hand, that law has meant some lost business for American firms, with some potentially serious consequences for larger U.S. economic interests and human rights themselves. For example, many Japanese and West German firms, under little comparable pressure from their governments, have moved into traditional U.S. markets. They are far less likely than their U.S. counterparts to seek reform from repressive regimes.

However legitimate the objections from the World Bank or big business may be, there is the overriding question of impact. How effective over time, is a policy that uses primarily negative means—a "no" vote on a loan or a freeze on trade—to elicit improved performance on human rights? Are more positive means—such as increased foreign aid to governments that use the funds to help meet the basic human needs of the poor or tax benefits to U.S. firms whose foreign subsidiaries provide social benefits to their employees—more likely to foster greater respect for human rights? Although most nations, like most individuals, will probably respond more readily to the carrot than to the stick, it is still impossible to make a definitive judgment, on the basis of the limited experience with the economics of human rights. To answer that question will require unraveling the riddle of reform. How and why does it happen? To what extent can outsiders reinforce the process? How can it provide the greatest and most lasting benefit to the greatest number of people? Such issues belong high on the agenda for inquiry in the 1980s.

* * *

Prescription for a principled approach

Quandaries of this sort begin to underscore not only the problems peculiar to the economics of human rights, but also the relationship among diplomacy, politics, and economics. That interaction is, in fact, crucial and illuminating. Traditional lines do blur. There is an increasing overlap between domestic and international concerns and between political and economic issues. An unprecedented U.S. court decision in 1978 dramatized the point. The Olin Corporation was ordered to pay $512,000 for charity programs in New Haven, Connecticut, as "reparations" for its illegal arms sales to South Africa. The Jackson-Vanik Amendment is another example of overlap. It illustrates a measure with domestic political motivation, economic content, and expected diplomatic effect.

Whatever the relation among the different parts of the human-rights question, there is fear that fundamental freedoms will not flourish and that consensus may be thinner than thought. Such fear need not, however, deter advocacy of human rights. Much can be done. And, more to the point, much *should* be done.

The case for making promotion of human rights an important factor in the formulation and execution of U.S. foreign policy rests on the following four main points stressed in this book:

《 Violations of human rights constitute a major global problem.
《 The global problem affects Americans individually and collectively.
《 The United States has a responsibility to promote human rights.
《 Promotion of human rights serves the U.S. national interest.

For those who accept those arguments, the issue before the United States is not *whether* to have a policy on human rights, but *what kind*. U.S. power—even if in relative decline, as Henry Kissinger and others argue—is still so pervasive that ostrich-like isolationism is not an option. When Uncle Sam winks at violations of human rights abroad, that disregard for human dignity has an effect as surely as does taking positive action in behalf of human rights. Further, given the sheer number, the brutality, the projected increase, and the international spillover of human-rights violations, the United States faces a problem that will not go away or leave Americans immune to impact.

Failure to deal actively with the causes and effects of the growing global problem of human rights may only compound the problem. There may be, as some recent experience suggests, a penalty for passivity. For example, past American disregard for racial discrimination in southern Africa accounts for much of the mounting tension and bloodshed there now. Failure to use U.S. influence to turn the tides of either totalitarianism or authoritarianism may mean increasing isolation for the United States in the world community. Failure to dissociate the United States from oppressive regimes may hurt the U.S., politically and economically, when and if foreign leaders more respectful of human rights come to power. Finally, indifference to expressed American values does violence to Americans' view of themselves and saps domestic support for U.S. foreign policy. Although consensus of the sort that died in the Vietnam war may be neither possible nor necessary now, the experience of the 1960s indicates that American diplomacy has most enduring effect when it reflects well on Americans and their ideals.

A foreign policy that stresses promotion of human rights is thus in order. Although it may not achieve all its stated objectives—for the reasons presented in Parts I and III—it at least holds out better prospects for helping shape the kind of world that accords with expressed American goals and concrete interests, than does capitulation to oppression. To facilitate effective promotion of human rights, several general principles should govern the implementation of U.S. policy.

A broad interpretation of human rights is necessary. That reading of human rights which includes the range set forth in the U.N. Universal Declaration is most consistent with the best in American humanitarian tradition and most consonant with long-run global developments. A more narrow or traditionally Anglo-Saxon recital of political and civil rights alone misses the point of what worries much of the world and many disaffected Americans. It also misses the crucial connection between access to political and economic opportunity and, as will be explored later, misses the needed chance to shift some national priorities. Attention solely to crimes against the security of person will not suffice. Such violations of human rights, although grim in their own grisly terms, are ultimately most significant as symptoms of an underlying abuse of economic and political power. Any U.S. policy based on concerns less sweeping than those most basic economic and political rights expressed in the Universal Declaration stands little chance of achieving significant global consensus. And, without an effort to use and build on standards that do reflect broader international concern, no U.S. action can have lasting effect.

Efforts to build on that basis may deal with either the *origin* of the idea of human rights or its current *validity*. Although the belief that every human being has recognized rights may derive primarily from the eighteenth-century Enlightenment in Europe, elements can be selected from antiquity and nonwestern cultures to legitimize stress on human rights. For example, the Koran enjoins generosity toward the destitute. Further attempts to develop a broader cross-cultural consensus for human rights should not focus so much on the roots of rights in any one century or culture as on their present and evolving relevance. The central question for policymakers is not when an idea began but what appeal it has now. Which means help most people today achieve their desired ends? Are perceptions of both means and ends changing? As with the ideas of liberal democracy or Marxist theory or modern science, the idea of human rights is raising more questions for more people. Is it necessary to sacrifice democracy for development? If so, is the end worth the means? Who wins—the individual or the state? Concern with human rights is a dynamic phenomenon, changing with the changing times.

Pursuit of human rights must also be seen as part of a long-term and perhaps inevitably incomplete process. For that reason, effective espousal of human rights, like attention to economic development, is not a policy that can be turned on and off like tap water. There must be continuity of commitment so that all concerned—including victims of violations, oppressive governments, U.S. allies, representatives of U.S. economic interests, and the American public—can plan ahead and keep their sights set on long-term goals. The Carter administration and its successors will thus have to take special pains to help assure continuing dedication to human dignity and to make clear how promotion of human rights serves Americans' long-term interests, albeit at some short-term cost. Like the proverbial journey of a thousand miles, it begins with a single step. Each release of a political prisoner and each meal to a starving child marks another step on a journey—not unlike that begun in 1776 by a small band of American dissidents who declared that all men are endowed with certain inalienable rights. Just as the Declaration of Independence was a revolutionary document that has yet to be fulfilled, so, too, is the Universal Declaration, with its attempt to improve the way all governments deal with their citizens, a revolutionary document with a growing appeal over time.

How long Jimmy Carter remains in the White House is important to the promotion of human rights, since he has placed unprecedented U.S. emphasis on the issue, but *not* essential. Even the most hard-nosed chief executive is likely to confront a new reality in the 1980s and beyond. "Human rights," in the words of one senior official at the Department of State, "now has a seat at the table." It has a political life of its own that cannot be reversed easily, because of U.S. domestic legislation and because of the proliferation of human-rights officers throughout much of the federal bureaucracy. It also has an international foundation that cannot be wholly eroded. For example, now that victims of violations know that they can appeal to respected nongovernmental organizations, the United Nations, world leaders, and the media, and that they can mobilize public opinion, they are not likely again to suffer in silence. The commitment to human rights of Pope John Paul II, as the charismatic leader of the world's 720 million Roman Catholics, attests *inter alia* to the fact that the United States is not alone in its advocacy of freedom. Former Soviet leader Josef Stalin once asked in a mocking question about the Pope near the end of World War II, "How many divisions does he have?" The answer for both the Pope and other influential forces behind world public opinion may be "Quite a few."

The key issue of implementation for U.S. policymakers is not direction, but degree. How much, realistically, can be done? The United States cannot take on promotion of all human rights all at once in all countries, given the awesome political and economic constraints on its resources. Nor should it. There may be no apparent solution to some of the problems outlined in previous discussion. Even though the relation between economic and political oppression may suggest to some an active campaign to overthrow dictators, prudence precludes dispatch of U.S. Marines forthwith or revival of the C.I.A.'s dirtiest tricks. This is a political fact of life because the citizens of the concerned countries can best achieve sustained change for themelves and because most Americans oppose that kind of direct intervention. The achievement of some goals, such as developing political will at home and abroad to fulfill economic and social rights, will require considerable patience and shift of perspective. Efforts to make people more aware of the opportunities open to them—points often made most effectively over time by such means as education and exchange programs—may have most influence. Some concerns, such as planning follow-up on the Helsinki Final Act or action at the next U.N. General Assembly, are more straightforward and can be tackled immediately.

The task before the United States is to differentiate among the categories of the ideal, the desirable, and the possible. Solidifying impressive gains already made and maintaining momentum would in itself be significant. To do so, however, requires a better choice of focus, timing, and perspective. U.S. policy on human rights will gain most credibility and have more impact if it starts with a sense of priority—What is most important?—and management—How can officials proceed effectively?

High on the list of priorities is the need to recognize that concentration on consistency misses the point. There can and should be consistent determination to take human rights into serious account for U.S. foreign policy. Yet stress on human rights must at all times be weighed against other factors. A rigid rubric for human rights can obscure the importance of other goals, some of which may have overarching global significance. For example, nuclear nonproliferation and military strength bear on that most fundamental human right—survival. Further, tactics must be tailored to time, place, and circumstance. As Allard Lowenstein, U.S. representative to the 1977 session of the U.N. Human Rights Commission, observed, "The world is at the same point in its history, but every country is at a different point in its history."[5] The diversity of national situations argues for a well-conceived case-by-case approach, albeit with the caveat that that method not amount to capitulation on more general commitment to human rights. The United States should undertake continuing reformulation and review of its programs to achieve greater respect for human rights in individual countries. Those programs should constitute plans for action that specify what major human-rights problems exist in each country, what can be done, how, and how fast—and how action vis-à-vis the human-rights situation in one country relates to comparable activity elsewhere. Although the United States can play an important role by encouraging those who promote human rights and by not supporting repression, its policymakers should operate according to the premise that their actions can, at most, reinforce the will of the people most concerned—the victims of violations.

Developing a case-by-case course of action need not preclude an overall U.S. strategy on human rights. Indeed, it should not. There must be more general objectives for U.S. policy, made clear to all practitioners of U.S. foreign policy and to their counterparts abroad. Those objectives should include trying to save particular indidividuals or groups from harm at the hands of their governments; reducing the most extreme abuses, such as officially sanctioned torture and murder; improving more general respect for human rights, with increasing regard for the promotion of economic and social rights; dissociating the United States from especially oppressive governments; and creating an international atmosphere more conducive to promotion of human rights than now exists. Although the United States should make clear its concern on all such counts, it should place greatest stress on those core rights that are critical to individual survival—such as prevention of arbitrary murder, torture, or starvation—and crucial to human dignity—such as blatant racial or sexual discrimination.

Better management of the human-rights issue in U.S. foreign policy depends, in part, on improved consultations within the U.S. government, and between Washington and other national capitals. The record of this last decade reflects poor communication between the U.S. Congress and the executive branch, for different reasons, under both a Republican and a Democratic administration. More consultation might help the U.S. government speak with a more coherent voice on human rights. Further, more consultation by the U.S. government with its national counterparts could help build on the international base that is essential for implementating the already existing legal framework on human rights. For example, until more nations consult more often and seriously about human-rights issues and take human-rights criteria into consideration in their bilateral and multilateral aid programs, U.S. economic tools in that regard will remain relatively weak instruments. Until more governments encourage private firms under their jurisdiction to take human rights into consideration in their decisions for investment and trade, U.S. human-rights legislation could cause both short- and long-term harm to American firms and lead to a congressional rollback on U.S. laws regarding international promotion of human rights. Without more multilateral determination to back up words with concerted action, there will not be much significant movement toward increased respect for human rights.

*   *   *

Roster of remaining issues

Effective U.S. management of the human-rights issue must also include more attention to unresolved or emerging questions. Raising the subject of human rights means lifting the lid on what amounts to a Pandora's box for American diplomacy. As suggested in this book, there are several diverse issues that deserve particular attention. They are important now and are likely to remain so for the foreseeable future.

There is, first, the question of information: how to get it, assess it and disseminate it. One of the ironies of the human-rights problem is the fact that, while the revolution in communications has made more people than ever before aware of violations of human rights, it has, at the same time, tempted governments to close more doors and borders. Dictators, angered by disclosures of violations in their domain, are clamping down on reporters. Cambodia under the Khmer Rouge may have been one of the most extreme examples of this crackdown on free access to and release of information. That trend, however, has been pronounced for some time in communist countries and is now growing in the Third World. There are instances of physical harassment. In 1977, a *Washington Post* reporter was accused of being a spy and thus beaten, kicked unconscious, and held incommunicado by the former Emperor Bokassa I of what was then called the Central African Empire. In 1979, the brutality of the Somoza government was brought home for Americans when the nightly news showed Bill Stewart, an ABC-TV correspondent, shot, point-blank, by a member of the Nicaraguan national guard. While leaders elsewhere have taken less extreme actions, they have made clear that they believe prerogatives of internal security and/or economic development preclude free-wheeling reports on their countries.

Against this backdrop, journalists must often choose between holding back facts or packing their bags. They face a situation—according to a UNESCO report on global communications released in early 1980—in which more and more governments regard information as a national resource. It is one that they are increasingly determined to protect. Expanded restrictions on information could hamstring human-rights advocates. They depend on access to information to learn about new victims of violations, and they need the media to help mobilize international outrage against repression. A free press is the last line of defense for human rights and the litmus test for the triumph of openness over oppression. The United States, together with other nations, should therefore take all possible steps—in the United Nations, in follow-up on the Helsinki Final Act, and elsewhere—to assure freedom of information.[6]

There is another side to the information issue. Most reports on human rights—whether prepared by the U.S. government, by other governments, or by multilateral organizations such as the United Nations or the Organization of American States—appear tainted politically. They lack credibility. There is thus the need, to the extent possible, to depoliticize the collection of information. Governments such as that in the United States, which prepare annual reviews of human-rights performance abroad, should stop writing report cards on each other. Instead, nongovernmental organizations should form a global data bank on human-rights violations and trends of performance. Such organizations—with links to the First, Second, and Third Worlds and *no* financing from any government—could provide the United Nations and other interested organizations and governments with reports that reflect needed scope and dispassionate assessment. Other efforts could be made on a regional basis. For example, a nongovernmental mechanism for systematic collection and assessment of complaints from victims of violations in C.S.C.E. signatory states could provide a significant step forward for depoliticization of the process begun by the Helsinki Final Act and fuller implementation of that document.

Second, stress on human rights underscores questions about the role of democracy in economic development. Spokesmen for many governments, as well as many academic commentators, argue that political liberty is a luxury that poor nations cannot afford. Therefore, economic development demands authoritarian or totalitarian rule and subordination of individual rights to the collective good.

The record from most of the Third World does not support that argument. For the most part, aggregate economic growth with impressive increases in Gross National Product has not translated into economic development that trickles down to the majority of citizens. Even when the national economic pie has grown larger, their relative and absolute slice has not. As the case of the Salvadorean peasant suggests, part of the reason lies in the relationship between economic and political repression. It is an issue which emphasis on human rights aptly joins. Even though political democracy is incomplete without economic democracy, the latter is impossible without the former. Democracy of either sort assumes that the individual need not be an expert to understand and articulate his hopes and requirements. Or, as the old saying goes, he who wears the shoe knows best where it pinches. It is thus insulting to citizens of the Third World, and inaccurate as well, to claim that only Western children of the Enlightenment care about individual dignity and can achieve it.

The fact that five hundred million of the earth's poor go to bed hungry is hard for most Americans to grasp. In the United States, *over*eating is a national obsession. Millions spend more on losing weight in one month than most persons in the Third World earn in one year. It is thus difficult to realize that starvation in Cambodia is not an isolated quirk of history, but part of a persistent global pattern. For Americans—and others—to agonize over pictures of starving Cambodians, but not try to reverse the economic and political causes of their plight, is to assure that next year yet another nation is host to hunger.

The challenge for U.S. policymakers is to facilitate genuine reform. There is still no clear understanding of how to achieve lasting and constructive change, whether in Afghanistan or Appalachia. There is much to be learned on many fronts in the 1980s about the "participatory democracy" that was the rhetorical vogue of the 1960s. Although emphasis on meeting basic human needs as one of several goals of U.S. foreign economic assistance may be a step in the right direction, there is little indication that U.S. policymakers know how to make foreign aid truly effective. How can it be channeled to those who need it most? How, in the absence of clearer impact on the needy, can (or should) American taxpayers be persuaded to allocate more money for foreign aid? How can recipient nations be engaged more effectively in achieving change? Indeed, to what extent is fundamental change possible, and to what degree would it affect present and future U.S. public and private interests? These are the sorts of questions that are often raised, but have yet to be resolved. They require attention, at the highest level of the U.S. government, if promotion of human rights is to have more than marginal effect.

Third, an activist, broad-based policy must deal with the question of at least two categories of victims of violations that are often overlooked. One is refugees and the other is women.

Whether political exiles without countries or economic outcasts without a means to livelihood, refugees constitute a large and growing problem. The number of refugees—estimated at twelve to thirteen million—could double over the next decade, as pressure related to both promotion and oppression of human rights builds. There is no comprehensive U.S. or international policy for dealing with the movement or displacement of persons—at least not of the scale indicated by recent developments in Southeast Asia and Africa and those possible elsewhere. There are lessons to be learned from the mass murder of Cambodians. To help avoid repeating such tragedy, the world community should adopt a sterner stance on genocide, perhaps including a new U.N. convention that provides sanctions against guilty regimes, and permit the U.N. High Commissioner for Refugees to intervene directly when whole communities are threatened with extinction or expulsion. The United States itself needs to improve its response to refugees, with more provision for long-term planning and a presidential coordinator with genuine latitude for action. Moreover, the issue of people forced to move needs to be addressed as an integral part of U.S. policy on human rights, both in terms of overall review of U.S. immigration law and in terms of its relation to economic development. On the latter point, for example, unless and until economic development in Mexico filters down to the majority, the flood of Hispanics into the United States will continue, and efforts to deal with illegal aliens will be a piecemeal palliative after the fact.

The United States, despite its disgraceful delay in ratifying the Equal Rights Amendment, has a relatively good record on furthering the rights of U.S. women. Where more attention *is* needed is in the Third World. There the United States should, as part of its overall human-rights policy and stress on basic human needs, put greater emphasis on the role of women in economic and political development. Until women like the Salvadorean *campesina* have an opportunity to learn about family planning, better health care, and nutrition and have access to general education or vocational training, they are not likely to break out of the cycle of pregnancy and poverty which compounds the population problem and economic underdevelopment of the Third World. Further, unless efforts are made to involve women in community action and politics, they are not likely to gain many economic advantages. U.S. efforts in behalf of women's rights, both by the government and by private organizations, could help meet the minimal goals set by the United Nations for the Decade for Women, 1976–85. Focus on fulfillment of rights for women will be essential to the long-term realization of rights for both men and women.

Fourth, there is the still-unanswered question of the proper role for U.S. business in the area of human rights. Is there, as many social activists charge, a legitimate issue of accountability? Do business firms have a moral responsibility to the community in which they operate? If so, for what?

The global reach of the American multinational corporation makes it an inevitable and powerful participant in the treatment of human rights, no matter what business executives may think of mixing morality with profit margins. Heads of major corporations and banks often have close working relationships with repressive rulers. Indeed, they often must, in order to do business in some countries. An estimated 30 percent of all world trade is handled by the multinationals. In addition to the power and *modus operandi* of many Fortune 500 firms, the U.S. Congress has extended its human-rights purview from the public to the private sector. Decisions based on current human-rights legislation help define when or if a deal can go through. There are indications from Senator Edward Kennedy and others that more such legislation may surface.

That said, neither the Congress nor the executive branch—not to mention the major corporations—has looked in depth at the implications of using the private sector to promote human rights. Before more important precedents are set, representatives from the executive branch and the Congress should consider the larger issues at play: to what extent should or can the U.S. government seek support from U.S. private business to help make official stress on international human rights more effective? Is there an inevitable contradiction between what remains of the free-enterprise system and the promotion of human rights in general and economic growth with equity in particular? Is one sovereign state justified in using economic power to try to affect what some consider the internal affairs of another? Can sanctions work? If so, where and with what consequences for whom? What does using economic instruments for political purposes do to the global system of trade and finance?

Such questions suggest that Americans and others should reassess current conventional wisdom about multinational corporations. Most discussion so far has generated more heat than help. Just as many business executives misunderstand or underestimate resentment against the large transnational firms, so, too, do many critics of the corporations react against them with too much emotion and too little information. Leaders from many developing nations view them as the twentieth-century equivalent of colonial trading companies, which enrich themselves and the metropole at the expense of the Third World.

Several points need to be made. Big is not necessarily bad. Nor do all corporations operate the same way in all countries. Some do sap the vital fluids from the societies of their host nations. Others play a uniquely constructive role in increasing standards of living for the poor. U.S. companies are not the only alleged villains of the piece. Third World multinationals, such as those based in Singapore, South Korea, or Taiwan, operate widely in Asia and the Mideast.

The likely long-term trend, if there is to be much increased respect for human rights, is for more overlap between private and public and between national and international actions. There is thus need—among government officials and academics and within the business community and international organizations—to probe whereof they speak and act. With the requisite homework done on the proper role for business in the promotion of human rights, there will be a better chance to avoid the extremes of either rash expropriation of U.S. property or callous exploitation of the poor by American firms, and so to proceed on a course most constructive for all concerned.

* * *

Relation between human rights and national interest

Important as the above questions are, there is yet another that deserves special attention by Americans. The issue: should promotion of human rights—in the broadest sense of political, civil, economic, social, and cultural rights—initate a larger debate on U.S. national priorities? Opponents of that perspective resist what they view as efforts to shove every general problem into the human-rights tent. They stress serious attention to the allegedly definable foreign-policy aspect of human rights and concentration on curtailing crimes against the security of person. Proponents of the wider view claim that the significance of human rights as an issue derives in part from the fact that it reflects, in microcosm, the diverse range of challenges before U.S. policy. The human-rights issue pervades traditional concerns about national security and domestic consensus, as well as the newer questions raised in North-South and East-West relations and debates about the "crisis of democracy" and "quality of life" within advanced industrial nations.

Although balance may well lie between the proverbial extremes, this book embraces the newer and more controversial view. Serious promo-

CONCLUSION 265

tion of human rights should lead to a redefinition of the U.S. national interest.

That process has begun. But just barely. "National security" remains a catch-all phrase that can mean all things to all people. There has been no probing debate of the concept since it emerged after World War II. No major figures in the Carter administration or the Congress challenge the underlying assumptions about how the United States should use its resources for the security of the nation or the world. Policymakers and politicians reflect and reinforce public-opinion polls which indicate that most Americans think security means having more and better weapons than the Soviet Union. Many commentators dismiss the failure of superior U.S. arms in Vietnam or the conquest of the Shah's arsenal and Somoza's bunker by aggrieved citizens as lapses in American *machismo*.

Thus, the questions about U.S. policy that open this decade may skirt the issues most crucial to the national interest. Members of Congress ask, not whether to cut the defense budget, but how much to raise it. They ask, not whether to increase allocations for the basic needs of the poor in America and elsewhere, but how to reduce such assistance. There are, of course, legitimate reasons to assure a strong and credible national defense and to curb budgetary excess. There are, at the same time, comparably compelling reasons to assure that money spent on the national defense achieves stated goals.

If only to be cost effective, advocacy of human rights must advance beyond such specific concerns as the release of political prisoners to more general questions. For example, is America's military stake in many authoritarian regimes as great as often argued—or does the very authoritarian nature of some U.S. allies undercut U.S. security? Siding with some dictators may prove necessary, even after re-examination of the relationship. No nation, including the United States, can choose its allies solely on the basis of shared values. On the other hand, assisting some oppressive leaders may not be the best way to ward off communist takeover; it may in fact be the worst. Most U.S. policymakers seem to prefer the short-term stability and possible long-run instability of tyrannical rule to the short-term instability and possible long-run stability of fundamental reform. It is time to shift postwar gears.

If review of long-standing relationships is in order, so, too, is reassessment of some newer ties. Greater attention to human rights has raised questions about increased U.S. dependence on several so-called emerging middle powers, among them Saudi Arabia and Brazil. Clearly, there are significant reasons for developing good relations with nations that have economic, strategic, or geopolitical importance. At the same time, balance here, as in other spheres of diplomacy, is prudent. Before linking the United States too closely with authoritarian regimes, there should be careful evaluation of the alleged stability of such governments, the options open for U.S. contacts in those countries, the range of U.S. commitments (particularly in the area of sophisticated weaponry), and the potential for anti-American backlash, should the governments in question fall.

Events in Iran suggest the danger of overdoing a marriage of convenience, where the long-range benefit is more apparent than real, and of overlooking what is really happening in the country concerned. The United States, through the Central Intelligence Agency, helped return Shah Mohammed Reza Pahlavi to power in 1953 and set up his secret police. Under pressure from the Kennedy administration, the Shah launched a series of reforms, dubbed grandiloquently the "White Revolution." Significant as it was in, for example, expanding rights for women and providing social services, there was still less to the program than the Shah led most to believe. Land reform brought little reward to the small farmer. More than half of the Iranian population remained illiterate.

U.S. actions in the 1970s served primarily to compound earlier misperceptions and mistakes. Much of the new wealth from oil went not to the poor but to the rich, and not for assuring equitable economic growth but for buying elaborate weapons systems. A meeting between former President Richard Nixon and the Shah in 1972—buttressed by Nixon's secretly authorizing the sale of any weapon, short of an atomic bomb, to Iran—helped lead to a buying binge worth billions of dollars. Throughout most of the 1970s, officials of the U.S. government ignored the shortcomings of the Shah because of the value placed on Iran's strategic position next to the Soviet Union, its oil, and its willingness to buy U.S. arms. Those sales served the dual purposes of shoring up the U.S. balance of payments and making the Shah the guardian of the Persian Gulf.

Senior officials during both the Nixon-Ford years and the first two years of the Carter administration knew little about what was simmering above and below the surface in Iran. There was an unspoken and self-imposed policy of not contacting opponents to the Shah, lest he be offended. Officers at the U.S. embassy in Teheran who questioned restrictions on contacts with opposition leaders or the Islamic establishment were told that critical information might be leaked and distorted by the Shah's enemies. Those signs of trouble that U.S. officials in Washington did detect, such as the reports of torture by the Iranian secret police publicized in congressional hearings and the press, they chose, for the most part, to ignore. Two tendencies grew and reinforced each other in the process: the inclination to view Iran through the Shah's imperial periscope and the propensity to equate U.S. interests with those of the Pahlavi dynasty. Thus, on the eve of the year that the Shah was to fall from power, President Carter, while in Teheran, called Iran "an island of stability." There was order because, he said, toasting the Shah, of the "love of your people for you."

Many critics of the Carter administration were to blame the president's human-rights policy for pushing the Shah from power. Although Carter's expressed support for human rights did lead many in Iran to believe that the Shah could no longer count on full U.S. support and thus did give increased courage to his opponents, that shift in American policy was not the critical factor in the Shah's downfall. The Shah toppled from the Peacock Throne primarily because of his own hubris. With mounting economic mismangement and corruption and no meaningful political outlet for cultural dislocation and economic grievances, he could not contain widespread and growing condemnation of his repressive rule. The answer, then, to the question "Who lost Iran?" is not Jimmy Carter, but the Shah himself.[7]

The answer to who lost because U.S. policymakers backed a loser may well be the American people. In the aftermath of the Shah's departure, there was concern about abandoned weaponry and sophisticated equipment, decreased means to verify SALT II, reduced supplies of oil, and increased uncertainty along what Brzezinski called the "arc of crisis" extending from Turkey to the Persian Gulf. There was predictably bitter anti-Americanism which surged to the surface with the seizure of the U.S. embassy in late 1979 and the ensuing crisis.

Such events underscore a fundamental question: is U.S. national interest best served by the *Realpolitik* espoused by Henry Kissinger or the stress on human rights—expressed but not fully practiced in the

Iranian case—by Jimmy Carter? "It is not clear," as one senior political appointee in the Carter administration said, "that getting on the Ayatollah's bandwagon would have gotten us off his death-list." It is, however, arguable that in Iran, as elsewhere, Americans would be better off, not with less emphasis on human rights, but with more.

Treatment of human rights relates to the nature of political change in much of the Third World and what the United States can or should do about it. Whether dictators make lasting allies and whether so-called liberal values bolster or destabilize developing nations are important issues for U.S. foreign policy in the 1980s.

Looking at what really lies behind violations of human rights in countries such as Iran may be important, not only because it provides insight into longer-term U.S. national security, but also because it may provide a sounder basis for reviewing the largely dormant North-South dialogue between developed and developing nations—and thus also serve American interests. Both U.S. emphasis on economic and social rights and Third World stress on the New International Economic Order deal with redistribution of resources. If the developed nations accede to the developing countries' demands for more assistance, the donors may require that their aid to developing nations reach the poor. U.S. policymakers should seize on the makings of a mutually advantageous bargain. The fact that more U.S. exports now go to developing countries than to Japan or Europe and that almost half of all U.S. direct foreign investment is in the Third World suggests a strong U.S. stake in the progress of poor countries. It is one that cannot be separated from U.S. national security and well-being. Whether the United States can afford stress on basic human needs depends on how or if Americans decide to reorder national and global priorities.

The contrast is striking between the amount of money spent on defense world-wide—now over $400 billion a year—and the less than $30 billion spent on the problems of energy, health, education, and food combined. Most to the point, that contrast, like the U.S. stake in Third World economic development, highlights the question of *real* security and sensible priorities. Excessive spending on military hardware may reduce, not increase, security because such outlays divert resources needed to alleviate the misery of more than one billion human beings.

The need to reassess national interest is no less urgent in the area of East-West relations than in the North-South context. The tendency of some U.S. officials to crow about what they call the "ideological offensive" gained from pressing for human rights in the Soviet Union and of some congressmen to cling to narrow concepts of linkage is a mistake. It not only makes leaders from developing nations believe that the U.S. human-rights campaign is warmed-over Cold War rhetoric; it obscures, more importantly, the overriding U.S. national interest in pursuing a rational route to *rapprochement* with the Soviet Union. The U.S. response to human rights in the U.S.S.R. should move beyond understandable focus on Jewish refuseniks to reflect the diverse concerns within the entire community of Soviet dissidents and broader and longer-term changes within Soviet and East European society.

No attention to pursuing human rights in East-West or North-South relations makes much sense without reference to what is happening close to home. For example, any transfer of resources, even if proclaimed in the name of human rights, seems doomed if leaders within the industrial nations will not or cannot look beyond their own immediate problems. Persistent inflation and slow economic growth may cripple many efforts to meet basic human needs at home, not to mention abroad. Terrorism by young extremists and counter-attacks by governments in Italy, the Federal Republic of Germany, and elsewhere may underscore the fragility of political and civil rights. There is a need to understand how deep the roots for human rights go in the so-called advanced democracies and what determination remains to nurture them.

The new perspective on national interest that stress on human rights might engender thus depends on the domestic underpinnings for diplomacy. Does U.S. reformist zeal in behalf of human rights reach into America's own backyard? Americans have stressed in public-opinion polls that they consider it most important to set a good example. Providing a better model might mean complementing the nation's considerable protection of political and civil rights with greater efforts to fulfill economic and social rights. The decay of a neighborhood such as the South Bronx can make a mockery of American declarations on economic and social rights elsewhere. There may be more Nightmare than Dream to the real-life statistics that stand on inner-city street corners (an estimated 40 to 60 percent of black and Hispanic teenagers are unemployed); the elderly who huddle alone, afraid and impoverished; and those subject to subhuman conditions in some U.S. prisons.

Just as there is no way to separate politics from economics in the practice of diplomacy, so, too, is there no neat divide between domestic and foreign affairs. Without sensitivity to that connection, there can be no lasting credibility, at home and abroad, for U.S. policy on human rights. If one of Jimmy Carter's original reasons for promoting human rights was to restore public consensus behind U.S. foreign policy, that venture could be either hoist with its own petard by failure to apply human-rights standards inside the United States, or used to establish an entirely new agreement on national goals.

Therein lie both the peril and the promise of U.S. policy on human rights. On the one hand, retreat into a narrow reading of human rights and refusal to address deprivation of human dignity at home could mean that traditionally espoused values fade into ambivalence. Americans may become their own worst enemy. On the other hand, forward movement on human rights could help the campaign that began as a product of reappraisal in the 1960s become the precursor of new priorities in the 1980s.

Rhetoric that rings out across the country every Fourth of July suggests that a Dream possesses the American people. They are special. They are part of a unique pact—a nation, in Abraham Lincoln's words, "conceived in liberty and dedicated to the proposition that all men are created equal." But Americans also have a history of struggle. Clashes between expressed ideals and less lofty interests mar their tradition. Where Americans have most often erred is in seeking uncritically to fulfill their Dream or to foist it inappropriately onto others. The lieutenant in Vietnam who said, "We had to destroy the village in order to save it," embodied the dark side of a distorted vision. Most Americans, however, believe that those who have given their lives for freedom elsewhere, opened their communities to the homeless, or given aid to the needy are more representative. In fact, Americans are probably, as historian Michael Kammen concludes, "people of paradox."

Promotion of human rights, pursued to its fullest potential, drives Americans to their roots. The issue forces them to confront their values, their deeds, and the reality of their nation's power. In more personal terms, the faces of the Cambodian refugee, the Soviet dissident, and the Salvadorean peasant bring Americans full circle to themselves and their own reflection. The face they see is their own.

That face mirrors the agony and the opportunity of a nation born with and bound to a Dream. Stripped of romanticized myth and makeup, there *is* a special claim to morality, but no unique title. And there is more. There is cause to follow the Dream. Promoting human rights as part of that venture can serve both pragmatism and principle, both hard-nosed interest and humanitarian impulse. The two are, in fact, related. There is also, given the resources of the nation and the often impressive resolve of the people, capacity to fulfill the Dream.

Carl Sandburg wrote: "The republic is a dream. Nothing happens unless first a dream."[8] Americans have such a vision, but have not fully decided how to realize it. Theirs is a nation that has yet, in its third century, to reveal its true nature. It is continuing to develop. The American Revolution is still, like a furled flag, unfolding. What Americans actually do to promote human rights at home and abroad, despite all the unanswered and unanswerable questions, will do much to disclose the real national character and destiny. Serious pursuit of human rights could compel Americans to reconsider what they believe and how much. It could open the door to a needed redefinition of national direction.

Americans say they are all for human rights, but are less clear on what they will pay for them. Old issues assume new significance. Who Americans are and what their policy against oppression may become depend, finally and fundamentally, on response to the question that launched the Republic: what price principle? Violations of human rights constitute a global nightmare. How Americans deal with that nightmare may determine what happens to their Dream.

Notes

1. *Amnesty International Report* 1978 (London: Amnesty International Publications, 1979), pp. 3–4.
2. Quoted by Mort Rosenblum, "Terror in Argentina," *The New York Review of Books*, vol. 23, no. 7 (October 28, 1976), 27.
3. Stanley J. Heginbotham, ed., "Human Rights and U.S. Foreign Assistance," study by the staff of the Library of Congress for the Senate Foreign Relations Committee, July 1979.
4. Quoted by *The New York Times*, April 2, 1978.
5. *Review of the United Nations Thirty-Third Commission on Human Rights*, Hearing before the Subcommittee on International Organizations of the Committee on International Relations, House of Representatives, Ninety-fifth Congress, First Session, May 19, 1977 (Washington, D.C.: U.S. Government Printing Office, 1977), p. 13.
6. For a helpful discussion of this issue, see Sean Kelly, *Access Denied: The Politics of*

Press Censorship (Beverly Hills, Calif.: Sage Publications, 1978). I am also indebted to Richard Blystone, correspondent for the Associated Press and Edward R. Murrow Fellow at the Council on Foreign Relations, 1977–78, for his insight into this subject and for arranging briefings with the highest officials of the Associated Press.

7. See the Bibliography for numerous articles that document this perspective and thus complement or reinforce views of U.S. officials expressed on background. Note also that, according to public-opinion polls taken in the United States in 1979, most Americans—while giving Carter only "fair" marks for his handling of the Iranian situation—agreed that the Shah had been his own worst enemy and that the U.S. should not have intervened to bail him out.

8. Carl Sandburg, "Washington Monument by Night."

Bibliography

Articles and Reports

Ajami, Fouad. "Human Rights and World Order Politics." *Alternatives*, vol. 3, no. 3 (March 1978), 351–83.

―――. "Human Rights: Sermons or Substance." *The Nation*, vol. 224, no. 13 (April 2, 1977), 389–90.

Apple, R. W., Jr. "Iran: Heart of the Matter." *The New York Times Magazine*, March 11, 1979, pp. 19, 101–2, 104–6.

Ball, George. "Asking for Trouble in South Africa." *Atlantic Monthly*, October 1977, pp. 43–51.

Baraheni, Reza. "Terror in Iran." *New York Review of Books*, vol. 23, no. 17 (October 28, 1976), 21–25.

Barghoorn, Frederick C. "Democratic Movement in the USSR." *Society*, vol. 13, no. 5 (July 1976), 59–74.

Barnet, Richard J. "Carter's Patchwork Doctrine." *Harper's*, (August 1977, pp. 27–34.

Berger, Peter L. "Are Human Rights Universal?" *Commentary*, vol. 64, no. 3 (September 1977), 60–63.

Bilder, Richard B. "Human Rights and U.S. Foreign Policy: Short-term Prospects." *The Virginia Journal of International Law*, vol. 14, no. 4 (Summer 1974), 597–609.

Birnbaum, Karl E. "Human Rights and East-West Relations." *Foreign Affairs*, vol. 55, no. 4 (July 1977), 783–99.

Bishop, Joseph W., Jr. "Can Democracy Defend Itself Against Terrorism?" *Commentary*, vol. 65, no. 5 (May 1978), 55–62.

Blumberg, Abraham. "Dissent in Russia." *Foreign Affairs*, vol. 52, no. 4 (July 1974), 781–98.

Bordeaux, Michael. "The Persecution of Christians in the USSR." *Case Studies on Human Rights and Fundamental Freedoms*, vol. 4. The Hague: Martinus Nijhoff, 1976, 537–68.

Bozeman, Adda B. "How to Think about Human Rights: the Human Factor in U.S.–Soviet Relations." *Proceedings of the National Security Affairs Conference—1977*. New York: National Strategy Information Center, Inc., 1977.

Brown, Seyom. "A Cooling-off Period for U.S.–Soviet Relations." *Foreign Policy*, no. 28 (Fall 1977), pp. 3–21.

Buckley, William F., Jr. "Mr. Carter's Discovery of Human Rights." *National Review*, vol. 29, no. 12 (April 1, 1977), 402.

———. "Pinochet and Human Rights," *National Review*, vol. 29, no. 10 (March 18, 1977), 350–51.

Buergenthal, Thomas. "Implementing the U.N. Racial Convention." *Texas International Law Journal*, vol. 12, nos. 2 and 3 (Spring/Summer 1977), 187–221.

———. "International and Regional Human Rights Law and Institutions: Some Examples of Their Interaction." *Texas International Law Journal*, vol. 12, nos. 2 and 3 (Spring/Summer 1977), 321–30.

———. "International Human Rights: U.S. Policy and Priorities," *The Virginia Journal of International Law*, vol. 14, no. 4 (Summer 1974), 611–21.

———. "The Revised O.A.S. Charter and the Protection of Human Rights." *American Journal of International Law*, vol. 69, no. 4 (October 1975), 828–36.

Bundy, William P. "Who Lost Patagonia? Foreign Policy in the 1980 Campaign." *Foreign Affairs*, vol. 58, no. 1 (Fall 1979), 1–27.

Chace, James. "How 'Moral' Can We Get?" *The New York Times Magazine*, May 22, 1977, pp. 38–49.

———. "Is a Foreign Policy Consensus Possible?" *Foreign Affairs*, vol. 57, no. 1 (Fall 1978), 1–16.

Cottam, Richard; Schoenbaum, David; Chubin, Shahram; Moran, Theodore H.; and Falk, Richard A. "The United States and Iran's Revolution." *Foreign Policy*, no. 34 (Spring 1979), pp. 3–34.

Deedy, J. "Human Rights." *Commonweal*, vol. 104, no. 8 (April 15, 1977), 226.

Drew, Elizabeth. "A Reporter at Large—Human Rights," *New Yorker*, July 18, 1977, pp. 36–62.

Dunner, Joseph. "Anti-Jewish Discrimination since the End of World War II." *Case Studies on Human Rights and Fundamental Freedoms*, vol. 1. The Hague: Martinus Nijhoff, 1976, 65–110.

Dushnyck, Walter. "Discrimination and Abuse of Power in the USSR." *Case Studies on Human Rights and Fundamental Freedoms*, vol. 2. The Hague: Martinus Nijhoff, 1976, 447–555.

Editors. "Torture as Policy: The Network of Evil." *Time*, August 16, 1976, pp. 31–34.

Emerson, Rupert. "The Fate of Human Rights in the Third World." *World Politics*, vol. 27, no. 2 (January 1975), 201–26.

Farer, Tom J. "The Laws of War 25 Years After Nuremberg." *International Conciliation*, no. 583 (May 1971), entire issue.

———. "United States Foreign Policy and the Protection of Human Rights:

Observations and Proposals." *The Virginia Journal of International Law*, vol. 14, no. 4 (Summer 1974), 623–51.

Fox, Donald T. "Report on Mission to El Salvador." For the International Commission of Jurists, September 1978.

Fraser, Donald M. "Freedom and Foreign Policy." *Foreign Policy*, no. 26 (Spring 1977), 140–56.

———. "Human Rights and U.S. Foreign Policy." *International Studies Quarterly*, vol. 23, no. 2 (June 1979), 174–85.

Gastil, Raymond D. "Pluralist Democracy and the Third World." *Worldview*, vol. 21, no. 10 (October 1978), 37–42.

Geyer, Georgie Anne. "From Here to Eternity." *Washington Post Magazine*, September 10, 1978, pp. 8–12, 14, 16–17.

Goodin, Robert E. "The Development-Rights Tradeoff: Some Unwarranted Economic and Political Assumptions." *Universal Human Rights*, vol. 1, no. 2 (April–June 1979), 31–42.

Green, James Frederick. "Changing Approaches to Human Rights: The United Nations, 1954 and 1974." *Texas International Law Journal*, vol. 12, nos. 2 and 3 (Spring/Summer 1977), 223–38.

Gupta, Jyotirindra. "A Season of Caesars: Emergency Regimes and Development Politics in Asia." *Asian Survey*, vol. 18, no. 4 (April 1978), 315–49.

Gushchin, Victor. "Human Rights in the Soviet Union—Putting the Record Straight." *New Times*, no. 1 (January 1976), pp. 18–22.

Hartmann, Betsy, and Boyce, James. "Bangladesh: Aid to the Needy?" *International Policy Report*, vol. 4, no. 1, May 1978.

Hawk, David. "Human Rights at Half-Time." *New Republic*, vol. 180, no. 14 (April 7, 1979), 21–23.

Henkin, Louis. "The United States and the Crisis in Human Rights." *The Virginia Journal of International Law*, vol. 14, no. 4 (Summer 1974), 653–71.

Hesburgh, Theodore M. "The Commission on Civil Rights—and Human Rights." *The Review of Politics*, vol. 34, no. 3 (July 1972), 291–305.

Hills, Denis. "Horror in Uganda." *New York Review of Books*, vol. 23, no. 14 (September 16, 1976), 21–23.

Hoffmann, Stanley. "The Hell of Good Intentions." *Foreign Policy*, no. 29 (Winter 1977–78), pp. 3–26.

Howe, Russell Warren. "Difficulties of Restraint, Arms and the Man from Plains." *The New Leader*, vol. 60, no. 16 (August 1, 1977), 4–6.

Hughes, Thomas L. "Carter and the Management of Contradictions." *Foreign Policy*, no. 31 (Summer 1978), pp. 34–55.

Johnson, Donald C. "Congress, the Executive, and Human Rights Legislation." *Foreign Service Journal*, vol. 53 (December 1976), 18–20,28.

Kedourie, Elie. "Is Democracy Doomed?" *Commentary*, vol. 62, no. 5

(November 1976), 39–43.

Kennan, George F. "Between Earth and Hell." *New York Review of Books*, vol. 21, no. 4 (March 21, 1974), 3–7.

Kissinger, Henry; Sakharov, Andrei, *et al.* "The Politics of Human Rights." *Trialogue*, no. 19 (Fall 1978), entire issue.

Kondracke, Morton. "Human Rights on Capitol Hill." *New Republic*, vol. 176, no. 15 (April 9, 1977), 11–12.

Korey, William. "The Future of Soviet Jewry: Emigration and Assimilation." *Foreign Affairs*, vol. 58, no. 1 (Fall 1979), 67–81.

———. "The Key to Human Rights—Implementation." *International Conciliation*, no. 570 (November 1968), entire issue.

Lacouture, Jean. "The Bloodiest Revolution." *New York Review of Books*, vol. 24, no. 5 (March 31, 1977), 9–10.

Laqueur, Walter. "The Issue of Human Rights." *Commentary*, vol. 63, no. 5 (May 1977), 29–35.

LeoGrande, William M. "The Revolution in Nicaragua: Another Cuba?" *Foreign Affairs*, vol. 58, no. 1 (Fall 1979), 28–50.

Lillich, Richard B. "Symposium—Human Rights, the National Interest, and U.S. Foreign Policy: Some Preliminary Observations." *The Virginia Journal of International Law*, vol. 14, no. 4 (Summer 1974), 591–96.

Manglapus, Raúl S. "Human Rights Are Not a Western Discovery." *Worldview*, vol. 21, no. 10 (October 1978), 4–6.

Marmorstein, Victoria E. "World Bank Power to Consider Human Rights Factors in Loan Decisions." *The Journal of International Law and Economics*, vol. 13, no. 1 (1978), 113–36.

Martin, David. "Amin's Butchery." *New York Review of Books*, vol. 23, no. 14 (September 16, 1976), 24–26.

McDougal, Myres S. "Human Rights and World Public Order: Principles of Content and Procedure for Clarifying General Community Policies." *The Virginia Journal of International Law*, vol. 14, no. 3 (Spring 1974), 387–421.

———; Lasswell, Harold D.; and Chen, Lung-chu. "Human Rights for Women and World Public Order: The Outlawing of Sex-based Discrimination." *American Journal of International Law*, vol. 69, no. 3 (July 1975), 497–533.

———. "The Protection of Aliens from Discrimination and World Public Order: Responsibility of States Conjoined with Human Rights." *American Journal of International Law*, vol. 70, no. 3 (July 1976), 432–69.

———. "The Right to Religious Freedom and World Public Order: The Emerging Norm of Non-Discrimination." *Michigan Law Review*, vol. 74, no. 865 (April 1976), 865–98.

Miller, Arthur S. "A Bill of Rights to Protect Our Liberties." *Political Quarterly*, vol. 47, no. 2 (April 1976), 137–48.

Moynihan, Daniel P. "The Politics of Human Rights." *Commentary*, vol. 64, no. 2 (August 1977), 19–26.

Pagels, Elaine. "Human Rights: Legitimizing a Recent Concept." *The Annals of the American Academy of Political and Social Science*, vol. 442 (March 1979), 57–62.

Possony, Stefan T. "Anti-Semitism in the Russian Orbit." *Case Studies on Human Rights and Fundamental Freedoms*, vol. 2. The Hague: Martinus Nijhoff, 1976, 407–44.

———. "From Gulag to Guitk: Political Prisons in the USSR Today." *Case Studies on Human Rights and Fundamental Freedoms*, vol. 1. The Hague: Martinus Nijhoff, 1976, 3–64.

Quinn, Kenneth M. "Cambodia 1976: Internal Consolidation and External Expansion." *Asian Survey*, vol. 17, no. 1 (January 1977), 43–54.

Rawls, Wendell, Jr. "Baby Doc's Haitian Terror." *The New York Times Magazine*, May 14, 1978, pp. 14–16, 32, 38, 42, 44.

Reddaway, Peter. "Dissent in the Soviet Union." *Dissent*, vol. 23, no. 2 (Spring 1976), 136–55.

Reich, Walter. "Diagnosing Soviet Dissidents." *Harper's*, August 1978, pp. 31–37.

———. "Grigorenko Gets a Second Opinion." *The New York Times Magazine*, May 13, 1979, pp. 18, 39–42, 44, 46.

Reisman, Michael. "The Pragmatism of Human Rights." *The Nation*, vol. 224, no. 18 (May 7, 1977), 554–58.

Riding, Alan. "Latin Church in Siege." *The New York Times Magazine*, May 6, 1979, pp. 32–34, 38, 40, and 42–44.

———. "National Mutiny in Nicaragua." *The New York Times Magazine*, July 30, 1978, pp. 12–15, 34, 39, 42, 46–47, 58–60.

Rosenblum, Mort. "Terror in Argentina." *New York Review of Books*, vol. 23, no. 7 (October 28, 1976), 26–28.

Rustin, Bayard. "Do Not Forget Us!" *Worldview*, vol. 21, no. 5 (May 1978), 9.

Sakharov, Andrei D. "How I Came to Dissent." *New York Review of Books*, vol. 21, no. 4 (March 21, 1974), 11–17.

Schlesinger, Arthur, Jr. "Human Rights and the American Tradition." *Foreign Affairs*, vol. 57, no. 3 (Winter 1978–79), 503–26.

Schwelb, Egon. "Entry into Force of the International Covenants on Human Rights and the Optional Protocol to the International Covenant on Civil and Political Rights." *American Journal of International Law*, vol. 70, no. 3 (July 1976), 511–19.

———. "The International Court of Justice and the Human Rights Clauses of the Charter." *American Journal of International Law*, vol. 66, no. 2 (April 1972), 337–51.

————. "The International Measures of Implementation of the International Covenant on Civil and Political Rights and the Optional Protocol." *Texas International Law Journal*, vol. 12, nos. 2 and 3 (Spring/Summer 1977), 141–86.

Shawcross, William. "Cambodia Under Its New Rulers." *New York Review of Books*, vol. 23, no. 3 (March 4, 1976), 24–27.

————. "The Third Indochina War." *New York Review of Books*, vol. 25, no. 5 (April 6, 1978), 15–22.

Shipler, David K. "Crisis for Russia's Dissidents." *The New York Times Magazine*, July 23, 1978, pp. 18–20, 30, 32, 34–35.

Shulman, Marshall. "On Learning to Live with Authoritarian Regimes." *Foreign Affairs*, vol. 55, no. 2 (January 1977), 325–38.

Smith, Timothy H., and Nesbitt, Prexy. "Raising Investors' Consciousness: The Campaign Against Investments." *Christianity and Crisis*, vol. 38, no. 3 (March 13, 1978), 58–61.

Sohn, Louis B. "The Human Rights Law of the Charter." *Texas International Law Journal*, vol. 12, nos. 2 and 3 (Spring/Summer 1977), 129–40.

————. "The Improvement of the UN Machinery on Human Rights." *International Studies Quarterly*, vol. 23, no. 2 (June 1979), 186–215.

St. Jorre, John de. "The Ugandan Connection." *The New York Times Magazine*, April 9, 1978, pp. 27–28, 82, 84, 86, 88.

Steel, Ronald. "Motherhood, Apple Pie and Human Rights." *New Republic*, vol. 176, no. 23 (June 4, 1977), 14–15.

————. "Foreign Affairs: So Far, So So." *Politicks*, vol. 1, no. 1 (October 25, 1977), 20.

Stoppard, Tom. "Prague: The Story of the Chartists." *New York Review of Books*, vol. 24, no. 13 (August 4, 1977), 11–15.

Styron, Rose. "America's Repressive Ally: Torture in Chile." *New Republic*, vol. 174, no. 12 (March 20, 1976), 3–20.

Szulc, Tad. "The Limits of Linkage." *New Republic*, vol. 176, no. 10 (March 5, 1977), 17–19.

Tardu, M. E. "The Protocol to the United Nations Covenant on Civil and Political Rights and the Inter-American System: A Study of Co-existing Petition Procedures." *American Journal of International Law*, vol. 70, no. 4 (October 1976), 778–800.

Thompson, Kenneth. "New Reflections on Ethics and Foreign Policy: The Problem of Human Rights." *Journal of Politics*, vol. 40, no. 4 (November 1978), 984–1010.

Thorne, Ludmilla. "Inside Russia's Psychiatric Jails." *The New York Times Magazine*, June 12, 1977, pp. 26–27, 30, 60, 62, 64, 68, 70–71.

Ullman, Richard H. "Human Rights and Economic Power: The United States versus Idi Amin." *Foreign Affairs*, vol. 56, no. 3 (April 1978), 529–43.

Van Dyke, Vernon. "Human Rights without Discrimination." *American Political Science Review*, vol. 67, no. 4 (December 1973), 1267.

Vogelgesang, Sandy. "Diplomacy of Human Rights." *International Studies Quarterly*, vol. 23, no. 2 (June 1979), 216–45.

———. "What Price Principle? U.S. Policy on Human Rights." *Foreign Affairs*, vol. 56, no. 4 (July 1978), 819–41.

Washburn, John. "Diplomacy without a Brief: Morality and Human Rights in Foreign Policy." *Foreign Service Journal*, vol. 54, no. 5 (May 1977), 7–9, 55.

Watts, William, and Free, Lloyd A. "Nationalism, Not Isolationism." *Foreign Policy*, no. 24 (Fall 1976), pp. 3–26.

Weissbrodt, David. "Human Rights Legislation and U.S. Foreign Policy." *Georgia Journal of International and Comparative Law*, vol. 7 (Summer 1977), 231–87.

———. "The Role of International Nongovernmental Organizations in the Implementation of Human Rights." *Texas International Law Journal*, vol. 12, nos. 2 and 3 (Spring/Summer 1977), 293–320.

Wicker, Tom. "Should American Business Pull Out of South Africa?" *The New York Times Magazine*, June 3, 1979 pp. 31, 33, 36–37, 72, 74, 76, 78.

Willey, Fay. "The Push for Human Rights." *Newsweek*, June 20, 1977, pp. 46–61.

Williams, Anne M. "The European Convention on Human Rights: A New Use?" *Texas International Law Journal*, vol. 12, nos. 2 and 3 (Spring/Summer 1977), 279–92.

Woods, Donald. "The Indictment." *New York Review of Books*, vol. 25, no. 7 (May 4, 1978), 23–29.

Books—General

Amnesty International. *Report on Torture*. New York: Farrar, Straus & Giroux, 1975.

Arendt, Hannah. *The Origins of Totalitarianism*. New York: Harcourt, Brace & World, 1966.

Beddard, Ralph. *Human Rights and Europe, A Study of the Machinery of Human Rights Protection of the Council of Europe*. London: Sweet & Maxwell, 1973.

Berger, Peter L. *Facing Up to Modernity*. New York: Basic Books, 1977.

Berlin, Isaiah. *Four Essays on Liberty*. New York: Oxford University Press, 1969.

Brown, Peter G., and MacLean, Douglas, eds., *Human Rights and U.S. Foreign Policy: Principles and Applications.* Lexington, Mass.: Lexington Books, 1979.

Buergenthal, Thomas, ed. *Human Rights, International Law, and the Helsinki Accord.* New York: Universe Books, 1977.

————, and Torney, Judith V. *International Human Rights and International Education.* Washington, D.C.: U.S. National Commission for UNESCO, 1976.

Buncher, Judith F., ed. *Human Rights and American Diplomacy, 1975–1977.* New York: Facts on File, 1977.

Carey, John. *International Protection of Human Rights.* Dobbs Ferry, N.Y.: Oceana Publications, 1968.

————. *U.N. Protection of Civil and Political Rights.* Syracuse, N.Y.: Syracuse University Press, 1970.

Chenery, Hollis, *et al. Redistribution with Growth.* London: Oxford University Press, 1974.

Claude, Richard P., ed. *Comparative Human Rights.* Baltimore: The Johns Hopkins University Press, 1976.

Cleveland, Harlan. *The Third Try at World Order: U.S. Policy for an Interdependent World.* New York: Aspen Institute for Humanistic Studies, 1977.

Cranston, Maurice. *What Are Human Rights?* New York: Taplinger Publishing Company, 1973.

Dominguez, Jorge; Rodley, Nigel; Wood, Bryce; and Falk, Richard. *Enhancing Global Human Rights.* New York: McGraw-Hill, 1979.

Drost, Pieter N. *Human Rights As Legal Rights.* Leyden: A. W. Sijthoff, 1965.

Eide, Asbjörn, and Schov, August, eds. *International Protection of Human Rights.* New York: John Wiley & Sons, 1968.

Fishlow, Albert; Diaz-Alejandro, Carlos F.; Fagen, Richard R.; and Hansen, Roger D. *Rich and Poor Nations in the World Economy.* New York: McGraw-Hill, 1978.

Frankel, Charles. *Morality and U.S. Foreign Policy.* New York: Foreign Policy Association, 1975.

Glaser, Kurt, and Possony, Stefan T. *Victims of Politics: the State of Human Rights.* New York: Columbia University Press, 1979.

Goldman, Robert K. *The Protection of Human Rights in the Americas: Past, Present, and Future.* New York: New York University Press, 1972.

Goulet, Denis. *The Cruel Choice: A New Concept in the Theory of Development.* New York: Atheneum, 1971.

Haas, Ernst B. *Global Evangelism Rides Again: How to Protect Human Rights without Really Trying.* Berkeley, Calif.: Institute of International Studies, 1978.

————. *Human Rights and International Action*. Stanford, Calif.: Stanford University Press, 1970.

Hammarberg, Thomas. *Amnesty International Report 1977*. London: Amnesty International Publications, 1977.

Hansen, Roger D. *Beyond the North-South Stalemate*. New York: McGraw-Hill, 1978.

Haq, Mahbub ul. *The Poverty Curtain: Choices for the Third World*. New York: Columbia University Press, 1976.

Heilbroner, Robert L. *An Inquiry into the Human Prospect*. New York: W. W. Norton & Company, 1974.

Henkin, Alice H., ed. *Human Dignity: the Internationalization of Human Rights*. New York: Aspen Institute for Humanistic Studies, 1979.

Henkin, Louis. *The Rights of Man Today*. Boulder, Colo.: Westview Press, 1978.

Horowitz, Irving Louis. *Genocide, State Power, and Mass Murder*. New Brunswick, N.J.: Transaction Books, 1976.

Huntington, Samuel P., and Nelson, Joan M. *No Easy Choice: Political Participation in Developing Countries*. Cambridge, Mass.: Harvard University Press, 1976.

International Commission of Jurists. *Human Rights in a One-Party State: International Seminar on Human Rights, Their Protection and the Rule of Law in a One-Party State*. London: Search Press, 1976.

Joyce, James A. *The New Politics of Human Rights*. New York: St. Martin's Press, 1979.

Kommers, Donald P. and Loescher, Gilburt D., eds. *Human Rights and American Foreign Policy*. Notre Dame, Ind.: University of Notre Dame Press, 1979.

Lappé, Frances Moore, and Collins, Joseph. *Food First: Beyond the Myth of Scarcity*. Boston: Houghton Mifflin Company, 1977.

Larsen, Egon. *A Flame in Barbed Wire: the Story of Amnesty International*. New York: W. W. Norton & Company, 1979.

Lauterpacht, Hersh. *An International Bill of the Rights of Man*. New York: Columbia University Press, 1945.

————. *International Law and Human Rights*. Hamden, Conn.: Archon Books, 1968.

Le Blanc, Lawrence. *The OAS and the Promotion and Protection of Human Rights*. The Hague: Martinus Nijhoff, 1977.

Luard, Evan, ed., *The International Protection of Human Rights*. New York: Frederick A. Praeger, 1967.

McGregor, Ian. *Human Rights*. London: B. T. Batsford, 1975.

McHale, John, and McHale, Magda Cordell. *Basic Human Needs: A Framework for Action*. New Brunswick, N.J.: Transaction Books, 1978.

Mellor, John W. *The New Economics of Growth*. Ithaca, N.Y.: Cornell University Press, 1976.

Miller, William, ed. *International Human Rights: A Bibliography, 1965–1969*. Notre Dame, Ind.: Center for Civil Rights, 1976.

————. *International Human Rights: A Bibliography, 1970–1976*. Notre Dame, Ind.: Center for Civil Rights, 1976.

Moore, Barrington, Jr. *Social Origins of Dictatorship and Democracy*. Boston: Beacon Press, 1966.

Morgenthau, Hans J. *Politics among Nations: The Struggle for Power and Peace*. New York: Alfred A. Knopf, 1961.

Morrison, Clovis C., Jr. *The Developing European Law of Human Rights*. Leyden, The Netherlands: A. W. Sijthoff—Leyden, 1967.

Nedjati, Zaim M. *Human Rights under the European Convention*. Amsterdam: North-Holland Publishing Company, 1978.

Niebuhr, Reinhold. *The Children of Light and the Children of Darkness*. New York: Charles Scribner's Sons, 1944.

————. *Moral Man and Immoral Society*. New York: Charles Scribner's Sons, 1932.

Okun, Arthur M. *Equity and Efficiency: The Big Tradeoff*. Washington, D.C.: The Brookings Institution, 1975.

Owen, David. *Human Rights*. New York: W. W. Norton & Company, 1978.

Paxman, John M., and Boggs, George T., eds. *The United Nations: A Reassessment—Sanctions, Peacekeeping, and Humanitarian Assistance*. Charlottesville, Va.: University Press of Virginia, 1973.

Pollack, Ervin H., ed. *Human Rights*. Buffalo, N.Y.: Jay Stewart Publications, 1971.

Pollis, Adamantia, and Schwab, Peter, eds. *Human Rights: Cultural and Ideological Perspectives*. New York: Frederick A. Praeger, Praeger Special Studies, 1979.

Robertson, Arthur H. *Human Rights in Europe*. Manchester, England: Manchester University Press, 1977.

————. *Human Rights in the World*. Manchester, England: Manchester University Press, 1972.

Robinson, Jacob. *Human Rights and Fundamental Freedoms in the Charter of the United Nations*. New York: Institute of Jewish Affairs, 1946.

Said, Abdul Aziz, ed. *Human Rights and World Order*. New Brunswick, N.J.: Transaction Books, 1978.

Schreiber, Anna P. *The Inter-American Commission on Human Rights*. Leyden, The Netherlands: A. W. Sijthoff—Leyden, 1970.

Schumacher, E. F. *Small Is Beautiful: A Study of Economics As If People Mattered*. New York: Harper & Row, 1976.

Sewell, John, *et al. The U.S. and World Development, Agenda 1977*. New York: Praeger Publishers, 1977.

Skinner, Burrhus Frederic. *Beyond Freedom and Dignity*. New York: Alfred A. Knopf, 1971.

Sohn, Louis B., and Buergenthal, Thomas. *Basic Documents on International Protection of Human Rights*. New York: Bobbs-Merrill, 1973.

————. *International Protection of Human Rights*. New York: Bobbs-Merrill, 1973.

Tinker, Irene, and Bramsen, Michele Bo, eds. *Women and World Development*. Washington, D.C.: Overseas Development Council, 1976.

Tucker, Robert W. *The Inequality of Nations*. New York: Basic Books, 1977.

Ullman, Richard H., *et al. Enhancing Global Human Rights*. New York: McGraw-Hill, 1978.

Van Dyke, Vernon. *Human Rights, the United States, and World Community*. New York: Oxford University Press, 1970.

Veenhoven, Willem A., ed. *Case Studies on Human Rights and Fundamental Freedoms*, vols. 1–5. The Hague: Martinus Nijhoff, 1976.

Walzer, Michael. *Just and Unjust Wars: Moral Argument with Historical Illustrations*. New York: Basic Books, 1977.

————. *Obligations: Essays on Disobedience, War, and Citizenship*. New York: Simon and Schuster, 1970.

Woito, Robert, ed. *International Human Rights Kit*. Chicago: World Without War Council, 1977.

Books—Specific Cases

Amalrik, Andrei. *Will the Soviet Union Survive Until 1984?* New York: Harper & Row, 1970.

Amnesty International. *Political Imprisonment in South Africa*. London: Amnesty International Publications, 1978.

————. *Prisoners of Conscience in the U.S.S.R.: Their Treatment and Conditions*. London: Amnesty International Publications, 1975.

Anderson, Thomas P. *Matanza: El Salvador's Communist Revolt of 1932*. Lincoln, Neb.: University of Nebraska Press, 1971.

Barron, John, and Paul, Anthony. *Murder of a Gentle Land: The Untold Story of a Communist Genocide in Cambodia*. New York: Reader's Digest Press, 1977.

Bloch, Sidney, and Reddaway, Peter. *Psychiatric Terror: How Soviet Psychiatry Is Used to Suppress Dissent*. New York: Basic Books, 1977.

Butler, William J. *Human Rights and the Legal System in Iran: Two Reports.* Geneva: International Commission of Jurists, 1976.

Capa, Cornell, and Stycos, J. Mayone. *Margin of Life.* New York: Grossman Publishers, 1974.

Chalidze, Valery. *To Defend These Rights: Human Rights and the Soviet Union.* New York: Random House, 1974.

Drinan, Robert F.; McAward, John J.; and Anderson, Thomas P. *Human Rights in El Salvador—1978.* Boston: Unitarian Universalist Service Committee, 1978.

Griffith, William E., ed. *The Soviet Empire: Expansion and Détente.* Lexington, Mass.: Lexington Books, 1976.

Hildebrand, George C., and Porter, Gareth. *Cambodia: Starvation and Revolution.* New York: Monthly Review Press, 1976.

International Commission of Jurists. *Uganda and Human Rights.* Geneva: International Commission of Jurists, 1977.

Morris, R.; Bowen, M.; Freeman, G.; and Miller, K. *Passing By: The United States and Genocide in Burundi.* Washington, D.C.: Carnegie Endowment for International Peace, Humanitarian Policy Studies, 1972.

Reddaway, Peter, ed. *Uncensored Russia: Protest and Dissent in the Soviet Union.* New York: American Heritage Press, 1972.

Rogers, Barbara. *White Wealth and Black Poverty: American Investments in Southern Africa.* Westport, Conn.: Greenwood Press, 1976.

Sakharov, Andrei D. *Sakharov Speaks.* New York: Alfred A. Knopf, 1974.

Shawcross, William. *Side Show: Kissinger, Nixon and the Destruction of Cambodia.* New York: Simon and Schuster, 1979.

Stern, Paula. *Water's Edge: Domestic Politics and the Making of American Foreign Policy.* Westport, Conn.: Greenwood Press, 1979.

Tökes, Rudolf L., ed. *Dissent in the U.S.S.R.* Baltimore: Johns Hopkins Press, 1975.

White, Alastair. *El Salvador.* New York: Praeger, 1973.

Congressional Hearings and Documents on Human Rights

Human Rights in the World Community: A Call for U.S. Leadership. March 27, 1974. (Report of the Subcommittee on International Organizations and Movements—hereafter referred to as IO)

International Protection of Human Rights: The Work of International Organizations and the Role of U.S. Foreign Policy. August 1; September 13, 19,

20, 27; October 3, 4, 10, 11, 16, 18, 24, 25; November 1; December 7, 1973. Before IO.

Human Rights in Chile (Part 1). December 9, 1973; May 7, 23; June 11, 12, and 18, 1974. Before IO and the Subcommittee on Inter-American Affairs.

Treatment of Israeli POW's in Syria and Their Status Under the Geneva Convention. February 26, 1974. Before IO.

Problems of Protecting Civilians Under International Law in the Middle East Conflict. April 4, 1974. Before IO.

Human Rights in Africa: Report by the International Commission of Jurists. June 13, 1974. Before IO.

Review of the U.N. Commission on Human Rights. June 18 and 20, 1974. Before IO.

Soviet Union: Human Rights and Detente. July 17 and 25, 1974. Before IO and Subcommittee on Europe.

Torture and Oppression in Brazil. December 11, 1974. Before IO.

Human Rights in South Korea and the Philippines: Implications for U.S. Policy. May 20, 22; June 3, 5, 10, 12, 17, 24, 1975. Before IO.

Human Rights in Chile (Part 2). November 19, 1974. Before IO and Subcommittee on Inter-American Affairs.

Human Rights in South Korea: Implications for U.S. Policy. July 31, August 5, December 20, 1974. Before IO and Subcommittee on Asian and Pacific Affairs.

Human Rights in Haiti. November 18, 1975. Before IO.

Human Rights in Chile. December 9, 1975. Before IO.

Chile: The Status of Human Rights and Its Relationship to U.S. Economic Assistance Programs. April 29; May 5, 1976. Before IO.

Psychiatric Abuse of Political Prisoners in the Soviet Union: Testimony by Leonid Plyushch. March 30, 1976. Before IO.

Human Rights in Indonesia and the Philippines. December 18 and May 3, 1976. Before IO.

Anti-Semitism and Reprisals against Jewish Emigration in the Soviet Union. May 27, 1976. Before IO.

Human Rights in the Philippines: Report by Amnesty International. September 15, 1976. Before IO.

Human Rights Issues at the Sixth Regular Session of the Organization of American States General Assembly. August 10, 1976. Before IO.

Religious Persecution in the Soviet Union. June 24 and 30, 1976. Before IO and Subcommittee on International Political and Military Affairs.

Human Rights in Iran. August 3 and September 8, 1976. Before IO.

Human Rights in Nicaragua, Guatemala, and El Salvador. June 8 and 9, 1976. Before IO.

Human Rights in India. June 23, 28, and 29, and September 16 and 23, 1976. Before IO.

Human Rights in Uruguay and Paraguay. June 17; July 27, 28; and August 4, 1976. Before IO.

Namibia: The United Nations and U.S. Policy. August 24 and 27, 1976. Before IO.

Human Rights in Argentina. September 28 and 29, 1976. Before IO.

Human Rights in North Korea. September 9, 1976. Before IO.

The Recent Presidential Elections in El Salvador: Implications for U.S. Foreign Policy. March 9 and 17, 1977. Before IO and Subcommittee on Inter-American Affairs.

Human Rights in East Timor and the Question of the Use of U.S. Equipment by the Indonesian Armed Forces. March 23, 1977. Before IO and Subcommittee on Asian and Pacific Affairs.

Human Rights Practices in Countries Receiving U.S. Security Assistance. Report Submitted to the House Committee on International Relations by the Department of State. April 25, 1977.

Human Rights in Cambodia. May 3, 1977. Before IO.

Review of the United Nations Thirty-third Commission on Human Rights. May 19, 1977. Before IO.

Human Rights in Taiwan. June 14, 1977. Before IO.

Human Rights in East Timor. June 28 and July 19, 1977. Before IO.

Human Rights in the International Community and in U.S. Foreign Policy, 1945–76. July 24, 1977. Report of the Subcommittee on International Organizations.

The Status of Human Rights in Selected Countries and the U.S. Response. July 25, 1977. Report of the Subcommittee on International Organizations.

Human Rights in Camboida. July 26, 1977. Before IO.

Human Rights Issues at the Seventh Regular Session of the Organization of American States General Assembly. September 15, 1977. Before IO.

Human Rights In Indonesia: A Review of the Situation with Respect to the Long-term Political Detainees. October 18, 1977. Before IO.

Human Rights in Iran. October 26, 1977. Before IO.

Country Reports on Human Rights Practices. February 3, 1978. Report Submitted to the Committee on International Relations of the U.S. House of Representatives and Committee on Foreign Relations of the U.S. Senate by the Department of State.

Human Rights in the Philippines: Recent Developments. April 27, 1978. Before IO.

Human Rights Conditions in Selected Countries and the U.S. Response. July 25, 1978. Prepared for IO by the Library of Congress.

Appendix

CHARTER OF THE UNITED NATIONS

WE THE PEOPLES OF THE UNITED NATIONS

determined

to save succeeding generations from the scourge of war, which twice in our life-time has brought untold sorrow to mankind, and to reaffirm faith in fundamental human rights, in the dignity and worth of the human person, in the equal rights of men and women and of nations large and small, and

to establish conditions under which justice and respect for the obligations arising from treaties and other sources of international law can be maintained, and

to promote social progress and better standards of life in larger freedom.

and for these ends

to practice tolerance and live together in peace with one another as good neighbours, and

to unite our strength to maintain international peace and security, and

to ensure, by the acceptance of principles and the institution of methods, that armed force shall not be used, save in the common interest, and

to employ international machinery for the promotion of the economic and social advancement of all peoples.

have resolved to combine our efforts

to accomplish these aims

Accordingly, our respective Governments, through representatives assembled in the city of San Francisco, who have exhibited their full powers found to be in good and due form, have agreed to the present Charter of the United Nations and do hereby establish an international organization to be known as the United Nations.

Article 1

The Purposes of the United Nations are:

1. To maintain international peace and security, and to that end: to take effective collective measures for the prevention and removal of threats to the peace, and for the suppression of acts of aggression or other breaches of the peace, and to bring about by peaceful means, and in conformity with the principles of justice and international law, adjustment or settlement of international disputes or situations which might lead to a breach of the peace;

2. To develop friendly relations among nations based on respect for the principle of equal rights and self-determination of peoples, and to take other appropriate measures to strengthen universal peace;

3. To achieve international co-operation in solving international problems of an economic, social, cultural, or humanitarian character, and in promoting and encouraging respect for human rights and for fundamental freedoms for all without distinction as to race, sex, language, or religion; and

4. To be a centre for harmonizing the actions of nations in the attainment of these common ends.

* * *

Article 55

With a view to the creation of conditions of stability and well-being which are necessary for peaceful and friendly relations among nations based on respect for the principle of equal rights and self-determination of peoples, the United Nations shall promote:

a. higher standards of living, full employment, and conditions of economic and social progress and development;

b. solutions of international economic, social, health, and related problems; and international cultural and educational co-operation; and

c. universal respect for, and observance of, human rights and fundamental freedoms for all without distinction as to race, sex, language, or religion.

Article 56

All Members pledge themselves to take joint and separate action in co-operation with the Organization for the achievement of the purposes set forth in Article 55.

* * *

UNIVERSAL DECLARATION OF HUMAN RIGHTS
Preamble

Whereas recognition of the inherent dignity and of the equal and inalienable rights of all members of the human family is the foundation of freedom, justice and peace in the world,

Whereas disregard and contempt for human rights have resulted in barbarous acts which have outraged the conscience of mankind, and the advent of a world in which human beings shall enjoy freedom of speech and belief and freedom from any fear and want has been proclaimed as the highest aspiration of the common people,

Whereas it is essential, if man is not to be compelled to have recourse, as a last resort, to rebellion against tyranny and oppression, that human rights should be protected by the rule of law,

Whereas it is essential to promote the development of friendly relations between nations,

Whereas the peoples of the United Nations have in the Charter reaffirmed their faith in fundamental human rights, in the dignity and worth of the human person and in the equal rights of men and women and have determined to promote social progress and better standards of life in larger freedom,

Whereas Member States have pledged themselves to achieve, in co-operation with the United Nations, the promotion of universal respect for and observance of human rights and fundamental freedoms,

Whereas a common understanding of these rights and freedoms is of the greatest importance for the full realization of this pledge,

Now, Therefore,
THE GENERAL ASSEMBLY
proclaims
THIS UNIVERSAL DECLARATION OF HUMAN RIGHTS as a common standard of achievement for all peoples and all nations, to the end that every individual and every organ of society, keeping this Declaration constantly in mind, shall strive by teaching and education to promote respect for these rights and freedoms and by progressive measures, national and international, to secure their universal and effective recognition and observance, both among the peoples of Member States themselves and among the peoples of territories under their jurisdiction.

Article 1. All human beings are born free and equal in dignity and rights. They are endowed with reason and conscience and should act towards one another in a spirit of brotherhood.

Article 2. Everyone is entitled to all the rights and freedoms set forth in this Declaration, without distinction of any kind, such as race, colour, sex, language, religion, political or other opinion, national or social origin, property, birth or other status.

Furthermore, no distinction shall be made on the basis of the political, jurisdictional or international status of the country or territory to which a person belongs, whether it be independent, trust, non-self-governing or under any other limitation of sovereignty.

Article 3. Everyone has the right to life, liberty and security of person.

Article 4. No one shall be held in slavery or servitude; slavery and the slave trade shall be prohibited in all their forms.

Article 5. No one shall be subjected to torture or to cruel, inhuman or degrading treatment or punishment.

Article 6. Everyone has the right to recognition everywhere as a person before the law.

Article 7. All are equal before the law and are entitled without any discrimination to equal protection of the law. All are entitled to equal protection against any discrimination in violation of this Declaration and against any incitement to such discrimination.

Article 8. Everyone has the right to an effective remedy by the competent national tribunals for acts violating the fundamental rights granted him by the constitution or by law.

Article 9. No one shall be subjected to arbitrary arrest, detention or exile.

Article 10. Everyone is entitled in full equality to a fair and public hearing by an independent and impartial tribunal, in the determination of his rights and obligations and of any criminal charge against him.

Article 11. (1) Everyone charged with a penal offence has the right to be presumed innocent until proved guilty according to law in a public trial at which he has had all the guarantees necessary for his defence.

(2) No one shall be held guilty of any penal offence on account of any act or omission which did not constitute a penal offence, under national or international law, at the time when it was committed. Nor shall a heavier penalty be imposed than the one that was applicable at the time the penal offence was committed.

Article 12. No one shall be subjected to arbitrary interference with his privacy, family, home or correspondence, nor to attacks upon his honour and reputation. Everyone has the right to the protection of the law against such interference or attacks.

Article 13. (1) Everyone has the right to freedom of movement and residence within the borders of each state.

(2) Everyone has the right to leave any country, including his own, and to return to his country.

Article 14. (1) Everyone has the right to seek and to enjoy in other countries asylum from persecution.

(2) This right may not be invoked in the case of prosecutions genuinely arising from non-political crimes or from acts contrary to the purposes and principles of the United Nations.

Article 15. (1) Everyone has the right to a nationality.

(2) No one shall be arbitrarily deprived of his nationality nor denied the right to change his nationality.

Article 16. (1) Men and women of full age, without any limitation due to race, nationality or religion, have the right to marry and to found a family. They are entitled to equal rights as to marriage, during marriage and as its dissolution.

(2) marriage shall be entered into only with the free and full consent of the intending spouses.

(3) The family is the natural and fundamental group unit of society and is entitled to protection by society and the State.

Article 17. (1) Everyone has the right to own property alone as well as in association with others.

(2) No one shall be arbitrarily deprived of his property.

Article 18. Everyone has the right to freedom of thought, conscience and religion; this right includes freedom to change his religion or belief, and freedom, either alone or in community with others and in public or private, to manifest his religion or belief in teaching, practice, worship and observance.

Article 19. Everyone has the right to freedom of opinion and expression; this right includes freedom to hold opinions without interference and to seek, receive and impart information and ideas through any media and regardless of frontiers.

Article 20. (1) Everyone has the right to freedom of peaceful assembly and association.

(2) No one may be compelled to belong to an association.

Article 21. (1) Everyone has the right to take part in the government of his country, directly or through freely chosen representatives.

(2) Everyone has the right of equal access to public service in his country.

(3) The will of the people shall be the basis of the authority of government; this will shall be expressed in periodic and genuine elections which shall be by universal and equal suffrage and shall be held by secret vote or by equivalent free voting procedures.

Article 22. Everyone, as a member of society, has the right to social security and is entitled to realization through national effort and international co-operation and in accordance with the organization and resources of each State, of the economic, social and cultural rights indispensable for his dignity and the free development of his personality.

Article 23. (1) Everyone has the right to work, to free choice of employment, to just and favourable conditions of work and to protection against unemployment.

(2) Everyone, without any discrimination, has the right to equal pay for equal work.

(3) Everyone who works has the right to just and favourable remuneration ensuring for himself and his family an existence worthy of human dignity, and supplemented, if necessary, by other means of social protection.

(4) Everyone has the right to form and to join trade unions for the protection of his interest.

Article 24. Everyone has the right to rest and leisure, including reasonable limitation of working hours and periodic holidays with pay.

Article 25. (1) Everyone has the right to a standard of living adequate for the health and well-being of himself and of his family, including food, clothing, housing and medical care and necessary social services, and the right to security in the event of unemployment, sickness, disability, widowhood, old age or other lack of livelihood in circumstances beyond his control.

(2) Motherhood and childhood are entitled to special care and assistance. All children, whether born in or out of wedlock, shall enjoy the same social protection.

Article 26. (1) Everyone has the right to education. Education shall be free, at least in the elementary and fundamental stages. Elementary education shall be compulsory. Technical and professional education shall be made generally available and higher education shall be equally accessible to all on the basis of merit.

(2) Education shall be directed to the full development of the human personality and to the strengthening of respect for human rights and fundamental freedoms. It shall promote understanding, tolerance and friendship among all nations, racial or religious groups, and shall further the activities of the United Nations for the maintenance of peace.

(3) Parents have a prior right to choose the kind of education that shall be given to their children.

Article 27. (1) Everyone has the right freely to participate in the cultural life of the community, to enjoy the arts and to share in scientific advancement and its benefits.

(2) Everyone has the right to the protection of the moral and material interests resulting from any scientific, literary or artistic production of which he is the author.

Article 28. Everyone is entitled to a social and international order in which the rights and freedoms set forth in this Declaration can be fully realized.

Article 29. (1) Everyone has duties to the community in which alone the free and full development of his personality is possible.

(2) In the exercise of his rights and freedoms, everyone shall be subject only to such limitations as are determined by law solely for the purpose of securing due recognition and respect for the rights and freedoms of others and of meeting the just requirements of morality, public order and the general welfare in a democratic society.

(3) These rights and freedoms may in no case be exercised contrary to the purposes and principles of the United Nations.

Article 30. Nothing in this Declaration may be interpreted as implying for any State, group or person any right to engage in any activity or to perform any act aimed at the destruction of any of the rights and freedoms set forth herein.

Index